THE
VICTORIAN
NOVEL

THE
MAGILL
BIBLIOGRAPHIES

THE VICTORIAN NOVEL

An Annotated Bibliography

LAURENCE W. MAZZENO
Dean of Humanities and Fine Arts
Mesa State College

SALEM PRESS

Pasadena, California   Englewood Cliffs, New Jersey

Library of Congress Cataloging-in-Publication Data

Mazzeno, Laurence W.
  The Victorian novel / Laurence W. Mazzeno.
      p.   cm. — (Magill bibliographies)
    ISBN 0-89356-653-5
    1. English fiction—19th century—History and
criticism—Bibliography. I. Title. II. Series.
Z2014.F4M39   1989
[PR871]
016.823 ' 8—dc20   89-10794
                                              CIP

4-19-90

CONTENTS

CONTENTS

EDITORIAL STAFF

ACKNOWLEDGMENTS

The author wishes to express sincere appreciation to colleagues in the Naval Academy English Department; particular thanks are due fellow Victorian scholars Natalie Michta, Laura Claridge, and especially Allan Lefcowitz and Eileen Tyler. The lion's share of initial proofing, editing, and re-checking of sources was handled with exceptional skill and a great deal of cheerful dedication by Ms. Chariti Davis, without whom this project could not have been completed.

THE
VICTORIAN
NOVEL

INTRODUCTION

The nineteenth century American writer and critic Henry James once observed that William Makepeace Thackeray's *The Newcomes* reminded him of a "loose baggy monster." The description has since been applied to many other novels of the Victorian era, works whose plots seem loosely constructed and whose amassed details often appear to have been added only to build suspense or evoke sentiment in readers. To James and to many critics of the early twentieth century, many of these "page turners" seemed merely attempts to pander to the public's penchant for sentimentality and its incipient thirst for adventure, mayhem, and external action, devoid of serious treatment of either character or theme.

Nevertheless, it is a fact that the general public in the nineteenth century adored their novelists: they waited eagerly for each new work by the inimitable "Boz," as Charles Dickens was known, and for those of his contemporaries George Eliot (pseudonym for Marian Evans), Thackeray, Anthony Trollope, Charles Reade, Wilkie Collins, and dozens of others, many of whose names and works have faded from memory. The nineteenth century reading public developed emotional attachments to their favorite characters, and novelists' careful use of sentimental language and setting, coupled with strident moral pronouncements about various social ills, insured a faithful clientele for their fiction. Appearing serially in magazines over twelve to twenty months, or issued in three or more thick volumes, Victorian novels kept readers coming back to the bookstores and lending libraries for the next installment of stories that played heavily on the heartstrings of those who became wrapped up in them.

Of course, not all the English novelists of the 1800's simply turned out potboilers for consumption by the populace at large. As the century progressed, more and more of the important figures working in the genre began to concentrate as much on individual characterization and the psychological development of their heroes and heroines as they did on the social ills against which they railed so effectively. Some became rebels of a sort, especially women novelists who wrote unabashedly about the plight of the woman in a male-dominated society, confronting head-on "the Woman Question"—that Victorian phrase used loosely to describe all the issues dealing with the status of women in a society that insisted on treating them as objects of veneration or of use rather than as fully developed human persons.

The corpus of nineteenth century novels now appears as a formidable body of literature to the student and scholar of the period. Estimates of the number of such works published during the years roughly defined as "the Victorian era" range in excess of forty thousand. Hundreds, even thousands, of men and women became writers—some amateurs who experimented with the genre as a means of casual entertainment for themselves and their readers, others seasoned professionals who made comfortable livings by churning out volume after volume for an avid readership whose attachment to their reading paralleled the twentieth century populace's addiction to television. For the first time in history, the novel became the province not only of the intellectual few but also of the masses at large. That phenomenon accounts for many of the conventions that grew up around the production of works of fiction. It also accounts for the novelists' reticence to tackle head-on certain subjects, especially those dealing with sexual relationships. In order for a novelist to make a living by his or her pen, it was necessary to pass rigid tests of censorship, imposed not by publishers but by a straight-laced middle class that, at its extreme, refused to allow the mention of any body parts, lest the mere reference to a person's physical attractiveness stir unwanted thoughts in tender breasts. Men such as Charles Mudie, who built the most influential lending library system in the country, demanded that every book on the shelves of his establishment be fit for the eyes of the tenderest maid—or for her ears, since many a Victorian family spent their evenings around the fireplace while Father read from some text intended to provide wholesome entertainment or sound advice for self-help or moral improvement.

For such readers, novels were considered no different from other works of instruction. Hence, the topicality of many of these works, the overzealousness of authors to deal stridently with moral transgressions that no longer seem so formidable, and the shoddiness of the handling of plot and characterization has caused hundreds, even thousands of them to languish unread on library shelves, or to have disappeared altogether.

A few remain, however, and have become part of the literary heritage of Western civilization, especially in Britain and America. Novelists such as Dickens and George Eliot, who were able to rise above the limitations imposed on them by a prudish reading public easily captivated by violent action and sentimentality, have become acknowledged as giants in their profession. They are not alone, however, in being recognized as writers of genius; in fact, the pantheon of significant Victorian novelists is relatively large. Besides Dickens and George Eliot, a group of writers including William Thackeray, Thomas Hardy, and George Meredith has maintained a steady readership among scholars and students, and has even attracted followings among contemporary publics outside the academic world. The same is true for certain of the works of Charles Kingsley, Benjamin Disraeli, Elizabeth Gaskell, Anthony Trollope, Wilkie Collins, and the Brontë sisters—Anne, Charlotte, and especially Emily, whose novel *Wuthering Heights* ranks with two or three of Dickens' works and Hardy's *Tess of the D'Urbervilles* as one of the most-taught Victorian novels in high schools and colleges in America. Other writers are remembered for only a few masterpieces, though the corpus of their work is significant; Anthony Trollope certainly falls into this category, as does George Meredith.

In the twentieth century, approximately five dozen titles form the basis for much of the study of the Victorian novel. Thousands of books and articles published in the last century provide assessments of both the technical merits of these novels as well as observations on the impact they had on the reading public. As the practice of criticism has become more specialized in recent decades, so has the analysis of Victorian fiction become more sharply focused, and constant revaluation of works once revered or discarded has caused a shift in the relative merits of both individual novels and of the men and women who wrote them.

Despite the altered emphasis new critical approaches or new cultural or political interests have given to various authors and novels, the works selected for inclusion in this bibliography have remained among the most-read and most studied in undergraduate classes on the novel or on Victorian literature. The principle adopted for selecting these works from among the many candidates has been primarily that of enduring popularity, as evidenced by continued accessibility in both scholarly and trade editions, repeated inclusion in course syllabuses, and frequent mention by scholars or students working in other areas of literary study. Many of these novels are consciously referred to as classics. Others, while not meriting that accolade, still remain the subject of fruitful research and criticism, and continue to give pleasure to both the casual reader and the professional scholar.

This bibliography is arranged alphabetically by author and title. For each author, a general bibliography is included, citing readily accessible works that discuss the author's life and achievements, often providing comparisons with contemporaries or with novelists of other periods. After each title, a number of citations point the student to books or chapters in books providing a detailed discussion of the individual novel. Every effort has been made to cite works that stand alone and that can be located in libraries to which undergraduate students have ready access. Care has been taken to survey several undergraduate libraries at universities and four-year colleges, as well as community-college libraries, to determine that some, if not all, of these texts can be obtained with relative ease. Some of the citations may be duplicated in standard reference works available in college and high-school libraries; however, students should find that the summaries following each citation will be helpful in determining if the individual book or chapter will be of value to their particular research project. These summaries are not intended as substitutes for the criticism itself; indeed, much of the subtlety of argumentation that makes these studies of value cannot be reproduced in brief synopses such as those included in this volume.

Though Queen Victoria reigned from 1837 to 1901, no attempt has been made to include every important novel written between these dates. Instead, the choice of authors and works has been made according to guidelines long established by scholars of the period to consider "Victorian" those writers who flourished during the years of the Queen's reign and shared certain cultural and social assumptions, as well as assumptions about the purpose and form of fiction. Hence, authors such as Oscar Wilde, Walter Pater, and Joseph Conrad are not represented because their works belong more properly to the period known as "Fin de Siecle"; their writings represent a decidedly modern spirit or technique that stands in sharp contrast to the works of Dickens, Eliot, or even Thomas Hardy. To give students using this bibliography some assurance that it will be of value, every novel by Dickens and George Eliot has been indexed, as have Thackeray's five major works, and five of Hardy's. In the case of some novelists such as Trollope, who were quite prolific but whose current popularity is limited, the selection of individual titles is severely restricted. To compensate for this limitation, however, more entries are included in the "General Studies" section of the bibliography for each author who fits this category.

The student will find that, in addition to works cited in this bibliography, a substantial body of critical material is available in professional journals devoted exclusively or in part to Victorian novelists or Victorian studies. Every attempt has been made to refrain from including citations to such journals, as the criticism in professional publications intended for teachers and practicing scholars is often too specialized to be of real use to the undergraduate. The graduate student or teacher who seeks either comprehensive coverage or a catalog of more specialized theoretical studies may be disappointed, since this collection is intentionally designed to offer a range of criticism whenever possible. Hence, some recent feminist, structuralist, poststructuralist, Marxist, and new historical studies are not included. In most cases, their omission is based on the limited accessibility of scholarly publications intended for professionals. Occasionally, however, one such study is indexed, so students may get a sense of such criticism; however, no one critical approach has been given primacy in this volume.

Should specialized study be required, students will find several reference works to be good starting places for beginning research. The Modern Language Association (MLA) publishes the annual *MLA International Bibliography*; this guide lists among its entries books or articles on Victorian novelists published during the calendar year. Authors are listed alphabetically in the section titled "English Literature, 1800-1899"; since 1982, individual works are listed alphabetically under the author's name, and citations for these works are grouped together to permit students and scholars to find references for specific works with greater ease. The Modern Humanities Association's *Humanities Index* (formerly *Humanities and Social Sciences Index*), also issued annually, provides similar citations; the bibliography is arranged alphabetically by author throughout individual volumes, without regard to the time in which a novelist published. Scholarly journals such as *Nineteenth Century Literature* (formerly *Nineteenth Century Fiction*) and *Novel*, both quarterly publications, are particularly good sources of material on individual authors or works. On occasion, these also provide controversial and well developed articles on the theory of fiction. Both are indexed in the *MLA International Bibliography*. Scholarship on Victorian writers is published regularly in journals such as *Victorian Studies*, *Victorian Newsletter*, *The Dickensian*, *Dickens Studies Annual*, *The George Eliot Fellowship Review*, *Brontë Society Transactions*, *The Thomas Hardy Yearbook*, the summer issue of *Studies in English Literature*, *Style*, and *Genre*.

General Studies

Allen, Walter. *The English Novel: A Short Critical History*. New York: E. P. Dutton, 1955.

Historical assessment of the development of the novel as an art form. Contains a valuable introduction on the art of the novel and a detailed discussion of all major Victorian novelists. Examines the social and cultural milieu in which they wrote and considers the influence of these novelists on the craft of writing and on the age. Substantial emphasis on technique, especially characterization.

Bartlett, Lynn C., and William R. Sherwood. *The English Novel: Background Readings*. New York: J. B. Lippincott, 1967.
A collection of supplementary readings, including excerpts from letters, prefaces, notebooks, and contemporary reviews, which illuminate the background of more than a dozen major Victorian works and provide sketches of the critical responses these novels provoked.

Batho, E. C., and Bonamy Dobree. *The Victorians and After, 1830-1914*. Vol. 4 in their *Introduction to English Literature*. 3d rev. ed. London: Cresset Press, 1962.
Among chapters that provide excellent background to the period as a whole, the editors include a chapter on fiction tracing the development of the novel from its role as a popular vehicle for entertainment to its position as a major art form; they also trace the movement of the novelists' concern with large social issues to interest in individual characters and psychological problems and processes.

Booth, Bradford. "Form and Technique in the Novel." In *The Reinterpretation of Victorian Literature*, edited by Joseph E. Baker. Princeton: Princeton University Press, 1950.
Attempts to explain the virtues and faults of Victorian novelists by focusing on the technical aspects of their work. Pays special attention to the ways various novelists invented or improved methods of narration, description, and characterization. Additional chapters in the volume give illuminating information on other literary forms popular during the period.

Brownstein, Rachel M. *Becoming a Heroine: Reading about Women in Novels*. New York: Viking Press, 1982.
Insightful analysis by a feminist critic of the implications of novels dealing with heroines as central characters; includes a discussion of several major Victorian figures. Examines the symbiotic relationship between the reading experience and real-life personality development.

Cecil, David. *Victorian Novelists: Essays in Revaluation*. Chicago: University of Chicago Press, 1935, rev. ed. 1958.
Study of Victorian novelists aimed at determining the qualities that give them

life beyond the age in which they were written. Posits several generalizations about subject and style common to all major figures of the period. Examines the careers of Charles Dickens, William Makepeace Thackeray, the Brontës, Elizabeth Gaskell, Anthony Trollope, and George Eliot. Useful corrective both to encomiums by earlier devotees and to harsh dismissals from modern novelists who elevate experimentation in form to paramount importance in judging a novel's value.

Drew, Elizabeth. *The Novel: A Modern Guide to Fifteen English Masterpieces*. New York: W. W. Norton, 1963.
Discusses works by five Victorian novelists as classics because their authors share a humanist tradition and hold similar beliefs about intellectual, ethical, and social issues. Offers valuable insight into ways different novelists convey individual and social values through their works.

Dunn, Richard J. *The English Novel: Twentieth Century Criticism*. Vol. 1. Chicago: Swallow Press, 1976.
Handy reference work listing citations of major authors and important novels of the Victorian period, organized alphabetically by author and title. Though the focus is primarily on criticism available in scholarly publications and specialized journals, the volume contains many citations that are readily accessible. Not annotated.

Ford, George, ed. *Victorian Fiction: A Second Guide to Research*. New York: Modern Language Association, 1978. A revised edition of Lionel Stevenson, ed., *Victorian Fiction: A Guide to Research* (Cambridge, Mass.: Harvard University Press, 1964.)
Both editions include an introductory essay surveying available resources for the study of Victorian fiction; essays on individual authors provide details about collections and bibliographies, as well as assessments of biographies and criticism.

Gelman, Robin. *The Novel in the Victorian Age*. Baltimore: Edward Arnold, 1986.
A general guide to Victorian fiction intended to provide a critical and cultural context for study of individual novelists and their works. Organized thematically, it focuses on such topics as "Aristocracy," "Definition of Self," and "The Age of Equipoise."

Gregor, Ian, ed. *Reading the Victorian Novel: Detail into Form*. New York: Barnes & Noble Books, 1980.
Collection of essays discussing individual texts or larger theoretical issues, all focusing on the way readers' reactions to, and opinions of, the Victorian novel are formed by the reading process itself. Attempts to explain both the difficulties and the satisfactions modern readers meet when reading Victorian fiction.

Karl, Frederick R. *A Reader's Guide to the Nineteenth Century Novel.* New York: Farrar, Straus & Giroux, 1964.

An introductory chapter tracing the history of the novel and sketching out a brief theory of fiction is followed by chapters focusing on works of major writers of the period. Also contains a good bibliography of both primary and secondary sources for these novelists.

Kettle, Arnold. *An Introduction to the English Novel*. Vol. 1. New York: Harper & Row, 1960.

Discusses works by several major Victorian novelists as illustrations of ways the writer solved a variety of problems faced by novelists of any period. The focus is on critical examination and evaluation of individual works: form, composition strategies, and treatment of character and theme; assesses the general merits and significance of the novels discussed.

Knoepflmacher, U. C. *Laughter and Despair: Readings in Ten Novels of the Victorian Era*. Berkeley: University of California Press, 1971.

Reads ten representative works to illustrate a general principle of Victorian fiction: the desire to overcome the despair brought on by loss of faith and removal of the props that sustained people's illusions about life. Uses the term "laughter" to describe techniques employed by novelists in battling this despair, such as comedy, sentimentalism, and happy endings. Concentrates on key scenes which suggest the various novels' balance between the extremes of laughter and despair. Offers penetrating analyses of individual works.

Levine, George. *The Realistic Imagination: English Fiction from Frankenstein to Lady Chatterly*. Chicago: University of Chicago Press, 1981.

Scholarly examination of the concept of realism, focusing on the ways novelists such as William Makepeace Thackeray, George Eliot, Anthony Trollope, and Thomas Hardy eventually succeeded in breaking out of conventional molds established by earlier generations of writers, only to have their methods become conventions against which twentieth century writers have rebelled.

Levine, Richard A., ed. *The Victorian Experience: The Novelists*. Athens: Ohio University Press, 1976.

Collection of essays intended to explain what "the Victorian experience" means to the twentieth century reader. In individual chapters, diverse critics review the corpus of several Victorian novelists, explaining how the experience of reading a particular author affects readers; offers reasons that these novelists still demand attention.

Russell, Norman. *The Novelist and Mammon: Literary Responses to the World of Commerce in the Nineteenth Century*. Oxford, England: Clarendon Press, 1986.

Surveys ways the burgeoning capitalist society influenced various nineteenth century novelists. Traces their reactions to important business events and scandals of the day; observes how heroes and villains of the world of commerce become subjects of fiction. Special attention is paid to the influence of such events and people on the work of Charles Dickens, Benjamin Disraeli, Anthony Trollope, and minor novelist Mrs. Catherine Gore.

Springer, Marlene. "Angels and Other Women in Victorian Literature." In *What Manner of Woman: Essays on English and American Life and Literature*, edited by Marlene Springer. New York: New York University Press, 1977.
Excellent overview of the way writers of the period portrayed women in literature; shows how there was a conscious effort to forge and maintain the notion that women were a subordinate sex, superior in morals but incapable of serving as men's equals in other spheres. Other essays in the volume examine the status of women in the literature of other periods.

Stevenson, Lionel, ed. *Victorian Fiction: A Guide to Research*. Cambridge, Mass.: Harvard University Press, 1964.
A collection of bibliographic essays on major and minor figures of the period. Each section sketches the history of critical inquiry into the life and works of individual authors and provides concise summaries of bibliographical, biographical, and editorial information published before the mid-1960's. A good starting point for readers wishing to get a sense of the issues important in a particular author's writings.

Sutherland, J. A. *Victorian Novelists and Publishers*. Chicago: University of Chicago Press, 1976.
Examines the way major nineteenth century publishing houses produced and marketed novels. Part 1 reviews the publishing trade in the middle decades of the century, and part 2 looks at several novelists and books popular in Victorian England to explore ways writers and publishers worked together to produce fiction.

Watson, George, ed. *The New Cambridge Bibliography of English Literature: Vol 3, 1800-1900*. Cambridge, England: Cambridge University Press, 1969.
A detailed reference listing of the works of all major Victorian novelists, including brief publication histories; also contains a selective listing of contemporary reviews and important nineteenth and twentieth century critical studies.

ANNE BRONTË

General Studies

Allott, Miriam. *The Brontës: The Critical Heritage*. London: Routledge & Kegan Paul, 1974.

Excerpts from contemporary reviews illustrating the reception Anne Brontë's novels received when first published; includes critical commentary about the reviews and reviewers, and materials on Anne Brontë's use of the pseudonym Acton Bell. Reprints opinions of Brontë's works by Margaret Oliphant, Algernon Charles Swinburne, Anthony Trollope, and others.

Bentley, Phyllis. *The Brontë Sisters*. Rev. ed. London: Longmans, Green, 1963.

Abbreviated, panoramic view of the life and works of each of the Brontës. A chapter on Anne Brontë offers summaries of her major works. Final chapter attempts to judge the Brontës' overall merits in comparison with other literary figures.

_____ . *The Brontës and Their World*. New York: Viking Press, 1969.

Biography written for the general reader rather than the scholar, giving much attention to family relationships and important friendships; sketches the publication history of the major novels. Heavily illustrated with photographs of family, homes, important locales, and facsimiles of pages from first editions.

Chitham, Edward. Introduction to *The Poems of Anne Brontë: A New Text and Commentary*. Totowa, N.J.: Rowman & Littlefield, 1979.

Attempts to demythologize the Brontës, especially Anne. Includes a brief biographical sketch, emphasizing her years as governess at Thorp Green, which provided background for her novels; discusses her relationship with William Weightman. Detailed account of her poetry.

Chitham, Edward, and Tom Winnifrith. *Brontë Facts and Brontë Problems*. London: Macmillan, 1983.

A collection of essays attempting to separate biographical fact from myth in the lives of all three sisters. Includes chapters on the problems of biography and the influence biography has on the way texts are read. Discusses the relationship between the Brontë sisters and their brother Branwell, and between them and Ellen Nussey.

Evans, Barbara, and G. L. Evans. *The Scribner Companion to the Brontës*. New York: Charles Scribner's Sons, 1982.

An encyclopedia covering the lives and works of the Brontës. Includes sections on Anne Brontë's novels, with commentary, plot synopses, and comments by her contemporaries. Also contains a section on juvenilia.

Ewbank, Inga-Stina. "Anne Brontë: The Woman Writer as Moralist." In her *Their Proper Sphere: A Study of the Brontë Sisters as Early-Victorian Female Novelists*. Cambridge, Mass.: Harvard University Press, 1966.
Examines Anne Brontë's works as attempts to speak about important moral and social issues without being bound by strictures imposed on women novelists in Victorian England. An introductory chapter provides material about the conventions and expectations from which Anne and her sisters struggled to escape.

Gerin, Winifred. *Anne Brontë*. London: Thomas Nelson, 1959.
The first full-length scholarly biography of Anne Brontë. Based on original records, anecdotes, and published sources. Generally sympathetic in dealing with Anne's personal relationships and her artistic endeavors. Illustrated with drawings by Anne and others in the family and with photographs of places important in her life.

Harrison, Ada, and Derek Stanford. *Anne Brontë: Her Life and Work*. London: Methuen, 1959.
Biographical portrait and study of both the poetry and fiction. Attempts to get beyond the impressions of Anne given by her sister Charlotte, from whom most biographical information comes. Discussion of the novels is slight in comparison with analysis of the poetry.

Karl, Frederick. "The Brontës: The Self Defined, Redefined, and Refined." In *The Victorian Experience: The Novelists*, edited by Richard Levine. Athens: Ohio University Press, 1976.
Examines the techniques used by Anne Brontë in her novels to explore the psychological depths of characters; points out parallels between Anne's works and those of her sisters.

Morrison, N. Brysson. *Haworth Harvest: The Story of the Brontës*. New York: Vanguard Press, 1969.
Highly readable biography concentrating on the lives of the three sisters, their friendships, and their work outside Haworth parsonage. Discusses the publication history of the novels.

Pinion, F. B. *A Brontë Companion*. New York: Harper & Row, 1975.
Contains a biographical sketch, critical commentary on the poems and novels, a description of the "Angria" and "Gondal" fantasies written by Anne and her sisters, a glossary of people and places in the novels, and a selected bibliography.

Scott, P. J. M. *Anne Brontë: A New Critical Assessment*. Totowa, N.J.: Barnes & Noble Books, 1983.
Scholarly, revisionist study of Anne Brontë's work, attempting to restore her stature by showing her accomplishments as a novelist; frequent comparisons to the works of her sisters. Believes that Brontë's work has often been ignored because it is overtly Christian.

Watson, Melvin. "Form and Substance in the Brontë Novels." In *From Jane Austen to Joseph Conrad*, edited by R. L. Rathburn and Martin Steinmann. Minneapolis: University of Minnesota Press, 1958.
Overview of all the novels written by the Brontë sisters, examining the ways form and substance are blended to form a unified artistic work. Finds that in neither of her fictional works does Anne achieve satisfactory mastery of her materials.

Williams, Merryn. "The Brontës." In *Women in the English Novel, 1800-1900*. New York: St. Martin's Press, 1984.
Comments that Anne Brontë was not the unassuming, religious woman her sister Charlotte considered her; rather, she was a feminist at heart, creating characters in her novels who challenged conventional roles for women in Victorian England.

Winnifrith, Tom. *The Brontës*. New York: Macmillan, 1977.
Critical study focusing largely on the novels of all three sisters; includes a biographical chapter to help establish differences between the novels and the lives of the women who wrote them.

Agnes Grey

Craik, W. A. *The Brontë Novels*. London: Methuen, 1968.
Explores autobiographical parallels and relationships to novels by Anne's sisters. Sees Anne using the character of the governess, a role with which she was familiar, as a means of examining the larger society. Notes how the pervasiveness of Brontë's moral stance throughout the novel colors both the narrative and the judgments rendered about characters.

Evans, Barbara, and G. L. Evans. *The Scribner Companion to the Brontës*. New York: Charles Scribner's Sons, 1982.
Commentary, plot synopsis, and contemporary criticism of the novel. Considers the novel less imbued with passion than any by Anne's sisters; sees its strength in its simple narration of the plight of governesses in a society that treats them unfairly.

Ewbank, Inga-Stina. "Anne Brontë: The Woman Writer as Moralist." In *Their Proper Sphere: A Study of the Brontë Sisters as Early-Victorian Female Novelists*. Cambridge, Mass.: Harvard University Press, 1966.
Careful analysis of techniques used in *Agnes Grey* to turn autobiography into fiction; notes both the successes and the failures, especially the tendency toward dullness in some scenes. Provides helpful comparisons with other contemporary novels featuring governesses, showing how this work differs in its clear attempt to highlight the special significance of life seen through a governess' eyes.

Gerin, Winifred. "Acton Bell." In her *Anne Brontë*. London: Thomas Nelson, 1959.
Detailed account of the composition and publication of the first edition of the novel, noting the Brontë sisters' plan to have it appear as part of a set including Charlotte's *The Professor* and Emily's *Wuthering Heights*. Insists that, despite autobiographical similarities, the heroine can stand as a fictional character of interest apart from the author.

——————. *The Brontës: Creative Work*. London: Longman, 1974.
Brief commentary on parallels between events in the novel and Brontë's life; cites several nineteenth century critical commentaries. Finds the novel limited in vision, but faithful to events Brontë wishes to report.

Halperin, John, and Janet Kunert. *Plots and Characters in the Fiction of Jane Austen, the Brontës, and George Eliot*. Hamden, Conn.: Archon Books, 1976.
Detailed summary of the plot of the novel, useful for identifying characters and obtaining a grasp of the relationships between incidents in the work. Contains a brief sketch of twenty-one characters who appear in the novel.

Pinion, F. B. *A Brontë Companion*. New York: Harper & Row, 1975.
Discusses the novel as Anne's attempt to expose the injustices done to governesses in Victorian society; notes her criticisms of education for women.

Scott, P. J. M. "*Agnes Grey*: Accommodating Reality." In his *Anne Brontë: A New Critical Assessment*. Totowa, N.J.: Barnes & Noble Books, 1983.
An explication of the novel, focusing on characterization and themes. Careful attention is paid to specific scenes. Argues that the novel is meant to show the necessity of giving all of oneself in relationships and to illustrate the damage thoughtless and selfish people do to others by failing to acknowledge the full human dignity each person possesses.

Winnifrith, Tom. *The Brontës*. New York: Macmillan, 1977.
Argues that insistence on an autobiographical reading prevents the possibility

of seeing the novel as a wide-ranging examination of the plight of governesses in general; attempts to explain the episodic nature of the work without resorting to its parallels with Anne Brontë's life.

The Tenant of Wildfell Hall

Chitham, Edward. "Diverging Twins: Some Clues to *Wildfell Hall*." In Edward Chitham and Tom Winnifrith's *Brontë Facts and Brontë Problems*. London: Macmillan, 1983.
Suggests *The Tenant of Wildfell Hall* may have been intended to serve as a corrective to the portraits of human nature presented in *Wuthering Heights*; notes parallels in characterization and scenes but highlights important differences in the way Anne resolves problems of love, marriage, and infidelity.

Craik, W. A. *The Brontë Novels*. London: Methuen, 1968.
Examines techniques of narration, pointing out parallels to other novels, especially eighteenth century masters of the form. Notes Anne Brontë's willingness to confront directly matters dealing with sexual relationships. Lengthy analysis of two major characters, Helen and Arthur Huntington.

Evans, Barbara, and G. L. Evans. *The Scribner Companion to the Brontës*. New York: Charles Scribner's Sons, 1982.
Commentary on the novel posits that it is better written than *Agnes Grey*; notes the absence of sentimentality in dealing with characters in circumstances that might lead a novelist to be sentimental. Outlines Brontë's multiple moral purposes for writing the book. Also includes plot synopsis and comments from nineteenth century critics.

Ewbank, Inga-Stina. "Anne Brontë: The Woman Writer as Moralist." In her *Their Proper Sphere: A Study of the Brontë Sisters as Early-Victorian Female Novelists*. Cambridge, Mass.: Harvard University Press, 1966.
Critical examination of Brontë's methods of narration, pointing out the problems caused by the multiple-narrator format she has adopted for this story. Notes the many scenes in which Brontë confronts subjects her contemporaries would have thought unsuitable for a work by a woman novelist. Stresses the success Brontë achieves in the psychological portrait of her heroine.

Gerin, Winifred. *The Brontës: Creative Work*. London: Longman, 1974.
Criticizes the novel as propaganda against drunkenness, not a work of art. Notes that nineteenth century critics damned the book for its coarseness in dealing with immoral subjects, especially since these were being handled by a woman. Quotes Brontë's rejoinders to this criticism.

—————————— . *"The Tenant of Wildfell Hall."* In her *Anne Brontë*. London: Thomas Nelson, 1959.

Emphasizes the circumstances surrounding the composition of the novel, especially the sufferings inflicted on Anne and her sisters by her brother Branwell; analyzes characterization in some detail. A subsequent chapter provides summary of critical reaction to this best-seller.

Halperin, John, and Janet Kunert. *Plots and Characters in the Fiction of Jane Austen, the Brontës, and George Eliot*. Hamden, Conn.: Archon Books, 1976.

Extensive summary of the action in the novel, providing details which help readers understand ways Brontë has used the tale-within-the-tale technique to portray her characters and illuminate the plight of her heroine. Also gives brief sketches of the major and minor figures appearing in the novel.

Pinion, F. B. *A Brontë Companion*. New York: Harper & Row, 1975.

Briefly surveys sources and contemporary criticism; more extensive analysis of plot and characterization. Criticizes Anne Brontë's method of narration but finds her a competent stylist.

Scott, P. J. M. *"The Tenant of Wildfell Hall*: Reality's Anarchism."* In his *Anne Brontë: A New Critical Assessment*. Totowa, N.J.: Barnes & Noble Books, 1983.

Acknowledges flaws caused by Brontë's treatment of motivation and her lack of control over her materials, yet sees the work as significant because the author attempts to deal with important Christian, moral issues. Considers the relationship Brontë creates between Helen Huntington and Gilbert Markham as a conscious riposte to her sister Emily's handling of Catherine and Heathcliff in *Wuthering Heights*.

Williams, Merryn. "The Brontës." In her *Women in the English Novel, 1800-1900*. New York: St. Martin's Press, 1984.

Remarks on Brontë's aim in the novel: to challenge conventional expectations for women, especially in respect to their relationships with men. Notes Brontë's questioning of the need for women to sacrifice themselves for family.

Winnifrith, Tom. *The Brontës*. New York: Macmillan, 1977.

Notes parallels between the novel and incidents in the life of Anne's brother Branwell, and similarities between this work and *Wuthering Heights*; argues that the autobiographical reading is too narrow. Discusses the story line that deals with marital infidelity, noting the reaction of both contemporary and later critics to Anne's willingness to confront the issue directly.

CHARLOTTE BRONTË

General Studies

Allott, Miriam. *The Brontës: The Critical Heritage*. London: Routledge & Kegan Paul, 1974.
Selections from contemporary reviews provide insight into the reception of the novels. Also contains critical commentary on the Brontë sisters' efforts to maintain their anonymity and their use of pseudonyms. Includes commentary on the novels from letters and published works of contemporaries such as Anthony Trollope and Margaret Oliphant.

Beer, Patricia. *Reader, I Married Him: A Study of the Women Characters of Jane Austen, Charlotte Brontë, Elizabeth Gaskell, and George Eliot*. London: Macmillan, 1974.
Discusses works of Charlotte Brontë as examples of the way women novelists depicted the social predicament of women during the period in which they wrote. Notes that Charlotte Brontë confronts social change and its implications in all her works. An introductory chapter summarizes the biographical influences on her novels.

Benson, Edward F. *Charlotte Brontë*. New York: Longmans, Green, 1932.
Scholarly study of Charlotte Brontë's life, using available primary and secondary sources; attempts to deal more evenhandedly with the novelist than had earlier biographers, many of whom intentionally suppressed unflattering information.

Bentley, Phyllis. *The Brontë Sisters*. Rev. ed. London: Longmans, Green, 1963.
Brief sketch of the lives of the Brontë sisters; contains a chapter outlining the work and achievements of Charlotte Brontë. A final chapter attempts to place the three sisters in the tradition of English letters.

_____ . *The Brontës and Their World*. New York: Viking Press, 1969.
Biography written for the general reader rather than the scholar, giving much attention to family relationships and to friendships between the Brontës and figures such as Elizabeth Gaskell and Ellen Nussey; sketches the publication history of the major novels. Heavily illustrated with photographs of portraits, homes, locales of interest, and facsimiles of first edition title pages.

Bloom, Harold, ed. *The Brontës*. Modern Critical Views Series. New York: Chelsea House, 1987.
Reprints essays from scholarly journals and chapters from earlier monographs

dealing with various aspects of Charlotte Brontë's artistry. Includes extensive analysis of her aesthetic theory and chapters on the major novels.

Bradby, Godfrey F. "Charlotte Brontë and Mr. Nicholls." In his *The Brontës and Other Essays*. Reprint. Freeport, N.Y.: Books for Libraries Press, 1967.
Largely biographical essay concerning the Reverend Arthur Bell Nicholls' courtship of Charlotte Brontë; reveals something of the strong family ties that influenced Charlotte's writings.

Chitham, Edward and Tom Winnifrith. *Brontë Facts and Brontë Problems*. London: Macmillan, 1983.
Essays dealing with the life and works of all three sisters, designed to separate fact from legend and examine the biographical context within which their poetry and prose was written. Includes a chapter on the relationship between the sisters and Ellen Nussey, with whom Charlotte was especially close, and an essay on the psychological underpinnings of Mr. Rochester in *Jane Eyre*.

Duthie, Enid L. *The Foreign Vision of Charlotte Brontë*. London: Macmillan, 1975.
Examines the way Brontë's early experiences as a governess in Brussels shaped her writings by providing details of characterization and setting as well as metaphors for expressing her ideas. Useful as a study of the way biography is transformed into art.

Evans, Barbara, and G. L. Evans. *The Scribner Companion to the Brontës*. New York: Charles Scribner's Sons, 1982.
Encyclopedic reference guide to the Brontë sisters' lives and writings; includes commentary and plot synopses of Charlotte's writings, a section on her juvenilia, and comments on her work by her contemporaries.

Ewbank, Inga-Stina. "Charlotte Brontë: The Woman Writer as an Author Only." In her *Their Proper Sphere: A Study of the Brontë Sisters as Early-Victorian Female Novelists*. Cambridge, Mass.: Harvard University Press, 1966.
Sketches the evolution of Charlotte Brontë's talents as a novelist as she developed a poetics of fiction based on a firm belief that the goal of the novelist was to represent the truth. Shows how all of her novels illustrate this principle while dealing in some way with the emotional and intellectual needs of her heroines.

Gregor, Ian, ed. *The Brontës: A Collection of Critical Essays*. Englewood Cliffs, N.J.: Prentice-Hall, 1970.
Collection of previously published essays dealing in part with Charlotte Brontë's major works. Includes a discussion of her use of the gothic, an article

on the role of imagination in *Villette*, and a comparative essay focusing on the place of love in *Jane Eyre* and *Wuthering Heights*.

Karl, Frederick R. "The Self Defined, Redefined, and Refined." In *The Victorian Experience: The Novelists*, edited by Richard A. Levine. Athens: Ohio University Press, 1976.
Explores methods the Brontë sisters employ to plumb the psychological depths of their characters while simultaneously creating a sense of mystery about them; shows how all three novelists often achieve their effect through techniques associated with Gothic fiction.

Martin, Hazel T. *Petticoat Rebels: A Study of the Novels of Social Protest of George Eliot, Elizabeth Gaskell, and Charlotte Brontë*. New York: Helios Books, 1968.
Views Charlotte Brontë as one of the few Victorian women novelists willing to rebel against the conventions imposed on female writers; shows how she deals with controversial topics such as religious and moral issues and with "the woman question" — women's rights to a free, productive life in society.

Moglen, Helene. *Charlotte Brontë: The Self Conceived*. New York: W. W. Norton, 1976.
Critical biography examining the interaction of Brontë's life experiences and her works. Pays special attention to the influence of the Romantic impulse in her life and writings, especially the Byronic; explores Brontë's life as an example of the formation of the modern female psyche.

Morrison, N. Brysson. *Haworth Harvest: The Story of the Brontës*. New York: Vanguard Press, 1969.
A biography of the lives of the Brontë family written for the general reader. Details their home lives and friendships outside the parsonage, especially Charlotte's association with Ellen Nussey and Elizabeth Gaskell. Discusses Charlotte's experiences in Belgium. Summarizes the publication history of the novels.

O'Neill, Judith, ed. *Critics on Charlotte and Emily Brontë*. Coral Gables, Fla.: University of Miami Press, 1968.
Collection of previously published essays on the lives and works of the two sisters. A good single source for obtaining an overview of Charlotte Brontë's artistic achievements.

Peters, Margot. *Unquiet Soul: A Biography of Charlotte Brontë*. Garden City, N.Y.: Doubleday, 1975.
Well researched, analytical biography, focusing on both the external circumstances of Brontë's tragic life and on the psychological burdens she was forced

to bear as a result of constraints placed on her as a woman in Victorian England. Individual chapters discuss the major novels in light of this issue.

Pinion, F. B. *A Brontë Companion*. New York: Harper & Row, 1975.
Includes a brief biography of Charlotte Brontë; critical commentary on her poetry and novels; a glossary of characters and settings in the novels; and a sketch of Brontë's nonfiction, especially her commentary on her own writings and her political and moral treatises. Also contains information on the fantasy writings of the three sisters, notes on Elizabeth Gaskell's biography of Charlotte, and a selected bibliography.

Qualls, Barry V. "The Terrible Beauty of Charlotte Brontë's 'Natural Supernaturalism.' " In his *The Secular Pilgrims of Victorian Fiction*. Cambridge, England: Cambridge University Press, 1982.
Views Brontë's works as a form of secular scripture, intended to fulfill the role that biblical texts played in earlier times as sources of moral guidance; sees the Victorian Age as relying on novelists to provide such guidance in their works.

Watson, Melvin. "Form and Substance in the Brontë Novels." In *From Jane Austen to Joseph Conrad*, edited by R. L. Rathburn and Martin Steinmann. Minneapolis: University of Minnesota Press, 1958.
Reviews the seven novels produced by the Brontë sisters, assessing the technical merits of each. Ranks Charlotte's *Jane Eyre* and Emily's *Wuthering Heights* as the only two in which the novelists manage to gain control over their materials to create lasting masterpieces.

Williams, Merryn. "The Brontës." In her *Women in the English Novel, 1800-1900*. New York: St. Martin's Press, 1984.
Surveys Brontë's major novels to show how the novelist dealt with the treatment of Victorian women as appendages to, or property of, the men in their lives. Observes that Lucy Snowe of *Villette* is one of the few Victorian heroines to pursue a career rather than marry.

Winnifrith, Tom. *The Brontës*. New York: Macmillan, 1977.
General survey of the works of Charlotte and her sisters, with emphasis on the novels. Discusses the relationship between the lives of the three novelists and their works to point out important differences; shows how imagination played as important a role as real-life experiences in the creation of all the major works.

Jane Eyre

Berg, Maggie. *Jane Eyre: Portrait of a Life*. Boston: Twayne, 1987.
Book-length analysis of the novel, providing information on historical context and critical reception. Reads the work as a conscious effort to portray Jane Eyre's life as a work of art; notes how Brontë consciously distances herself from the text and uses references to art as a means of defining her heroine in this fictional autobiography.

Craik, W. A. *The Brontë Novels*. London: Methuen, 1968.
Close reading of the text to show how this novel compares favorably with *Wuthering Heights* and others of its genre—the conventional love story—in that Brontë is able to display the passions of her characters finely. Discusses both major and minor characters, focusing on their functions in the story.

Evans, Barbara, and G. L. Evans. *The Scribner Companion to the Brontës*. New York: Charles Scribner's Sons, 1982.
Includes criticism by Brontë's contemporaries and a plot summary. Commentary suggests the novel is especially strong in characterization and plotting, following the traditions of the romance; sees Brontë's particular interest in the figure of the governess in Victorian England as a motivating principle in her depiction of the heroine.

Gerin, Winifred. *The Brontës: Creative Work*. London: Longman, 1974.
Sketches the main elements of the plot and notes the unfavorable reaction the novel received during the nineteenth century from those who thought it offended standards of propriety. Notes Brontë's willingness to treat men and women as equals in matters of passion, and suggests this as being the basis for much of the hostile reaction.

Griffin, Gail. "The Humanization of Edward Rochester." In *Men by Women*, edited by Janet Todd. New York: Holmes & Meier, 1981.
Sees Rochester's actions in incarcerating his first wife as an attempt to imprison his own illicit impulses; finds the novel a working-out of the triangular relationship between the man and the two women whose qualities he admires yet simultaneously fears.

Halperin, John, and Janet Kunert. *Plots and Characters in the Fiction of Jane Austen, the Brontës, and George Eliot*. Hamden, Conn.: Archon Books, 1976.
Careful synopsis of the action of the novel, allowing readers to gain a sense of the major events and understand the importance of various details. Also includes thumbnail sketches of more than forty characters who appear in the work.

Karl, Frederick R. "The Brontës: The Outsider as Protagonist." In his *A Reader's Guide to the Nineteenth Century Novel*. New York: Farrar, Straus & Giroux, 1964.
   Detailed explication of the novel's major themes, focusing on both the love story and the social injustices which concern Brontë. Heavy emphasis on character analysis, especially of the heroine.

Linder, Cynthia A. *Romantic Imagery in the Novels of Charlotte Brontë*. London: Methuen, 1978.
   Examination of character, setting, and incident to determine the success with which Brontë fused elements of the Romantic tradition to form a coherent narrative. Shows how Brontë uses external objects as correlatives for her heroine's inner feelings.

Martin, Hazel T. *Petticoat Rebels: A Study of the Novels of Social Protest of George Eliot, Elizabeth Gaskell, and Charlotte Brontë*. New York: Helios Books, 1968.
   Considers Brontë's heroine as a totally new kind of woman in fiction, one who asserts her right to love whomever she chooses, on her own terms. Notes the consternation the novel caused by upsetting conventional notions of male-female relationships in Victorian England.

Martin, R. B. *The Accents of Persuasion: Charlotte Brontë's Novels*. London: Faber & Faber, 1966.
   Examines the novel as a study of the maturation of its central characters, Jane and Rochester. Careful analysis of key scenes shows how Jane achieves stability and grows in genuine love for Rochester. Notes importance of setting and use of elements from the tradition of the romance.

Moglen, Helene. "*Jane Eyre*: The Creation of a Feminist Myth." In her *Charlotte Brontë: The Self Conceived*. New York: W. W. Norton, 1976.
   Suggests that because Jane has no inherent status or power, she is free of the conventions normally imposed on women in Victorian England; hence, she can test the limits to which a woman might be able to go in seeking self-fulfillment. The novel is a revelation of Jane's testing her inner strength against social constraints.

Pinion, F. B. *A Brontë Companion*. New York: Harper & Row, 1975.
   Careful plot analysis, frequently drawing parallels between details of Brontë's life and events in the novel. Discusses Brontë's use of sensational elements, her handling of religious questions, and her method of narration.

Roberts, Doreen. "*Jane Eyre* and 'The Warped System of Things.' " In *Reading the Victorian Novel: Detail into Form*, edited by Ian Gregor. New York: Barnes & Noble Books, 1980.

Accounts for the strong reaction readers have to Brontë's works by examining the style of this novel, showing how it provides a turbulent reading experience which upsets the reader's sense of balance; illustrates how characters act passionately, and how readers are polarized in their opinion of these characters by Brontë's narrative method.

Tillotson, Kathleen. *Novels of the Eighteen Forties*. Oxford, England: Clarendon Press, 1954.
Suggests that the novel is Brontë's greatest achievement because in it she masters the autobiographical strains that make up the basis of the work; examines the work as a phenomenon of the decade in which it was published.

Winnifrith, Tom. *The Brontës*. New York: Macmillan, 1977.
Notes fluctuation in critical assessments of the work; explains how weaknesses in handling characterization are offset by careful control of the story through devices such as recurring patterns of imagery. Argues that Brontë's aim throughout is to show the difficulties of balancing competing forces of altruism and selfishness.

_____ "Charlotte Brontë and Mr. Rochester." In Edward Chitham and Tom Winnifrith's *Brontë Facts and Brontë Problems*. London: Macmillan, 1983.
Reproduces a hitherto unpublished poem from a Brontë manuscript to show similarities between its hero and Rochester. Speculates on the autobiographical nature of both works, strengthening earlier writers' claims that *Jane Eyre* is heavily indebted to Brontë's real-life experiences.

Shirley

Beer, Patricia. *Reader, I Married Him: A Study of the Women Characters of Jane Austen, Charlotte Brontë, Elizabeth Gaskell, and George Eliot*. London: Macmillan, 1974.
Sees the novel as Brontë's examination of the status of women in her society; notes the feminist leanings of the author, whose heroine has many of the characteristics of a proto-feminist leader.

Craik, W. A. *The Brontë Novels*. London: Methuen, 1968.
Critical examination of Brontë's use of third-person point-of-view and its effects on the way she is able to control her materials and manipulate the reader. Notes parallels with *Jane Eyre* but acknowledges the greater complexity of plot and the greater number of characters; discusses characterization at length. Points out problems Brontë had in connecting plot and theme.

Evans, Barbara, and G. L. Evans. *The Scribner Companion to the Brontës*. New York: Charles Scribner's Sons, 1982.

In addition to a plot summary, list of characters, and comments from Brontë's contemporaries, this volume provides an analysis of the novel as a kind of documentary of the effects of social changes as England moved from an agrarian to an industrial economy. Notes the concurrent importance of the love story in the work; considers Brontë successful in creating characters with deft verbal sketches.

Gerin, Winifred. *The Brontës: Creative Work*. London: Longman, 1974.

Attributes many of the failures of composition to the tragic circumstances which occurred in the Brontë family while Charlotte was writing the novel. Considers the work faulty in both plotting and characterization.

Halperin, John, and Janet Kunert. *Plots and Characters in the Fiction of Jane Austen, the Brontës, and George Eliot*. Hamden, Conn.: Archon Books, 1976.

Plot summary detailing the action and offering insight into the characters' motivations; useful for readers wishing to grasp the complex relationships among the many characters who appear in the novel. Also provides brief descriptions of over fifty characters.

Linder, Cynthia A. *Romantic Imagery in the Novels of Charlotte Brontë*. London: Macmillan, 1978.

Attempts to explain the ways this novel differs from *Jane Eyre* in both intent and composition; argues the work is best judged on its own terms, as a social novel aimed at exploring the theme of feminism through the character of Shirley Keeldar, whose attributes mirror those of the Romantic hero.

Martin, Hazel T. *Petticoat Rebels: A Study of the Novels of Social Protest of George Eliot, Elizabeth Gaskell, and Charlotte Brontë*. New York: Helios Books, 1968.

Extensive examination of the social background informing the novel: marriage customs and conventions that, coupled with limits placed on the kinds of employment unmarried women could seek, drive Brontë to create a heroine whose actions are a vivid protest against those strictures.

Martin, R. B. *The Accents of Persuasion: Charlotte Brontë's Novels*. London: Faber & Faber, 1966.

Observes the tension between romance and realism within the work. Sees similar tensions between pairs of characters, especially Caroline Helstone and Shirley Keeldar, who illustrate a central issue of the novel: the problem of women's status in society.

Moglen, Helene. "*Shirley*: Feminism and Power." In her *Charlotte Brontë: The Self Conceived*. New York: W. W. Norton, 1976.

Rejects earlier criticism faulting Brontë for loose construction or flaws in plotting and characterization; sees the novel as a mature attempt to deal directly with an important social issue, the oppression of women by society through various agencies and organizations.

Pinion, F. B. *A Brontë Companion*. New York: Harper & Row, 1975.
Concentrates on background and composition, especially Brontë's attempts to satisfy criticism leveled against *Jane Eyre*. Discusses problems with the novel's unity and with the contrived happy ending.

Winnifrith, Tom. *The Brontës*. New York: Macmillan, 1977.
Careful review of the story line, showing how Brontë deals with issues such as the plight of governesses and, through a study of these young women's fortunes, the limitations imposed on women as a group in Victorian society. Reviews Brontë's method of creating pairs of characters in conflict with one another.

Villette

Craik, W. A. *The Brontë Novels*. London: Macmillan, 1968.
Discusses the technical merits and flaws in characterization, plotting, handling of dialogue and setting. Considerable discussion of the heroine, who is considered similar in psychological temperament to Charlotte Brontë herself.

Evans, Barbara, and G. L. Evans. *The Scribner Companion to the Brontës*. New York: Charles Scribner's Sons, 1982.
Considers Brontë especially adept at re-creating the scenes of Brussels as a backdrop for the novel; also notes the wider range of characters than in any previous Brontë novel. Finds the portrait of Lucy Snowe particularly poignant as a study of mental collapse and recovery.

Gerin, Winifred. *The Brontës: Creative Work*. London: Longman, 1974.
Details the hardships and tragedies in Brontë's life which find their way into the novel. Sees its themes of isolation and despair springing from Brontë's resignation to a life of sorrow. Surveys the characters in the novel to show how Brontë realized her intention through them.

Halperin, John, and Janet Kunert. *Plots and Characters in the Fiction of Jane Austen, the Brontës, and George Eliot*. Hamden, Conn.: Archon Books, 1976.
Synopsis of the major story line, focusing on the significance of individual incidents as they relate to the heroine. Contains more than thirty abbreviated character sketches.

Linder, Cynthia A. *Romantic Imagery in the Novels of Charlotte Brontë*. London: Methuen, 1978.

Concentrates on Brontë's complex structure to explain how the novel succeeds in dealing with the tragedy of Lucy Snowe's love affair. Shows Brontë effectively using the opposition of organizations such as the Church to her heroine's love for a married man to raise that love to the level of Romantic passion, which is considered greater than any other feeling.

Martin, R. B. *The Accents of Persuasion: Charlotte Brontë's Novels*. London: Faber & Faber, 1966.

Considers the novel a statement on the inevitability of suffering; posits that Brontë accepts the notion without rancor. Notes the importance of Christianity within the work. Careful examination of characterization and plotting, showing Brontë's focus remains throughout on seeing her heroine come to some understanding of herself.

Moglen, Helene. "*Villette*: The Romantic Experience as Psychoanalysis." In her *Charlotte Brontë: The Self Conceived*. New York: W. W. Norton, 1976.

Views this as Brontë's most autobiographical novel, in which she tries through the medium of fiction to make sense of her own life: both the past, with its psychologically devastating affair with Constantine Heger, and the present, with its isolation. Sees the sad ending as Brontë's uncompromising acceptance of life as it really is.

Pinion, F. B. *A Brontë Companion*. New York: Harper & Row, 1975.

Extensive analysis of characters, especially the heroine; notes Brontë's use of personal experiences and previously written materials (from *The Professor*), but cites examples where she injects her imaginative power to control and shape her materials.

Winnifrith, Tom. *The Brontës*. New York: Macmillan, 1975.

Discusses the heavy autobiographical strain of the work, which may explain some of its structural flaws. Detailed analysis of the plot shows how Brontë achieves some success in characterization, especially with Paul Emmanuel. Discusses the importance of fate in the novel.

EMILY BRONTË

General Studies

Allott, Miriam. *The Brontës: The Critical Heritage*. London: Routledge & Kegan
Paul, 1974.
Excerpts from criticism by Brontë's contemporaries, including critical commentary on *Wuthering Heights*. Discusses the influence the Brontës' family life
at Haworth Parsonage had on Emily's writings.

Bentley, Phyllis. *The Brontë Sisters*. London: Longmans, Green, 1963.
Short overview of the lives of all three Brontë sisters; an individual chapter
provides a review of Emily's work, focusing on *Wuthering Heights*. Concluding
chapter offers an assessment of the Brontë sisters' place in the English literary
tradition.

_____ . *The Brontës and Their World*. New York: Viking Press, 1969.
Biography written for the general reader rather than the scholar, giving details
of family relationships; sketches the publication history of *Wuthering Heights*.
Heavily illustrated with photos of family homes, important locales in the
novels, and portraits.

Benvenuto, Richard. *Emily Brontë*. Boston: Twayne, 1982.
Biographical and critical study of Brontë's works. Includes chapters on the
Gondal saga, the poetry, and *Wuthering Heights*. Also includes a selected
bibliography of criticism.

Bloom, Harold, ed. *The Brontës*. New York: Chelsea House, 1987.
Anthology of previously published articles and chapters from books; includes
essays on Brontë's narrative technique in *Wuthering Heights* and a comparative essay focusing on the aesthetic theories of Emily and her sister
Charlotte.

Bradby, Godfrey F. "Emily Brontë." In his *The Brontës and Other Essays*. Reprint.
Freeport, N.Y.: Books for Libraries Press, 1967.
Sketches the inner struggles Brontë faced living with her father and siblings at
Haworth and the ways she displayed her rebellion through her imagination in
her poetry and in *Wuthering Heights*.

Chitham, Edward, and Tom Winnifrith. *Brontë Facts and Brontë Problems*.
London: Macmillan, 1983.

A collection of essays highlighting the biographical and psychological background of works by all three Brontës. Attempts to separate misinformation from fact. Five chapters are devoted almost exclusively to Emily's poetry and prose, including one on the history of the composition of *Wuthering Heights*.

Evans, Barbara, and G. L. Evans. *The Scribner Companion to the Brontës*. New York: Charles Scribner's Sons, 1982.

An encyclopedia covering the lives and works of the Brontë family, focusing on novels of the sisters. Includes sections on family members, juvenilia (especially the Angria and Gondal stories), and selections on Emily's publications, including a synopsis and a list of characters and places in her novel.

Ewbank, Inga-Stina. "Emily Brontë: The Woman Writer as Poet." In her *Their Proper Sphere: A Study of the Brontë Sisters as Early-Victorian Female Novelists*. Cambridge, Mass.: Harvard University Press, 1966.

Assesses Brontë's literary career against a larger background: the status of women writers in Victorian England. Notes how, in both her poetry and prose, Brontë deals less with specifically feminist issues than with questions touching on human feelings in general: loneliness, freedom, enslavement, conformity, and rebellion.

Gregor, Ian, ed. *The Brontës: A Collection of Critical Essays*. Englewood Cliffs, N.J.: Prentice-Hall, 1970.

Essays excerpted from journals and monographs; more than half are devoted to analysis of *Wuthering Heights*, including studies discussing the novel's structure, examining the importance of particular images, and comparing Brontë's handling of the love story with her sister Charlotte's treatment of the same issue in *Jane Eyre*.

Karl, Frederick R. "The Brontës: The Self Defined, Redefined, and Refined." In *The Victorian Experience: The Novelists*, edited by Richard A. Levine. Athens: Ohio University Press, 1976.

Discusses the way Emily and her sisters sought to enclose their characters in isolated worlds (both inner and outer), simultaneously revealing the psychological depths of their creations; points out similarities of technique in various novels by the three sisters.

Morrison, N. Brysson. *Haworth Harvest: The Story of the Brontës*. New York: Vanguard Press, 1969.

Biography aimed at the general reader, detailing the lives of the Brontës; discusses their home life and their relationships outside the parsonage. Notes the influence of their personal experiences on their work.

O'Neill, Judith, ed. *Critics on Charlotte and Emily Brontë*. Coral Gables, Fla.: University of Miami Press, 1968.

Anthology of criticism by nineteenth and twentieth century reviewers and scholars, excerpted from previously published works; selections outline Emily Brontë's aesthetic theory and discuss the structure, characterization, and themes of *Wuthering Heights*.

Pinion, F. B. *A Brontë Companion*. New York: Harper & Row, 1975.

Contains a biographical sketch; details the fantasy world created by Emily and her sisters. Critical analysis of Emily's poems and of *Wuthering Heights*; notes on the characters and the setting of the novel. An appendix outlines a possible source of the work. Contains a selected bibliography of secondary sources.

Watson, Melvin. "Form and Substance in the Brontë Novels." In *From Jane Austen to Joseph Conrad*, edited by R. L. Rathburn and Martin Steinmann. Minneapolis: University of Minnesota Press, 1958.

General assessment of the technical merits of the seven Brontë novels, focusing on the writers' ability to achieve an appropriate blend of form and substance. Finds *Wuthering Heights* and *Jane Eyre* the only two in which that combination is fully successful.

Williams, Merryn. "The Brontës." In her *Women in the English Novel, 1800-1900*. New York: St. Martin's Press, 1984.

Brief commentary on Emily Brontë's oblique handling of issues dealing with the status of women in Victorian society. Reads *Wuthering Heights* as an exploration of the impact of patriarchal values on both men and women.

Winnifrith, Tom. *The Brontës*. New York: Macmillan, 1977.

Scholarly assessment of the Brontë sisters' novels, presented in the context of their lives and their other works, such as juvenilia and poetry. Special emphasis on the differences between the lives of the writers and events depicted in the novels.

Wuthering Heights

Benvenuto, Richard. "*Wuthering Heights*: Finding the Uses of Creation." In his *Emily Brontë*. Boston: Twayne, 1982.

Sees the novel as Brontë's attempt to examine timeless psychological qualities of human existence. Shows how the structure of the book parallels this psychological dimension, with its divisions and attempts at unifying opposites. Explains the function of Nelly Dean in the work.

Craik, W. A. *The Brontë Novels*. London: Methuen, 1968.
Focuses on major characters in the novel, illustrating how they defy conventional moral standards yet maintain readers' sympathies. Detailed examination of numerous scenes displays Brontë's ability to portray powerful human feelings that exist in everyone but are often repressed.

Daleski, H. M. "*Wuthering Heights*: The Whirl of Contraries." In his *The Divided Heroine: A Recurrent Pattern in Six English Novels*. New York: Holmes & Meier, 1984.
Explication of the novel as exemplar of a particular pattern used to illustrate problems of self-division common to human experience: the love triangle in which one woman genuinely loves both men who seek her affections. Considers the second half of the novel an antidote to the disintegration that results from Catherine's disastrous passion for Heathcliff in the first half.

Evans, Barbara, and G. L. Evans. *The Scribner Companion to the Brontës*. New York: Charles Scribner's Sons, 1982.
Ranks the novel with *War and Peace* as the two best at portraying the human emotions associated with love and hate. Sees the groundswell of criticism arising because readers cannot determine Brontë's attitude toward her characters, and because her men and women, seemingly ill-matched, have such passion for each other.

Ewbank, Inga-Stina. "Emily Brontë: The Woman Writer as Poet." In her *Their Proper Sphere: A Study of the Brontë Sisters as Early-Victorian Female Novelists*. Cambridge, Mass.: Harvard University Press, 1966.
Excellent brief summary of critical attitudes toward the novel. Uses Brontë's poetry to illustrate the thesis that, despite the preponderance of critical commentary refuting the notion, Brontë does wish her characters to be judged by moral standards. Provides detailed analysis of narrative techniques to show how Brontë provides grounds for such judgment.

Gerin, Winifred. *The Brontës: Creative Work*. London: Longman, 1974.
Explains Brontë's themes and methods of composition by noting similarities between the novel and the poetry Brontë was writing at the same time. Considers the novel's primary aim the exploration of eternal questions about human life and values; claims it is not tied exclusively to nineteenth century social or moral concerns.

Gose, Elliot B. *Imagination Indulged: The Irrational in the Nineteenth-Century Novel*. Montreal: McGill-Queens University Press, 1972.
Traces the fairy-tale elements in the novel, noting how Brontë gives such details symbolic significance. Detailed character analysis shows Brontë bridging the gap the between fairy tale (romance) and the realism expected of novelists.

Halperin, John, and Janet Kunert. *Plots and Characters in the Fiction of Jane Austen, the Brontës, and George Eliot*. Hamden, Conn.: Archon Books, 1976.
Summary of the novel, carefully presented to emphasize both the strength of characterization and the importance of the two narrators; also provides descriptions of major characters, offering highly detailed biographical sketches of Heathcliff, Catherine, and Lockwood.

Karl, Frederick R. "The Brontës: The Outsider as Protagonist." In his *A Reader's Guide to the Nineteenth Century British Novel*. New York: Farrar, Straus & Giroux, 1964.
Detailed analysis of major characters in the novel, especially Heathcliff. Compares the novel both to its predecessors and to selected twentieth century works to show its anomalous nature as a tale containing elements of various fictional traditions such as the gothic and the existential novel.

Kiely, Robert. *The Romantic Novel in England*. Cambridge, Mass.: Harvard University Press, 1972.
Sees the work as the finest Romantic novel in English. Traces Brontë's use of conventions of Romanticism; illustrates her ability to handle her subject without overtly calling attention to that tradition. Detailed examination of structure and character.

Knoepflmacher, U. C. "*Wuthering Heights*: A Tragicomic Romance." In his *Laughter and Despair: Readings in Ten Novels of the Victorian Era*. Berkeley: University of California Press, 1971.
Discusses Brontë's use of the narrator Lockwood as a means of giving readers a familiar point of entry into the strange world of the major characters in the story. Traces the ways Brontë makes use of conventions of the comic tradition to ground her novel in reality.

Miller, J. Hillis. *The Disappearance of God: Five Nineteenth Century Writers*. Cambridge, Mass.: Belknap Press, 1963.
Considers Brontë's attempts to deal with a world in which traditional notions of God no longer hold currency. Sees *Wuthering Heights* as the novelist's struggle to reveal her private vision of the world while trying to keep her vision from the public. Emphasizes parallels with religious tracts.

Paris, Bernard J. " 'Hush, hush! He's a human being': A Psychological Approach to Heathcliff." In *Men by Women*, edited by Janet Todd. New York: Holmes & Meier, 1981.
Uses contemporary psychological theory to argue that Brontë's bestial hero is actually a human being reacting in frustration to hurts inflicted on him by others. Stresses the importance of the genuine love Heathcliff feels for Catherine as a motivating factor for all his actions.

Parker, Patricia. "The (Self) Identity of the Literary Text." In her *Literary Fat Ladies: Rhetoric, Gender, Property*. New York: Methuen, 1987.
Uses poststructuralist literary theory to explore reasons that the novel has received such attention from formalist critics and from those concerned with explaining the social and cultural implications of Heathcliff's plight. Emphasis on critical conceptions of reading dynamics and textuality.

Phelps, Gilbert. *A Reader's Guide to Fifty British Novels, 1600-1900*. New York: Barnes & Noble Books, 1979.
Brief biographical sketch and plot summary. Critical commentary argues that the novel is essentially a tragedy in prose; focus is on the seemingly natural qualities of the characters, whose passion and actions extend beyond the bounds of the realistic.

Pinion, F. B. *A Brontë Companion*. New York: Harper & Row, 1975.
Discusses sources and style. Detailed analysis of plot, setting, and characters; explains the significance of violence and of the extraordinary within the work.

Sale, William M., ed. *Wuthering Heights*. New York: W. W. Norton, 1963.
A Norton Critical Edition of the novel containing essays on a variety of topics: explanations of Brontë's method of creation, analyses of the structure of the work, and discussions of the function and effects of multiple narrators. Also provides excerpts of contemporary reviews.

Vogler, Thomas A., ed. *Twentieth-Century Interpretations of Wuthering Heights*. Englewood Cliffs, N.J.: Prentice-Hall, 1968.
Handy collection of excerpts and short articles providing a wide spectrum of critical commentary illuminating Brontë's methods of narration, characterization, description, and development of themes.

Winnifrith, Tom. *The Brontës*. New York: Macmillan, 1977.
Deals with the inadequacy of earlier readings of the novel by pointing out the complexity of the relationships among the characters in the story, especially the bond between Catherine and Heathcliff. Includes some discussion of the way setting is used to suggest differing value systems.

——————— . "*Wuthering Heights*: One Volume or Two?" In Edward Chitham and Tom Winnifrith's *Brontë Facts and Brontë Problems*. London: Macmillan, 1983.
Speculates on the possibility that Brontë may have originally planned a longer novel and then reduced it to its one-volume size to fit as part of a three-volume set with her sisters' works.

WILKIE COLLINS

General Studies

Ashley, Robert. "Wilkie Collins." In *Victorian Fiction: A Guide to Research*, edited by Lionel Stevenson. Cambridge, Mass.: Harvard University Press, 1964.
Brief, useful bibliographical essay summarizing scholarship written before 1962. Contains a review of criticism, a summary of important biographies and biographical essays, notices of editions and collections of letters, and information on available bibliographies of Collins' writings.

Beetz, Kirk H. *Wilkie Collins: An Annotated Bibliography, 1889-1976*. Metuchen, N.J.: Scarecrow Press, 1978.
Annotated list of criticism covering all of Collins' major works. Entries are organized under such topics as "Biographical," "Assessments of Collins' Life and Works," "Influences on Collins." Both monographs and periodical articles are cited. Useful for those wishing to explore particular subjects in greater detail.

Blair, David. "Wilkie Collins and the Crisis of Suspense." In *Reading the Victorian Novel: Detail into Form*, edited by Ian Gregor. New York: Barnes & Noble Books, 1980.
Uses Collins' work, especially *Armadale* (1866), to illustrate the ways Victorian writers of thrillers manipulate their readers; shows how mystery and suspense affect the reader's apprehension of a work and outlines the relationship between the details of a novel and its formal structure.

Davis, Nuel Pharr. *The Life of Wilkie Collins*. Urbana: University of Illinois Press, 1956.
Full-length scholarly biography, explaining the relationship between events of Collins' life and his fiction. Relies heavily on the testimony of Collins' contemporaries to construct a portrait of the novelist as a writer and a man. Contains an insightful introduction by noted scholar Gordon N. Ray.

Elwin, Malcolm. *Victorian Wallflowers*. Port Washington, N.Y.: Kennikat Press, 1934.
Biographical sketch of Collins, focusing on his relationship with Charles Dickens and exploring their collaborative efforts while working on various magazines. Brief mention of Collins' major works, with some assessments of *The Woman in White* and *The Moonstone*.

Hughes, Winifred. "Wilkie Collins: The Triumph of the Detective." In her *The Maniac in the Cellar: Sensation Novels of the 1860s*. Princeton, N.J.: Princeton University Press, 1980.
Sees Collins advancing the art of the sensation novel by exploring its philosophical implications in his works. Shows how, without losing sight of his primary purpose (to tell a captivating story), Collins is able to achieve artistic merit through control of his materials.

Lonoff, Sue. *Wilkie Collins and his Victorian Readers: A Study in the Rhetoric of Authorship*. New York: AMS Press, 1982.
Explores the ways Collins was influenced by his readers; shows how reader reaction affected his plotting, characterization, and choice of settings. Separate chapters focus on the importance of certain readers (such as Charles Dickens), Collins' concern for reader response, his views toward subjects such as women. Includes a detailed exegesis of *The Moonstone* as an example of Collins' method of composition.

Marshall, William H. *Wilkie Collins*. New York: Twayne, 1970.
Critical review of Collins' work as a novelist, focusing on the major publications; shows Collins has often been oversimplified by his critics. A concluding chapter provides a general assessment of Collins' achievements. Includes a chronology and a selected bibliography of criticism.

Page, Norman. *Wilkie Collins: The Critical Heritage*. Boston: Routledge & Kegan Paul, 1974.
Commentary on the major works is given in excerpts from nineteenth century reviews of Collins' novels, and from letters written by Collins' contemporaries. Contains a bibliography of primary and secondary sources.

Peterson, Audrey. "Wilkie Collins and the Mystery Novel." In her *Victorian Masters of Mystery*. New York: Frederick Ungar, 1984.
Biographical sketch highlighting many of the problems scholars have had in collecting information about Collins. Surveys early works, showing Collins' growth as a suspense novelist. Detailed discussions of *The Woman in White* and *The Moonstone*.

Robinson, Kenneth. *Wilkie Collins: A Biography*. New York: Macmillan, 1952.
Carefully researched, full-scale life study, illustrated with photos and facsimiles of manuscripts. Individual chapters discuss Collins' relationship with Charles Dickens and provide commentary on the major novels.

Sayers, Dorothy. *Wilkie Collins: A Critical and Biographical Study*, edited by E. R. Gregory. Toledo, Ohio: Friends of the University of Toledo Libraries, 1977.

Partially completed biography of Collins by an admirer famous in her own right as a mystery writer; carefully researched and based on manuscripts, letters, and records from Collins' day. In the introduction, the editor explains Sayers' debt to Collins.

Williams, Merryn. "The Male Image of Women." In her *Women in the English Novel, 1800-1900*. New York: St. Martin's Press, 1984.
Brief survey of Collins' major novels reveals his unconventional attitude toward women: he had genuine respect for their intelligence and capabilities, and often made them the strongest, most resourceful characters in his fiction.

The Moonstone

Hughes, Winifred. "Wilkie Collins: The Triumph of the Detective." In her *The Maniac in the Cellar: Sensation Novels of the 1860s*. Princeton, N.J.: Princeton University Press, 1980.
Demonstrates how Collins' concern for form led him to create this novel, the first detective thriller. Shows that Collins' need to find reason in the chance occurrences of life can be satisfied within the limits of this genre. Sees the novel as a retreat from attempts to solve universal moral problems; in this work, Collins contents himself with solving a single intellectual conundrum.

Lonoff, Sue. "*The Moonstone* and Its Audience." In her *Wilkie Collins and His Victorian Readers: A Study in the Rhetoric of Authorship*. New York: AMS Press, 1982.
Uses the novel to explore the way Collins considered his readers' desires when he was creating fiction. Reviews the genesis of the work, considering both the events of Collins' life and the literary sources that inspired him. Examines Collins' methods of plotting and critiques the structure, noting the complex, subtle system of symbols Collins interweaves throughout this detective story.

Marshall, William. "The Major Novels, 1868-70." In his *Wilkie Collins*. New York: Twayne, 1970.
Offers an explanation for the novel's popularity as a work of detective fiction. Suggests that it is also a serious study of the workings of the unconscious. Finds Collins' method of using several narrators particularly suited to the kind of psychological depths he wished to explore in this work.

Miller, D. A. "From *roman policier* to *roman-police*: Wilkie Collins' *The Moonstone*." In his *The Novel and the Police*. Berkeley: University of California Press, 1988.

Intriguing, sophisticated analysis of the novel as an example of the way a community responds to the presence of outside forces that impose their power on it. Sees the community within the novel overcoming the organized police through their collective powers to police themselves and restore order. Also investigates Collins' method of narration, employing techniques of poststructuralist literary theory, especially that of Mikhail Bakhtin.

Page, Norman. *Wilkie Collins: The Critical Heritage*. Boston: Routledge & Kegan Paul, 1974.
Excerpts from six reviews published immediately after the novel was released; also contains comments on the novel by Charles Dickens, who criticizes its lack of structure. Other reviews note Collins' mastery of suspense.

Peterson, Audrey. "Wilkie Collins and the Mystery Novel." In her *Victorian Masters of Mystery*. New York: Frederick Ungar, 1984.
Assessment of characters in the novel, especially the detective, Sergeant Cuff. Also reviews Collins' use of various devices to create suspense within the work, especially buried information, guilt of the least likely suspect, and ironclad alibis.

Robinson, Kenneth. *Wilkie Collins: A Biography*. New York: Macmillan, 1952.
Reviews the highly stressful conditions under which Collins composed the weekly installments of the novel for *All the Year Round* magazine. Critical analysis focuses on the work as the first detective novel; reviews Collins' sources and his use of multiple narrators.

The Woman in White

Davis, Nuel Pharr. *The Life of Wilkie Collins*. Urbana: University of Illinois Press, 1956.
Within the context of a larger biographical narrative, Davis provides an extensive sketch of the genesis of the novel and of Collins' method of composition. Notes the effects of the novel's tremendous popularity and the many allusions to it in the works of Collins' contemporaries.

Hughes, Winifred. "Wilkie Collins: The Triumph of the Detective." In her *The Maniac in the Cellar: Sensation Novels of the 1860s*. Princeton, N.J.: Princeton University Press, 1980.
Discusses the ways Collins uses foreshadowing, premonition, and happenstance to create suspense but also to suggest a governing intelligence behind the events occurring in the work. Details the conflict both in action and in moral outlook between the central male characters, Hartright and Count Fosco.

Marshall, William. "The Major Novels, 1860-66." In his *Wilkie Collins*. New York: Twayne, 1970.
Extensive character analysis, especially of the villain, Count Fosco, who is compared to Satan in John Milton's *Paradise Lost*. Notes Collins' ability to give psychological depth to his characters, an aspect largely achieved by constructing the tale as a compilation of records, diaries, and other fragments which give rise to dramatic irony.

Miller, D. A. "*Cage aux folles*: Sensation and Gender in Wilkie Collins' *The Woman in White*." In his *The Novel and the Police*. Berkeley: University of California Press, 1988.
Demonstrates ways the novel works upon the nerves of the readers; stresses the importance of sensations generated by the reading experience itself, claiming the creation of such feelings is one of Collins' major goals for the work. Discusses the subtext of male domination in the novel, ranging far afield to gather examples from other works to show how this novel challenges accepted norms of male domination in ways that make readers uncomfortable.

Page, Norman. *Wilkie Collins: The Critical Heritage*. Boston: Routledge & Kegan Paul, 1974.
Excerpts from letters by George Meredith, Charles Dickens, and Edward FitzGerald. Selections from twelve reviews, including ones by Margaret Oliphant, William Makepeace Thackeray, and Henry James.

Peterson, Audrey. "Wilkie Collins and the Mystery Novel." In her *Victorian Masters of Mystery*. New York: Frederick Ungar, 1984.
Traces Collins' use of various plotting and narrative devices to create suspense in the novel. Brief character analysis. Also reviews the immediate success of the work and points out parallels between it and Robert Browning's *The Ring and the Book*.

Phelps, Gilbert. *A Reader's Guide to Fifty English Novels 1600-1900*. New York: Barnes & Noble Books, 1979.
Brief biographical sketch and plot summary. Critical commentary outlines Collins' use of gothic conventions and his reliance on sensationalism to heighten the reader's interest; outlines ways in which this novel is a prototype of detective fiction.

Robinson, Kenneth. *Wilkie Collins: A Biography*. New York: Macmillan, 1952.
Discusses the genesis of the novel and its immediate popular success, both in serial form and as a book. A brief analysis stresses Collins' ability to create believable characters.

CHARLES DICKENS

General Studies

Bloom, Harold, ed. *Charles Dickens*. New York: Chelsea House, 1987.
Fourteen previously published essays provide a spectrum of criticism covering three decades. Includes selections on most of the major novels as well as chapters from texts or articles focusing on topics common throughout Dickens' fiction.

Brown, Ivor. *Dickens and his World*. New York: Henry Z. Walck, 1970.
Short presentation of the essentials of Dickens' life, followed by a discussion of the Victorian literary scene. Surveys the works of various nineteenth century writers; sketches the social and political climate, and the growth of materialism. Heavily illustrated; especially good for high school students as an introduction to Dickens and his times.

Cockshut, A. O. J. *The Imagination of Charles Dickens*. New York: New York University Press, 1962.
Through a study of the major novels, attempts to account for Dickens' position as both a popular cult figure in the nineteenth century and as a writer of truly classic fiction. Examines Dickens' works chronologically, with separate chapters devoted to seven of the novels (*Dombey and Son*, *David Copperfield*, *Bleak House*, *Hard Times*, *Little Dorrit*, *Great Expectations*, and *Our Mutual Friend*).

Collins, Philip. *Dickens and Crime*. Bloomington: Indiana University Press, 1962.
Scholarly investigation of Dickens' fascination with crime and criminals. Surveys the occurrences of criminals, criminal activities, and the consequences of crime in Dickens' works. Highlights the novelist's portrayal of famous prisons such as Newgate, the Marshalsea, and the Bastille; discusses his attitude toward the courts and the police; and reviews his treatment of the character of the murderer.

——————— , ed. *Dickens: The Critical Heritage*. Boston: Routledge & Kegan Paul, 1971.
Selections from reviews of Dickens' works by his contemporaries; excerpts from letters and diaries of important literary figures and from many others who knew Dickens personally. Valuable starting point for those interested in the critical history of Dickens' works or those wishing to gain insight into Dickens' stature in his own day. An appendix provides information on the sale of Dickens' works during his lifetime.

_____ . *Dickens: Interviews and Recollections*. 2 vols. Totowa, N.J.:
Barnes & Noble Books, 1981.
Excerpts from letters, reminiscences, biographies, and other sources, providing
a sketch of Dickens, his work, and his impact on society. Selections are from
works written by men and women who knew the novelist or saw him in
person. Arranged chronologically to give readers a sense of the impression
Dickens made as he grew older and more famous.

Dyson, A. E. *The Inimitable Dickens: A Reading of the Novels*. London: Macmillan, 1970.
Separate chapters provide critical assessments of the novels beginning with
Dickens' fourth work, *The Old Curiosity Shop*. Places emphasis on analysis of
characterization, which Dyson considers Dickens' special strength. Attempts
to account for Dickens' impact on succeeding generations and to justify the
claim that Dickens deserves the title he gave himself, "inimitable," the most
notable writer in English.

Fielding, Kenneth J. *Charles Dickens: A Critical Introduction*. London: Longman,
1958, enlarged ed. 1965.
Comprehensive review of Dickens' career as a novelist; individual chapters
analyze the major novels, integrating important details from Dickens' life into
the narrative and providing brief sketches of the production of each work.

Ford, George H. *Dickens and His Readers: Aspects of Novel-Criticism Since 1836*.
Princeton, N.J.: Princeton University Press, 1955.
Scholarly account of the reception of Dickens' novels by his contemporaries
and by readers in the following decades. Examines the ways Dickens' reputation has been influenced by changing tastes in reading and by development of
new literary theories. Organized to facilitate examination of various qualities
(humor, sentimentality, social criticism). Indispensable for a broad understanding of the impact of Dickens as a novelist.

Ford, George H., and Lariat Lane, Jr., eds. *The Dickens Critics*. Westport, Conn.:
Greenwood Press, 1972. Originally published by Cornell University Press,
1961.
Collection of previously published material assembled to present an overview
of critical approaches to Dickens' major works. Each novel is discussed in at
least one selection. Essays aim primarily at answering questions of criticism
rather than focusing on biography, sociology, or bibliography; all attempt to
discern what the reader apprehends from reading the novels and explain how
Dickens' artistry contributes to creating that effect.

Giddings, Robert, ed. *The Changing World of Charles Dickens*. Totowa, N.J.:
Barnes & Noble Books, 1983.

Collection of essays dealing with individual novels and with issues common to several works, such as the crowd in the novels, Dickens' attitude toward social progress, and the novelist's influence on others. Also contains a chapter on film adaptations of Dickens' works, and a chapter discussing his career as a dramatist and stage reader.

Gomme, A. H. *Dickens*. Literature in Perspective Series. London: Evans Brothers, 1971.
Part of a series aimed at presenting writers and their work to a general audience. Individual chapters sketch Dickens' life; analyze several of the novels in detail; and examine the characteristics of his fiction, including his use of language, reliance on mystery and coincidence, melodrama, and sentimentality.

House, Humphry. *The Dickens World*. London: Oxford University Press, 1942.
A scholarly sourcebook tracing the background of Dickens' work. Examines the milieu in which the works were written—the history of the period, the topography, and the institutions against which Dickens railed—to show how Dickens transformed this environment into fiction. By examining source documents such as newspapers and periodicals, House is able to illustrate how closely Dickens often followed factual accounts in his portrait of society.

Johnson, Edgar. *Charles Dickens: His Tragedy and Triumph*. 2 vols. New York: Simon & Schuster, 1952.
The most significant and comprehensive biographical study done in the twentieth century. Through Dickens' letters, memoranda, and published writings, and from the memoirs and letters of his contemporaries, Johnson constructs a well-rounded portrait of the novelist. Carefully interwoven into the text is criticism of the fiction; however, Johnson does not overstress the biographical influence on the works.

Karl, Frederick R. "Charles Dickens: The Victorian Quixote." In his *A Reader's Guide to the Nineteenth-Century Novel*. New York: Farrar, Straus & Giroux, 1964.
A review of Dickens' major works; attempts to explain Dickens' popularity and his reasons for adopting the various techniques which make the works distinctive. Examines the moral outlook informing the novels.

MacKenzie, Norman and Jeanne MacKenzie. *Dickens: A Life*. New York: Oxford University Press, 1979.
A well-researched biography based on previously published life studies and on a scholarly edition of Dickens' letters published in the 1970's. Focuses on

the novelist's personal development and the influence of his life on his work. Four major sections trace Dickens' rise to fame, examine his years of great productivity and great optimism, explore the period of disenchantment with his own life and with society, and discuss his final years as a living national institution.

Miller, J. Hillis. *Charles Dickens: The World of His Novels*. Cambridge, Mass.: Harvard University Press, 1959.
Analysis of Dickens' novels as works of art. Explores the way the novelist contributed to shaping his countrymen's artistic and social conscience through his art. Attempts to account for Dickens' creative genius. The major focus is on six novels (*Pickwick Papers*, *Oliver Twist*, *Martin Chuzzlewit*, *Bleak House*, *Great Expectations*, and *Our Mutual Friend*), with brief discussions of the other works.

Nelson, Harland S. *Charles Dickens*. Boston: Twayne, 1981.
Useful critical introduction to Dickens' methods as a writer. Offers a way to understand the fiction by analyzing the elements of a typical novel; discusses one work, *Bleak House*, in detail. Includes a chronology of Dickens' life and an annotated selected bibliography of criticism.

Nisbet, Ada. "Charles Dickens." In *Victorian Fiction: A Guide to Research*, edited by Lionel Stevenson. Cambridge, Mass.: Harvard University Press, 1964.
Lengthy bibliographical essay containing valuable information on manuscripts, collections of letters, and editions of Dickens' works. Also provides summaries of critical studies published before 1962 that discuss Dickens' career and his individual novels. Useful guide to research on particular works or on topics of interest; separate sections include "Craftsmanship," "Self-Revelation," "Imagination and Symbolism."

Patten, Robert L. *Charles Dickens and his Publishers*. Oxford: Clarendon Press, 1978.
Carefully researched, scholarly account of Dickens' relationship with his various publishers. Offers valuable insight into the way the demands of the trade of novelwriting influenced Dickens' works. Serves as a useful biography of Dickens-as-writer, detailing events immediately related to his practice of the craft of fiction.

Praz, Mario. *The Hero in Eclipse in Victorian Fiction*. Translated by Angus Davidson. New York: Oxford University Press, 1956.
Discusses the bourgeois tendencies in Dickens' works. Lengthy analysis of the novelist's attitudes toward social reform and his tendencies to favor the

sensational and theatrical over realistic portraits of the contemporary scene.
Points out examples of Dickens' ability to create the picturesque.

Price, Martin, ed. *Dickens: A Collection of Critical Essays*. Englewood Cliffs, N.J.:
Prentice-Hall, 1967.
Anthology of critical essays by diverse hands, reprinted or excerpted from
earlier studies. Seven focus on individual novels, five provide thematic analysis
of topics such as heroes and heroines, Dickens' view of the world, and the
novelist's changing attitude toward society.

Quiller-Couch, Sir Arthur. *Charles Dickens and Other Victorians*. New York: G. P.
Putnam's Sons, 1925.
Lengthy essay constructed from lecture notes, giving a general assessment of
Dickens' status as the greatest Victorian novelist. Individual sections attempt
to account for his popularity and its effect on his work, describe his talents for
plotting and characterization, and analyze his ability to combine realistic detail
with surrealistic atmosphere.

Rooke, Patrick. *The Age of Dickens*. New York: G. P. Putnam's Sons, 1970.
Historical survey of the Victorian social, political, and business milieu that
shaped the work of Dickens and his fellow writers. Sketches the influence of
improvements in engineering and science. Briefly notes events in Dickens'
novels which mirror important issues. Illustrated; particularly good as background reading for those with little knowledge of the period.

Slater, Michael. *Dickens and Women*. Stanford, Calif.: Stanford University Press,
1983.
Wide-ranging study of Dickens' response to the concept of femaleness and the
interrelationships between men and women in the novels. Examines biographical evidence as well as all of the major novels to determine Dickens' perceptions of women and their role in society, and discusses the novelist's strategies
for presenting women in his fiction.

Steig, Michael. *Dickens and Phiz*. Bloomington: Indiana University Press, 1978.
Interpretative study of the relationship between Dickens and his principal
illustrator, Hablot K. Browne. Details the ways Browne's drawings are actually
commentaries on the texts, not simply graphic representations of specific
scenes. Includes more than one hundred working sketches and finished illustrations from the original editions.

Stewart, Garrett. *Dickens and the Trials of Imagination*. Cambridge, Mass.: Harvard University Press, 1974.
Perceptive study of Dickens' imaginative vision. Through a review of several

of the novels, Stewart examines the many stylistic devices Dickens employs to vivify his essentially romantic vision of life. Extensive discussions of *Pickwick Papers* and *Our Mutual Friend*.

Stoehr, Taylor. *Dickens: The Dreamer's Stance*. Ithaca, N.Y.: Cornell University Press, 1965.
Systematic study of Dickens' manner of composition, using techniques of Freudian dream theory. Develops a theoretical framework for such an analysis, then examines six novels to show how applying techniques of dream theory can account for the power of the works, help explain Dickens' manner of presentation, and make clear his world view.

Williams, Merryn. *Women in the English Novel, 1800-1900*. New York: St. Martin's Press, 1984.
Reviews the female characters in Dickens' novels to show the author's attitudes toward women in society. Notes Dickens' high respect for women and his desire to expose the cruelty inflicted on women by spouses and families; shows the novelist's interest in the effects of psychological cruelty.

Wilson, Angus. *The World of Charles Dickens*. New York: Viking Press, 1970.
Illustrated biography written for the general reader. Emphasis is on the people who influenced Dickens personally, and on the way events of his life provided material for the fiction and essays. Also contains excellent brief critical analyses of the major novels.

Wilson, Edmund. "Dickens: The Two Scrooges." In his *The Wound and the Bow*. Boston: Houghton, Mifflin, 1941.
Excellent introductory essay on Dickens' life and works, emphasizing the novelist's stance as a rebel in society. Notes Dickens' affinity for the criminal elements. Discusses his growing tendency to criticize society in his novels; shows his gradual loss of faith in middle class values as a source for restoring dignity to human relationships and social institutions. Special attention is paid to *Bleak House*, *Little Dorrit*, *Our Mutual Friend*, and *The Mystery of Edwin Drood*.

Barnaby Rudge

Butt, John, and Kathleen Tillotson. "*Barnaby Rudge*: The First Projected Novel." In their *Dickens at Work*. London: Methuen, 1959.
Explains why Dickens delayed work on this novel for five years after determining its subject and theme; details several changes that occurred as a result of this delay, and other alterations caused by Dickens' need to adapt the novel

for weekly serialization. Includes some examples of passages excised from Dickens' manuscript version before publication; summarizes Dickens' use of historical source materials.

Collins, Philip. *Dickens and Crime*. Bloomington: Indiana University Press, 1962.
Examines the novel to expose Dickens' ambivalence toward prisons and prisoners. Notes his fascination with those who stand outside the law; although he does not side with them, he does not praise the authorities either. Nevertheless, he does not advocate revolutions such as the Gordon Riots as a means of reforming society.

Davis, Earle. *The Flint and the Flame: The Artistry of Charles Dickens*. Columbia: University of Missouri Press, 1963.
Scattered comments throughout Davis' study of Dickens' techniques remark on his handling of various literary devices in this novel: plotting; use of gothic conventions; Romantic characterization, in which heroes and villains take on mythic qualities or represent natural virtues and vices; and the use of historical events and panoramic descriptions to illustrate social or moral themes.

Dyson, A. E. "*Barnaby Rudge*: The Genesis of Violence." In his *The Inimitable Dickens: A Reading of the Novels*. London: Macmillan, 1970.
Argues for the significance of the novel within the Dickens canon; attempts to account for the failure of the work to interest Dickens' contemporaries. Extensive analysis of major characters, with special emphasis on the figure of Gabriel Varden. Notes Dickens' disillusionment with the past and his growing distaste for the rising spirit of materialism.

Fielding, Kenneth J. *Charles Dickens: A Critical Introduction*. London: Longman, 1958, enlarged ed. 1965.
Emphasizes the background of the novel, including Dickens' reasons for choosing to tell this story. Compares the work to its immediate predecessors: the works of Edward Bulwer-Lytton, Harold Ainsworth, and Walter Scott. Briefly notes Dickens' attempts to expose the evils of the old social order, dispelling notions that he longed for the supposed serenity of the past.

Hollingsworth, Keith. "The Newgate Theme of *Barnaby Rudge*." In his *The Newgate Novel, 1830-1847*. Detroit: Wayne State University Press, 1963.
Brief discussion of the relationship of this novel to similar works emphasizing criminal elements of society. Points out how Dickens uses the historical event of the Gordon Riots of 1770 to highlight contemporary problems, especially the harsh laws governing imprisonment and capital punishment.

Johnson, Edgar. "The Neglected and Misused." In his *Charles Dickens: His Tragedy and Triumph*. Vol. 1. New York: Simon & Schuster, 1952.

Though acknowledging the passion which Dickens generates in his description of the mob, Johnson calls this novel Dickens' least successful. He attributes the defects to poor characterization. Nevertheless, he considers the novel a cogent portrayal of the causes and consequences of officials in organized society neglecting the needs of the poor.

Lucas, John. *The Melancholy Man: A Study of Dickens' Novels*. Reprint. Totowa, N.J.: Barnes & Noble Books, 1980.
Praises Dickens' attempt to examine an explosive social crisis from a variety of perspectives. Believes that Dickens is ultimately forced to side with those in authority because they are trying, albeit often unsuccessfully, to preserve something of value from the past. Dickens does not want the past annihilated, but he is harsh on figures of the aristocracy who do not fulfill their responsibility to deal justly with others.

Magnet, Myron. *Dickens and the Social Order*. Philadelphia: University of Pennsylvania Press, 1985.
Monograph-length analysis of the novel, focusing on the way Dickens explores the nature of aggressiveness both in individuals and in social institutions. Seven chapters examine individual characters and take a close look at the novelist's portrayal of the Gordon Riots; believes that Dickens sees civilization as a force serving to neutralize man's naturally aggressive instincts.

Marcus, Steven. "Sons and Fathers." In his *Dickens: From Pickwick to Dombey*. New York: Basic Books, 1965.
Considers the novel better than most previous critics had; believes that Dickens handles the historical materials well, and draws clear parallels between the Gordon Riots and the Chartist movement of the novelist's own day. Sees the central conflict between the idyllic past and the violent present; traces the relationships between five fathers and sons in the novel, showing how these familial estrangements dramatize the conflict between past and present values. Believes Dickens found the conflict irreconcilable, but refused to side with the revolutionaries.

Miller, J. Hillis. *Charles Dickens: The World of His Novels*. Cambridge, Mass.: Harvard University Press, 1959.
Brief comments on the novel link it with *The Old Curiosity Shop* and *Nicholas Nickleby* as works in which Dickens concentrates on creating grotesque characters, and in which he deals with individuals discovering a place for themselves in society. Notes Dickens' rejection of revolution as a viable means of achieving justice in an unjust society; Dickens opts instead for reforming society from within.

Patten, Robert. *Dickens and His Publishers*. Oxford: Clarendon Press, 1978.
Commentary on Dickens' long-standing plan to write this novel, his eventual
success at completing the project, and his growing unrest with Richard
Bentley, his publisher at the time. .

Rice, Thomas J. "The Politics of *Barnaby Rudge*." In *The Changing World of
Charles Dickens*, edited by Robert Giddings. Totowa, N.J.: Barnes & Noble
Books, 1983.
Discusses in detail the parallels between the novel and events contemporary
with Dickens' composing it; notes that, though historical in some respects, the
work actually reflects Dickens' concern over the resurgence of Chartism and
the cries of no-Popery which rang out again in the 1840's. Reinterprets the
actions of the major figures as emblematic of the contemporary political tur-
moil which spurred Dickens to complete the novel.

Steig, Michael. *Dickens and Phiz*. Bloomington: Indiana University Press, 1978.
Brief summary of the way Hablot K. Browne illustrated the monthly installments of the novel in *Master Humphrey's Clock*. Notes how Dickens' changing
conceptions of various characters are mirrored in the illustrations; also discusses Browne's use of added details in the drawings that call attention to the
moral issues which the text raises.

Stone, Harry. "From *Pickwick* to *Chuzzlewit*: Fairy Tales and the Apprentice Novels." In his *Dickens and the Invisible World*. Bloomington: Indiana University
Press, 1979.
Explores Dickens' use of fairy-tale techniques, showing how several characters, including Barnaby, his father, and Hugh, are modeled on archetypal
figures from the world of fantasy and folklore. Notes that the fanciful qualities
of the novel seem to conflict with the realistic presentation of many events:
many of its supernatural and gothic effects are not well integrated into its
realistic structure.

Bleak House

Butt, John, and Kathleen Tillotson. "The Topicality of *Bleak House*." In their
Dickens at Work. London: Methuen, 1957.
Considers the novel a tract for the times. Reviews external sources, especially
the London *Times*, which chronicle the major issues Dickens discusses in the
novel (the evils of Chancery, the need for sanitary reform, parliamentary indifference to reform movements); shows these issues were present in the minds of
his contemporaries. Also reveals how many characters in the novel are

drawn from real life or are created to represent types of figures that were in the public eye while Dickens was composing the work.

Cockshut, A. O. J. *The Imagination of Charles Dickens.* New York: New York University Press, 1962.

Sketches the functions of various characters in the novel, especially Skimpole and Krook, to show how Dickens attacks the legal system, symbolized vividly by the image of the fog. Discusses reasons for the inclusion of the melodramatic story of the Dedlocks, a portion of the novel Cockshut finds unsuccessful.

Collins, Philip, ed. *Dickens: The Critical Heritage.* Boston: Routledge & Kegan Paul, 1971.

Excerpts from ten sources. Includes entries from Henry Crabbe Robinson's diary; George Henry Lewes' letter to Dickens advising him of his responsibility to his readers; passages from five reviews in popular British periodicals; John Stuart Mill's stinging criticism of the novel in a letter to Harriet Martineau; and John Ruskin's sardonic exposé of Dickens' penchant for sensationalism and violence, excerpted from his article in the popular journal *The Nineteenth Century.*

Davis, Earle. "The Social Microcosmic Pattern." In his *The Flint and the Flame: The Artistry of Charles Dickens.* Columbia: University of Missouri Press, 1963.

Calls the novel the first of Dickens' "dark" masterpieces in which the novelist exposes the ills of his society. Shows how Dickens uses all of his time-tested fictional techniques, including farce, caricature, melodrama, the Gothic, and sentimentality to serve his central theme: the castigation of the legal system, a corrupt and moribund institution affecting the lives of people at every level of society. Discusses the importance of multiple plots; comments on Dickens' use of dual narrators.

Dyson, A. E. *The Inimitable Dickens; A Reading of the Novels.* London: Macmillan, 1970.

Stresses the importance of plotting, and of the elements of the Romance in the work. Notes the impersonality of evil against which an unusually large number of good characters struggle. Details the way Dickens symbolically weaves a web that eventually traps all of his characters, citing the importance of coincidence in bringing many of them together with startling results. Explores the use of dual narrators, giving primacy to Esther as a capable and exceptionally good woman. Shows Dickens' conviction that evils such as Chancery can be overcome.

Fielding, Kenneth J. *Charles Dickens: A Critical Introduction.* London: Longman, 1958, enlarged ed. 1965.

Considers this one of Dickens' best constructed works, noting how every character and every incident revolves around the Court of Chancery and the lawsuit that forms the central interest in the work. Notes the criticism some of Dickens' contemporaries had for the way the novelist handles certain elements of the tale at the expense of realism. Suggests Dickens' social criticisms should not be taken as serious satire but rather as entertaining burlesque.

Fielding, Kenneth J., and A. W. Brice. "*Bleak House* and the Graveyard." In *Dickens the Craftsman: Strategies of Presentation*, edited by Robert B. Partlow. Carbondale: Southern Illinois University Press, 1970.
Examines the topicality of several incidents in the novel, showing how Dickens could transform materials of current concern into fiction of interest to posterity. To prove this thesis, the authors trace Dickens' longtime involvement in efforts to bring about sanitary reform, detailing ways his immediate grounding in real-world issues gives his prose an intensity and a realism which strikes a universal chord of sympathy in readers.

Ford, George H. "Self-Help and the Helpless in *Bleak House*." In *From Jane Austen to Joseph Conrad*, edited by R. C. Rathburn and Martin Steinmann, Jr. Minneapolis: University of Minnesota Press, 1958.
Analysis of the social assumptions underlying Dickens' portraits of his heroes and villains. Finds two kinds of characters existing in the work: those who are helpless, and those who can help both themselves and others. Illustrates how, by pairing characters, Dickens reveals the importance of acting to improve oneself and society; stresses the importance of work as a means by which people achieve goodness.

Gose, Elliott B. *Imagination Indulged: The Irrational in the Nineteenth-Century Novel*. Montreal: McGill-Queens University Press, 1972.
Highlights Dickens' use of fairy-tale motifs within the work. Also discusses the importance of alter egos for characters within the novel, a technique Dickens uses to illustrate the psychological duality of human nature, in which conscious and unconscious elements of the personality are often in conflict.

Harvey, W. J. "Chance and Design in *Bleak House*." In *Dickens: A Collection of Critical Essays*, edited by Martin Price. Englewood Cliffs, N.J.: Prentice-Hall, 1967.
Detailed structural analysis of the novel, concentrating on Dickens' use of two narrators. Highlights the dual perspective achieved through this technique, seeing the world of Chancery from within (through Esther) and from without (through the omniscient narrator). Also examines Dickens' use of coincidence and chance as a technique for furthering the plot and illuminating themes.

Hornback, Bert. "The Other Portion of *Bleak House*." In *The Changing World of Charles Dickens*, edited by Robert Giddings. Totowa, N.J.: Barnes & Noble Books, 1983.

Intriguing reading of the novel stressing the importance of knowledge and ignorance. Catalogs the many times characters in the work confront the problems of knowledge and ignorance; sees Jo as by far the most pathetic character because he is the most ignorant. Points out that Esther proves to be limited and ineffectual in achieving any real knowledge of events happening around her, or about her own past. In contrast with Esther, the omniscient narrator tries to impose his knowledge on the reader.

Johnson, Edgar. "The Anatomy of Society." In his *Charles Dickens: His Tragedy and Triumph*. Vol. 2. New York: Simon & Schuster, 1952.

Reads the novel as Dickens' condemnation of an unjust and corrupt society which crushes human energies. Sees the major images—the fog, the Court of Chancery, and the spider's web—reflecting that theme. Faults Dickens for using Esther as a narrator and for weak characterization in the novel. Praises the stridency of his attack on the corruption of society, realized through characters who symbolize its evils, and revealed both through descriptions of setting and through the rhetoric of satire and invective.

Karl, Frederick R. *A Reader's Guide to the Nineteenth-Century Novel*. New York: Farrar, Straus & Giroux, 1964.

Treats the novel as Dickens' attack on the injustices of the legal system which should protect the citizenry, but instead destroys it. Traces the pervasiveness of greed—for money or for self-aggrandizement—that causes people to destroy others.

Korg, Jacob, ed. *Twentieth-Century Interpretations of Bleak House*. Englewood Cliffs, N.J.: Prentice-Hall, Inc., 1968.

Collection of ten previously published articles and selections from longer works offering a variety of interpretations of the novel. Includes criticism focusing on the structure, style, and major symbols of the work, and on the relationship of the novel to other literary masterpieces.

Larson, Janet L. "Biblical Readings in the Later Dickens: The Book of Job According to *Bleak House*." In her *Dickens and the Broken Scripture*. Athens: University of Georgia Press, 1985.

Lengthy analysis of the novel as a revision of the Book of Job. Shows how the work shares with its biblical predecessor a questioning spirit regarding human existence; notes that both have dual narrators who offer differing perspectives on the world. Detailed analysis of chapters 1 and 32 displays the way Dickens modifies or subverts biblical platitudes. Also provides a detailed examin-

ation of Esther Summerson, showing how Dickens relies on the Book of Esther
and the Book of Job to give resonance to his problematical heroine.

Leavis, Q. D. *"Bleak House*: A Chancery World." In F. R. Leavis and Q. D. Leavis'
    Dickens the Novelist. New Brunswick, N.J.: Rutgers University Press, 1979.
    Argues that Chancery is Dickens' metaphor for Man in Victorian Society.
    Shows through a sketch of the plot how Dickens exposes his major theme: the
    innate tendencies of man to act litigiously and to engage in social warfare.
    Discusses opportunities the novelist sees for men to turn away from such a
    society; only selfless professional service seems to offer hope. Includes a
    sympathetic treatment of Sir Leicester Dedlock, a stinging critique of Skimp-
    ole, and psychological analyses of Esther, Tulkinghorn, and Vholes. Short
    appendixes discuss the role of the doctor in Victorian fiction and examine the
    relationship between Dickens and social reformer Henry Mayhew.

Lucas, John. *The Melancholy Man: A Study of Dickens' Novels*. Reprint. Totowa,
    N.J.: Barnes & Noble Books, 1980.
    Describes the many ways Dickens uses this novel as a satiric commentary on
    his own society and its institutions: the law, organized religion, and the educa-
    tional system. Shows how Dickens forces readers to confront the unpleasant
    side of society; demonstrates how he portrays society as atomistic, a condition
    that bodes ill for all men. Analyzes the way Dickens uses the imagery of
    disease to reinforce his portrait of a corrupt society. A separate appendix
    discusses the novelist's use of contradictions within the work.

Miller, J. Hillis. *Charles Dickens: The World of His Novels*. Cambridge, Mass.:
    Harvard University Press, 1959.
    Considers the novel Dickens' greatest statement about the possibilities of
    bringing order to chaos and warding off entropy. Skillful assessment of the
    opening chapter as a metaphor for Dickens' method throughout: the juxtaposi-
    tion of disparate entities existing under cover of a single prevailing presence.
    Shows how various characters order their worlds, only to fail; in contrast,
    Esther accepts Divine Providence while doing what she can to set things right
    for herself and others. Sees the Court of Chancery as emblematic of the world
    at large: an interlocking system where one person's actions affect the lives of
    all others.

Nelson, Harland S. *Charles Dickens*. New York: Twayne, 1981.
    Methodical analysis of the novel, divided into separate sections summarizing
    the action. Examines the point of view, especially Dickens' use of dual narra-
    tors; remarks on the intricacies of plotting, structure, and chronology; and
    explores Dickens' methods of characterization and use of humor. Also dis-

cusses the way the author's stance in the novel parallels that of the Old Testament prophets: Dickens appears intent on warning society of the potential for disaster if human dignity is not recognized by social institutions.

Patten, Robert L. *"Bleak House* and the Literary Croesus." In his *Charles Dickens and His Publishers*. Oxford, England: Clarendon Press, 1978.
Traces the business background of the novel's publication; contains an especially detailed account of Dickens' publishers' advertising campaign. Shows the immense success of the novel, measured by readership—an interesting observation in light of its mixed reception by contemporary reviewers.

Steig, Michael. *"Bleak House* and *Little Dorrit*: The Iconography of Darkness." In his *Dickens and Phiz*. Bloomington: Indiana University Press, 1978.
Extensive analysis of the illustrations done by Hablot K. Browne for the monthly installments of the novel in progress. Explores the sources of Browne's technique, showing how he uses the drawings to link his own interpretation of Dickens' satiric treatment of the law with earlier artists' renditions of similar subjects. Notes, too, how Browne's use of different techniques for etching complement the darker side of the tale; his "dark plates" reflect the mystery surrounding the Dedlocks' story.

Stoehr, Taylor. *Dickens: The Dreamer's Stance*. Ithaca, N.Y.: Cornell University Press, 1965.
Sees Dickens' use of dual narrators as an example of his reliance on techniques of the dream as an organizing and informing principle in his novels. Focusing on the effects of this technique, Stoehr shows how the use of two narrators allows for distortion, displacement, and isolation of competing emotional elements. Provides detailed analysis of Esther and revealing summaries of other characters, especially Richard Carstone and Tulkinghorn.

Storey, Graham. *Charles Dickens: Bleak House*. New York: Cambridge University Press, 1987.
Informative monograph examining the novel from a variety of viewpoints. Discusses the historical and intellectual background; the function of the double narrative; Dickens' use of language and his portrait of social groups; and the function of irony in the work. Separate chapters discuss the critical reception of the novel and its place in the European literary tradition.

Zabel, Morton Dauwen. *"Bleak House."* In *The Dickens Critics*, edited by George Ford and Lariat Lane, Jr. Westport, Conn.: Greenwood Press, 1972.
Examines the way Dickens constructs his elaborate plot and introduces his many characters while maintaining a constant focus on his central concern: the exposure of the disease and corruption in his society, identified with the law.

Claims the novel achieves the status of a fable of society in a time of crisis. Discusses the sources of Dickens' genius as a writer, using this work to illustrate the novelist's imaginative vision and his control of his materials.

A Christmas Carol

Cazamian, Louis. "Implicit Social Comment in Dickens' Novels." In his *The Social Novel in England, 1830-1850: Dickens, Disraeli, Mrs. Gaskell, Kingsley*. Boston: Routledge & Kegan Paul, 1973.
Discusses the Cratchit family as an example of the kind of poor family for which Dickens had great admiration. Notes how they bear up well under the dual burdens of poverty and grief, exemplifying the "spirit of Christmas" that Dickens cherished.

Davis, Earle. "From Alternation to Pattern: The Technique of Contrast." In his *The Flint and the Flame: The Artistry of Charles Dickens*. Columbia: University of Missouri Press, 1963.
Though recognizing Dickens' use of the fairy-tale style of composition, Davis stresses the economic and political undercurrents of the tale. Scrooge is an embodiment of laissez-faire economics, a believer that Benthamite principles for regulating the poor will work. The three ghosts show how Scrooge differs from those who are generous with workers, and warn of the consequences to society if men like Scrooge fail to reform.

Fielding, Kenneth J. " 'Christmas Books' and *Dombey and Son*" In his *Charles Dickens: A Critical Introduction*. London: Longman, 1958, enlarged ed. 1965.
Brief commentary on the genesis of the story, noting Dickens' interest in philanthropy. Points out the story's graphic presentation of the needy and cites its dual purpose as a plea for benevolence and a warning of the consequences of ignoring want and ignorance.

Johnson, Edgar. "Selfishness and the Economic Man." In his *Charles Dickens: His Tragedy and Triumph*. Vol. 1. New York: Simon & Schuster, 1952.
Reads the story as a parable of social redemption. Considers Dickens' vision of the Spirit of Christmas not particularly religious; rather, it is a belief that men should treat one another with dignity and kindness at all times. Notes the dark undercurrent within the story: neglecting the poor leads to disastrous consequences.

Lucas, John. *The Melancholy Man: A Study of Dickens' Novels*. Reprint. Totowa, N.J.: Barnes & Noble Books, 1980.
Reads the story as Dickens' fable of Utilitarianism: Scrooge is the living ex-

ample of a man who follows Benthamite principles. Discusses Dickens' handling of the consequences of such a life, focusing on the sense of isolation Scrooge experiences by reducing every human relationship to a business exchange. Views the Cratchits as representative of the countervailing force in society and the hope for mankind.

Patten, Robert L. *Charles Dickens and His Publishers*. Oxford, England: Clarendon Press, 1978.
Discussion of the production of "A Christmas Carol" as a venture Dickens expected would clear him of many debts. Outlines the novelist's personal involvement in bringing out the first edition; charts sales figures and Dickens' profits from the successive printings demanded by an avid reading public.

Stone, Harry. "*A Christmas Carol*: Giving Nursery Tales a Higher Form." In *Charles Dickens*, edited by Harold Bloom. New York: Chelsea House, 1987.
Outlines the way Dickens uses the formulas and conventions of fairy tales to his best advantage in creating a story with social and moral significance. Points out parallels between Scrooge and the reader, noting that the reader feels relief and hope in Scrooge's release from the prison of himself to the paradise of shared community experience. Traces the allegorical significance of the Spirits, and shows how Dickens achieves his best success in sketching key scenes that convey his message.

David Copperfield

Barnes, Samuel G. "Dickens and Copperfield: The Hero as Man of Letters." In *The Classic British Novel*, edited by Howard M. Harper and Charles Edge. Athens: University of Georgia Press, 1972.
Traces the influence of Thomas Carlyle on Dickens' thought; shows how Carlyle's writings affected the novelist in his formative years and especially during the 1840's. Demonstrates how the Carlylean ideology of work and insistence on personal reformation forms the basis for judging characters in *David Copperfield*.

Buckley, Jerome H. "Dickens, David, and Pip." In his *Seasons of Youth: The Bildungsroman from Dickens to Golding*. Cambridge, Mass.: Harvard University Press, 1974.
Considers the novel an example of the *Bildungsroman*; the work is David's autobiography, not Dickens'. Posits that only two events of the author's life actually play a major part in the work. David appears Wordsworthian in reviewing the turbulent emotional events of his life in a moment of tranquility. Shows how the pattern of the novel illustrates an issue common to Victorian literature: the crisis of faith, made vivid in Thomas Carlyle's *Sartor Resartus*.

Butt, John, and Kathleen Tillotson. "*David Copperfield* Month by Month." In their
Dickens at Work. London: Methuen, 1957.
Reproduces Dickens' monthly number plans for the novel, showing how the
author envisioned his work and how he planned to achieve unity through
careful balancing of scenes among the major characters. Scholarly commentary remarks on the changes Dickens made as he composed the text of these
monthly installments.

Carabine, Keith. "Reading *David Copperfield*." In *Reading the Victorian Novel:
Detail into Form*, edited by Ian Gregor. New York: Barnes & Noble Books,
1980.
Examines the various kinds of experience a reader may have as a result of
witnessing both the changing perspective of the main character and Dickens'
apparent ambivalence toward his hero. Shows how Dickens consciously unset-
tles readers' expectations, especially those who encountered the novel serially
as it was first published; readers are forced to suspend judgment of the hero
until the end of the story.

Cockshut, A. O. J. *The Imagination of Charles Dickens*. New York: New York
University Press, 1962.
Attempts a balanced assessment in the face of what Cockshut sees as a difficult
barrier: the general applause of readers throughout the decades since the novel
appeared. Carefully examines David, Uriah, and Steerforth, and explores several key scenes within the work to show how Dickens weaves autobiography
and fantasy together to create what he called his favorite work.

Collins, Philip, ed. *Dickens: The Critical Heritage*. Boston: Routledge & Kegan
Paul, 1971.
Contains comments from five reviews published in 1850-1851, when the novel
was first making an impact on the English reading public. A sixth selection,
from an essay by Matthew Arnold, cites the novel as an example of superior
contemporary literature, praising Dickens' characterization and his social
conscience.

Davis, Earle. "First Person: David Copperfield." In his *The Flint and the Flame:
The Artistry of Charles Dickens*. Columbia: University of Missouri Press, 1963.
Examines the way Dickens uses autobiography and invention and carefully
balances his multiple plots to create a truly great novel. Detailed analysis of the
plot reveals Dickens' mastery of various literary techniques. Discusses the
novelist's method of presenting a portrait of love through three contrasting love
triangles. Highlights the importance of earlier works, especially Henry Fielding's *Tom Jones*, in forming Dickens' concept for this epic in prose.

Dunn, Richard J. "David Copperfield's Carlylean Retailoring." In *Dickens the Craftsman: Strategies of Presentation*, edited by Robert B. Partlow. Carbondale: Southern Illinois University Press, 1970.

Comparison of David Copperfield with Diogenes Teufelsdroch of Thomas Carlyle's *Sartor Resartus* shows how Dickens is indirectly influenced by Carlylean thought. Claims both heroes are on a quest for self-discovery and self-definition. Traces David's relationships with other characters to explain how Dickens' hero comes to find self-satisfaction through an integration of self-knowledge and a loving heart.

——————— . *Approaches to Teaching Dickens' David Copperfield*. New York: Modern Language Association, 1984.

Varied collection of essays and excerpts designed for teachers but of great use to students in understanding the novel. Essays deal with the work's autobiographical elements, its relationship with Dickens' other novels, and its links to novels by other Victorians; some selections provide close textual analysis. Also contains excellent bibliographical information on secondary sources.

Dyson, A. E. "*David Copperfield*: The Favourite Child." In his *The Inimitable Dickens: A Reading of the Novels*. London: Macmillan, 1970.

Begins with a discussion of the many names by which the hero is called, to show how this outward diversity reflects the many aspects of a single homogenous figure. Argues that one of Dickens' main concerns is with sexual relationships and marriage; notes the difficulties of dealing with the former in Victorian England. Shows how few marriages or families in the work are really typical; ultimately finds Dickens championing marriage as an institution where love and concern for one's partner as a friend is better than sexual attraction in solidifying relationships.

Fielding, Kenneth J. *Charles Dickens: A Critical Introduction*. London: Longman, 1958, enlarged ed. 1965.

Explains the importance of the autobiographical elements as a means of giving Dickens some control over his characters and over the structure of the work. Praises Dickens' comic characters, especially Miss Mowcher, but faults the novelist for his portraits of the more serious figures.

Johnson, Edgar. "His Favorite Child." In his *Charles Dickens: His Tragedy and Triumph*. Vol. 2. New York: Simon & Schuster, 1952.

Explores autobiographical elements in the work to show how Dickens transformed events of his own early life into a novel capturing the universal experience of childhood. Points out parallels between the Micawbers and Dickens' real parents. Also examines the function of other characters in the work.

Leavis, Q. D. "Dickens and Tolstoy: The Case for a Serious View of *David Copperfield*." In F. R. Leavis and Q. D. Leavis' *Dickens the Novelist*. New Brunswick, N.J.: Rutgers University Press, 1979.

Points out significant parallels between the novel and Leo Tolstoy's *War and Peace* to show ways the Russian was influenced by Dickens: Dickens shows a mastery of insight into the nature of love, recognizing that the impulse transcends Victorian conventions and restrictions. Detailed analysis of specific scenes and characters, especially David and Steerforth, explores the novelist's handling of the issues of love and happiness. In three short appendixes Leavis examines the novel's relation to *Oliver Twist* and *Jane Eyre*, the characterization of Dora, and the exposure scenes.

Lucas, John. *The Melancholy Man: A Study of Dickens' Novels*. Reprint. Totowa, N.J.: Barnes & Noble Books, 1980.

Argues that Dickens uses his own past as material to shape a novel about the growth of an individual to maturity. Notes parallels to the poetry of William Wordsworth and Alfred, Lord Tennyson, which Lucas says helped form Dickens' ideas about childhood, growth, and human relationships (especially those involving love and marriage). Extensive analysis of David's relationships with the many father- and mother-figures in the book; especially detailed critique of Steerforth.

Lutman, Stephen. "Reading Illustrations: Pictures in *David Copperfield*." In *Reading the Victorian Novel: Detail into Form*, edited by Ian Gregor. New York: Barnes & Noble Books, 1980.

Briefly outlines the importance of illustrations to Victorian novelists, especially Dickens. Suggests that the illustrations in *David Copperfield* form an important complement to the text, giving an objective portrait of the action (contrasting with the first-person point of view), and serving as visual cues for understanding character development. Heavily illustrated.

Miller, J. Hillis. *Charles Dickens: The World of His Novels*. Cambridge, Mass.: Harvard University Press, 1959.

Sees in the novel a key to understanding Dickens' creative genius: his retention of a childlike viewpoint which spurs his imagination when confronted with the injustices of modern society. Notes the importance of memory; cites the many references to it, claiming David's task is to organize his memories into his autobiographical narrative. Reviews the way Dickens allows David to achieve a happy end even though he constantly defies the forces of providence.

Patten, Robert L. "*David Copperfield* and the Cheap Edition." In his *Charles Dickens and His Publishers*. Oxford, England: Clarendon Press, 1978.

Careful presentation of available information about Dickens' conception for this novel, and about his trials in writing it. The sales receipts of the monthly installments of *David Copperfield* are compared to those of *Dombey and Son* (which actually sold better); comments from correspondence indicate Dickens' continuing enthusiasm for the novel as he moved through the composition process.

Sadoff, Dianne. "Language Engenders: *David Copperfield* and *Great Expectations*." In *Charles Dickens*, edited by Harold Bloom. New York: Chelsea House, 1987.
Treats this novel as an example of Dickens' attempts to deal with the psychological issue of fatherhood and sonship in his fiction. Sees the fatherless figure of David writing his own account and creating himself through his autobiographical narrative; concurrently, Dickens, one step removed from his creation, achieves the same re-creation of his own scarred childhood through his fiction.

Spilka, Mark. "*David Copperfield* as Psychological Fiction." In *Dickens: Modern Judgments*, edited by A. E. Dyson. London: Macmillan, 1968.
Discusses the novel as an example of psychological fiction in which the hero attempts to overcome the pain and fears associated with childhood. Notes how Murdstone represents for David a vengeful father figure, Steerforth a helpful surrogate parent, and Dora a replacement for the mother David never had. Also shows how the twentieth century novelist Franz Kafka modeled his works on Dickens' masterpiece.

Steig, Michael. "*David Copperfield*: Progress of a Confused Soul." In his *Dickens and Phiz*. Bloomington: Indiana University Press, 1978.
Serious, detailed examination of Hablot K. Browne's illustrations for the monthly installments of the work. Shows how the drawings illuminate the relationships among characters and highlight the feelings and attitudes of the principal figures in the novel. Through an examination of the drawings, offers a reading of the novel as David's search for an accommodation to the women in his life.

Stone, Harry. "*David Copperfield*: The Fairy-Tale Method Perfected." In his *Dickens and the Invisible World*. Bloomington: Indiana University Press, 1979.
Extensive discussion of Dickens' reliance on elements of fairy-tale literature to lend a special aura to his otherwise realistic account of David's growing up. The technique allows readers to see David's development as heroic, even though he is a deeply flawed character whose undisciplined attitudes and inveterate romanticism often lead to near-disastrous consequences.

Westburg, Barry. *The Confessional Fiction of Charles Dickens*. DeKalb: Northern
Illinois University Press, 1977.

Two chapters illustrate how this novel shares with *Oliver Twist* and *Great
Expectations* a common mode of presentation: the confession, which Westburg
defines as an attempt to describe the significance of an individual's life by
making sense of fragmented experiences. The novel focuses on the significance
of time in shaping an individual's life; David Copperfield defends himself by
making sense of his past. Distinguishes between autobiography and confession, calling the latter a conscious fiction with wider implications for portraying the process of development all human beings undergo.

Dombey and Son

Butt, John, and Kathleen Tillotson. "*Dombey and Son*: Design and Execution." In
their *Dickens at Work*. London: Methuen, 1957.

Discusses Dickens' careful planning for this novel. Relies on the number plans
he drafted before composing the work, and on letters to John Forster, to show
how the novelist sustained interest in his characters and ensured audience
acceptance of his work. Details the changes Dickens was forced to make in his
plan due to limitations of space and the need to highlight his theme, the fatal
consequences of pride. Brief but highly informative explication of the cover
illustration used on each of the monthly installments.

Cockshut, A. O. J. *The Imagination of Charles Dickens*. New York: New York
University Press, 1962.

Examines the novel's major characters, especially Bagstock, and the principal images Dickens uses to convey his portrait of contemporary society. Discusses Mr. Dombey's self-centeredness and his hypocrisy. Also highlights
Dickens' penetrating if sometimes flawed treatment of imperialism and prostitution, outgrowths of the industrial society which produced men like
Dombey.

Collins, Philip, ed. *Dickens: The Critical Heritage*. Boston: Routledge & Kegan
Paul, 1971.

Excerpts from eight sources provide appraisals by Dickens' contemporaries.
Included are brief comments by Edward FitzGerald, part of a review by Dickens' close friend John Forster, and a selection from a parody of the novel in the
journal *The Man in the Moon*.

Davis, Earle. "From Alternation to Pattern: The Technique of Contrast." In his *The
Flint and the Flame: The Artistry of Charles Dickens*. Columbia: University of
Missouri Press, 1963.

A mixed review of the novel. Praises Dickens for following John Forster's advice to stick to the plan he had set out for the work and for keeping his focus on his major theme: the destructive effects of capitalistic selfishness and overweening pride. Faults the novelist, however, for the lack of contrasting action which would offer relief from the insistent tone of his condemnation of that pride, and for artificial characterization (especially Paul and Edith).

Dyson, A. E. "*Dombey and Son*: Cobwebs to Sunlight." In his *The Inimitable Dickens: A Reading of the Novels*. London: Macmillan, 1970.
Claims this novel lacks the warmth and humor of Dickens' previously published works. Extensive discussion of Mr. Dombey as a representative of the rising merchant class: men who are sincere but so totally focused on ascending in stature and fulfilling personal goals that they bring about their own destruction (psychologically and literally). Though recognizing Dickens' attempt to show the saving power of love, considers the novelist's personal attachment to his character Florence a major weakness.

Fielding, Kenneth J. *Charles Dickens: A Critical Introduction*. London: Longman, 1958, enlarged ed. 1965.
Briefly sketches Dickens' handling of the characters, especially Edith Dombey, and discusses his attempts to illustrate the evils of money and egocentric pride. Major focus is on the composition of the work; discusses Dickens' plan for the novel and outlines his method of composition, a technique he used in most of his subsequent works.

Gomme, A. H. "Four Great Novels." In his *Dickens*. London: Evans Brothers, 1971.
Highlights the importance of money and of Mr. Dombey's will as the stultifying elements preventing the development of meaningful human relationships. Detailed character analysis focuses on Mr. Dombey, his wife Edith, and Toots, who is judged one of Dickens' best comic creations.

Johnson, Edgar. "The World of Dombeyism." In his *Charles Dickens: His Tragedy and Triumph*. Vol. 1. New York: Simon & Schuster, 1952.
Judges the novel the first masterpiece of Dickens' mature period. Notes it is the first in which Dickens performs an anatomy of middle-class society; Dombey is emblematic of the class that squeezes out all feeling from human relationships, reducing them to economic exchanges. The book traces what Dickens sees as the inevitable conclusion of such a stance.

Larson, Janet L. "Traditional Dickens: Biblical Schemes and New Worlds in *Dombey and Son*." In her *Dickens and the Broken Scripture*. Athens: University of Georgia Press, 1985.
Traces Dickens' use of biblical allusions in the novel. Also notes the influ-

ence of Thomas Carlyle's writings. Demonstrates Dickens' belief that the Bible had lost its efficacy in leading men to goodness. Extensive analysis of the death of Paul Dombey; detailed discussion of Florence. Also provides a sketch of the clientele of the Midshipman Tavern as an alternative to the world represented by Mr. Dombey. Includes a good discussion of the wave imagery.

Leavis, F. R. "The First Major Novel: *Dombey and Son*." In F. R. Leavis and Q. D. Leavis' *Dickens the Novelist*. New Brunswick, N.J.: Rutgers University Press, 1979.
Noting the significance of this book as the first in which Dickens consciously sought to develop his theme systematically, Leavis quotes extensively from the text and offers penetrating analysis of the novelist's techniques in order to account for his artistry. Believes the secret to Dickens' success lies in his ability to adapt the techniques of poetry to the novel. An appendix details Dickens' debt to Tobias George Smollett in his portrait of Captain Cuttle.

Lucas, John. *The Melancholy Man: A Study of Dickens' Novels*. Reprint. Totowa, N.J.: Barnes & Noble Books, 1980.
Notes ways the novel deals with a society whose members are consumed by thoughts of materialism; argues that this portrait of a world in transition is reinforced throughout by references to time. The other major images, the railroad and the sea, present opposing views of time and progress. Provides a detailed sketch of Mr. Dombey, with briefer analyses of Mrs. Skewton and Carker. Also discusses the importance of the destruction of Stagg's Garden as a metaphor for the fate of institutions of the past which stand in the way of progress.

Marcus, Steven. "The Changing World." In his *Dickens: From Pickwick to Dombey*. New York: Basic Books, 1965.
Extended criticism of the novel as Dickens' first great unified work of art. Sees as Dickens' main concern the impact of change on society, symbolized by the railroad and the sea; notes, too, the many references to time that constantly reinforce the importance of change. Provides extensive comparison of Mr. Dombey and Carker, who represent moral opposites: the unfeeling man of will who defies the forces of nature, and the man of feeling who is totally debased by sensate experience. Sees Florence as the single redeeming character, whose love offers some hope for saving both her father and the society he represents.

Miller, J. Hillis. *Charles Dickens: The World of His Novels*. Cambridge, Mass.: Harvard University Press, 1959.
Discussion of the importance of the novel in the Dickens canon both as a climax of his interest in parent-child relations and as his exploration of relations between upper and lower classes. Describes Dickens' use of the notion of

"habit" as a form of isolation for individuals who divorce themselves from social concerns. Remarks on the irony of the Dombey children's plight: they are isolated within the family circle, outcasts even though living with their parents.

Patten, Robert L. *"Dombey and Son*, 'the greatest success.' " In his *Charles Dickens and His Publishers*. Oxford, England: Clarendon Press, 1978.
Extensive review of the business side of the book's production. Charts the remarkable sales figures of the monthly installments, showing what Dickens received from the sale of these periodical releases. Also details Dickens' business dealings with his publishers during the period when he was writing the novel.

Smith, Grahame. "The Middle Years." In his *Dickens, Money, and Society*. Berkeley: University of California Press, 1968.
Analysis of Mr. Dombey and Florence as opposites whose conflict forms the central interest of the novel. Mr. Dombey is incapable of having personal relationships because he sees all interactions in terms of competition; hence, he is isolated from society. Florence, with her intense love for her father, represents hope because she values communal associations rather than competitive ones. Rates the novel less successful than those in which Dickens rises above the personal level of tragedy to a comprehensive review of the tragedy of his entire society.

Steig, Michael. *"Dombey and Son*: Iconography of Social and Sexual Satire." In his *Dickens and Phiz*. Bloomington: Indiana University Press, 1978.
Examination of the many illustrations Hablot K. Browne prepared for the monthly installments and for the completed novel. Shows how the illustrations depict visually the most important topics in the work: the effect of Mr. Dombey on his children and his involvement in a world of conflicts centering on power and sex. Believes the illustrations help interpret the text, complementing it directly with its presentation of power-hungry men victimizing those with whom they come in contact, especially women.

Stone, Harry. *"Dombey and Son*: The New Fairy-Tale Method." In his *Dickens and the Invisible World*. Bloomington: Indiana University Press, 1979.
A lengthy chapter discusses Dickens' use of elements of the fairy tale within the novel. Shows how fantasy literature provides models for characterization and serves as a pervasive force throughout the work. Argues the novel has a dual purpose: to analyze the psychology of a Victorian businessman and simultaneously to present a fable of contemporary life. Elements of the folktale tradition provide Dickens a means of vivifying this fable.

Tillotson, Kathleen. *Novels of the Eighteen-Forties*. Oxford, England: Clarendon Press, 1954.
Analyzes the novel from the perspective of the period in which it was written; notes the control Dickens has over his materials, the result of careful planning that is not evident in his earlier works. Sees this as the first novel in which Dickens focuses on the inner conflict of characters as a central concern.

Great Expectations

Barzilai, Shuli. "Dickens' *Great Expectations*: The Motive for Moral Masochism." In *Charles Dickens*, edited by Harold Bloom. New York: Chelsea House, 1987.
Uses the tools of psychological criticism to explain the reasons for Pip's preoccupation with his guilt. Notes how Pip, Estella, and Miss Havisham are linked so closely that they become almost interchangeable versions of the same self; hence, by analogy, what the reader learns of Estella and Miss Havisham applies to Pip as well. Traces the importance of spider imagery in helping the reader understand the methods by which the characters entrap and eventually punish themselves.

Buckley, Jerome H. "Dickens, David, and Pip." In his *Seasons of Youth: The Bildungsroman from Dickens to Golding*. Cambridge, Mass.: Harvard University Press, 1974.
Analyzes the novel as Dickens' second (after *David Copperfield*) and more successful effort at the *Bildungsroman*. Extensive discussion of Pip's growth to mature self-awareness and acceptance of himself as he overcomes the temptations of avarice and social status. Considers Pip closely allied to Dickens himself in temperament and self-awareness.

Cockshut, A. O. J. *The Imagination of Charles Dickens*. New York: New York University Press, 1962.
Examines the novel as Dickens' attempt to criticize his own life through Pip's story. Argues Dickens is never comfortable dealing with people like Miss Havisham and Magwitch who, excluded from society by force or choice, try to influence those within the mainstream. Sees difficulties in Dickens' narrative method; believes he could not settle on an appropriate perspective from which Pip should relate his life to the reader.

Collins, Philip, ed. *Dickens: The Critical Heritage*. Boston: Routledge & Kegan Paul, 1971.
Reprints extracts from five reviews published shortly after the novel appeared, to provide a sense of the British public's favorable reaction to the work. Margaret Oliphant's criticisms of the novel in her *Blackwood's* essay sound a dissenting note.

Dyson, A. E. "*Great Expectations*: The Immolation of Pip." In his *The Inimitable Dickens: A Reading of the Novels*. London: Macmillan, 1970.
Reverses traditional readings of the novel. Argues that the work is not a social critique of the evils of snobbery; rather, it is the personal tragedy and triumph of Pip, who is actually quite normal in his reaction to the people and circumstances he encounters. As such, he earns the reader's sympathy throughout the work, even when he is clearly wrong in his dealings with others.

Fielding, Kenneth J. *Charles Dickens: A Critical Introduction*. London: Longman, 1958, enlarged ed. 1965.
Judges this novel Dickens' best, because in it the novelist is in complete control of his materials. The work is both an attack on the notion that money will bring happiness, and a moral fable promoting Christian virtues. Notes Dickens' growing ability to create believable female characters.

Gomme, A. H. *Dickens*. London: Evans Brothers, 1971.
Compares the novel with *Martin Chuzzlewit* and *David Copperfield* to show how Dickens' greater control of plotting and narrative technique in *Great Expectations* allows him to unite plot and theme more closely than in any other of his works. Discusses the ways Pip deceives himself about his importance until he is forced to recognize the source of his fortune, an event that finally leads him to self-knowledge.

Johnson, Edgar. "The Tempest and the Ruined Garden." In his *Charles Dickens: His Tragedy and Triumph*. Vol. 2. New York: Simon & Schuster, 1952.
Reviews the major events in the story to show Pip's growing snobbery, his disillusionment upon learning the source of his wealth, and his transformation into a man who comes to appreciate others for what they are. Reads the novel as emblematic of Dickens' view of the great expectation all of Victorian society had: to live at ease at the expense of others' labor. Notes parallels between Pip and Dickens, but stresses these are psychological, not autobiographical.

Karl, Frederick R. *A Reader's Guide to the Nineteenth-Century Novel*. New York: Farrar, Straus & Giroux, 1964.
Traces the ironic stance underlying Dickens' portrayal of character and incident in the novel. Considers this work an advance over *David Copperfield* in its control of techniques of fiction. Highlights Dickens' treatment of snobbery.

Leavis, Q. D. "How We Must Read *Great Expectations*." In F. R. Leavis and Q. D. Leavis' *Dickens the Novelist*. New Brunswick, N.J.: Rutgers University Press, 1979.

Insists the novel should not be reduced to sentimentalism. Examines a Dickens short story which uses similar characters and a similar theme to illustrate the novelist's method of dealing with the problems of identity and social responsibility characterizing Pip's life. Penetrating analysis of Dickens' subtle handling of Pip as narrator and as a character in his own story; discusses the novelist's handling of social values through characterization and dramatic conflict. Focuses on Dickens' treatment of shame and guilt, two qualities whose interaction influences Pip's behavior. Argues that the happy ending is appropriate.

Lucas, John. *The Melancholy Man: A Study of Dickens' Novels*. Reprint. Totowa, N.J.: Barnes & Noble Books, 1980.
Reads the novel as an exploration of the way an individual comes to define the important events in his life. Stresses the significance of the three points of view: the young Pip, the older Pip criticizing his younger self, and the reader, who must judge both. Explains how Pip's excessive guilt is not justified; others help build his false expectations. Sees the novel depicting the human dilemma of commitment versus freedom. Excellent brief character analyses of Wemmick and Jaggers.

Miller, J. Hillis. *Charles Dickens: The World of His Novels*. Cambridge, Mass.: Harvard University Press, 1959.
Using Pip as an example, offers an anatomy of the archetypal Dickens hero: initially an outcast who considers himself a parasite on the social establishment, forced to choose between withdrawing from the world or entering the mainstream of society. Traces the many ways people manipulate others; focuses on Miss Havisham's efforts to do so. Also provides extended analysis of the way Pip deceives himself about his good fortune. Shows how Pip finally acts responsibly toward Magwitch, indicating Dickens' belief in love and sacrifice as the means for individuals to achieve dignity and self-satisfaction.

Patten, Robert L. *Dickens and His Publishers*. Oxford, England: Clarendon Press, 1978.
Intriguing account of the serial publication history of the work, explaining its genesis in terms of economic necessity: Dickens wanted to shore up sales of his magazine *All the Year Round*. Focuses on the immense popularity of the novel in Victorian England as evidenced by its sales in a variety of forms: copies of the magazine sold while the story was running serially, bound volumes bought by libraries, and subsequent editions issued in Dickens' lifetime.

Phelps, Gilbert. *A Reader's Guide to Fifty British Novels, 1600-1900*. New York: Barnes & Noble Books, 1979.

Plot summary and biographical sketch, followed by critical comments high-lighting Dickens' mastery in handling patterns of imagery. Posits the major theme of the work is the power of selfless love to overcome virtually any difficulty.

Pickrel, Paul. "*Great Expectations.*" In *Dickens: A Collection of Critical Essays*, edited by Martin Price. Englewood Cliffs, N.J.: Prentice-Hall, 1967.
Argues that Dickens is a symbolist poet *manqué*, and this novel is a study of a hero's struggles to view the world poetically. Sees Pip's story as a fantasy governed by two characters from the realm of the fantastic: Magwitch and Miss Havisham. Against this background of fantasy, Pip must operate in a moral universe that holds him accountable for his actions as he struggles to attain his great expectations.

Sadoff, Diane. "Language Engenders: *David Copperfield* and *Great Expectations.*" In *Charles Dickens*, edited by Harold Bloom. New York: Chelsea House, 1987.
Deals with both novels as examples of Dickens' attempts to come to grips with the psychological issue of fatherhood and sonship. Notes the novelist's close association with his characters as children, showing how Pip is really a part of Dickens himself. Claims the novel is about the power of language; characters who tell the tale create a self-identity and achieve authority and status in the world.

Smith, Grahame. "The Years of Achievement." In his *Dickens, Money, and Society*. Berkeley: University of California Press, 1968.
Sees ties between this novel and other European masterpieces in which the hero undertakes a spiritual pilgrimage. Traces Dickens' method of working out the relationship between greed and class consciousness in intensely personal terms. Perceptive analysis of the handling of love interests; shows how Pip's growing affection for Magwitch provides a radical reversal of his personality and offers him a chance for salvation through self-knowledge.

Stange, G. Robert. "Expectations Well Lost." In *The Dickens Critics*, edited by George H. Ford and Lariat Lane, Jr. Westport, Conn.: Greenwood Press, 1972.
Reads the novel as a moral fable, tracing Pip's development through three phases from his first moment of self-awareness to his acceptance of his lot in life. The action moves from the country to the city, paralleling Pip's movement from innocence to experience; his return to the country after his illusions are lost is seen as a movement of acceptance. Discusses fire and star imagery; also analyzes the function of Jaggers.

Stoehr, Taylor. *Dickens: The Dreamer's Stance*. Ithaca, N.Y.: Cornell University Press, 1965.

Extensive analysis of the structure of the novel, focusing on the way the three major landmarks of the work (the forge, Satis House, and Newgate) are emblematic of both the external options open to Pip in his choice of life-styles, and of the deeper psychological forces warring within Pip's subconscious for control of his personality.

Stone, Harry. *Dickens and the Invisible World*. Bloomington: Indiana University Press, 1979.
Devotes two chapters to an analysis of the novel. The first traces Dickens' creative genius in fixing on the subject of the work, especially his growing awareness of the possibilities presented by a character such as Miss Havisham. The second details the ways the novelist uses elements of the fairy tale to shape the novel by underscoring its moral complexities and uniting its autobiographical, social, and factual elements in a concise tale raised to the level of myth. The novel is seen as a fable of man's quest to fulfill his desires, and of the ultimate meting out of just rewards.

Westburg, Barry. *The Confessional Fictions of Charles Dickens*. DeKalb: Northern Illinois University Press, 1977.
Discusses the novel as the third in which Dickens explores the mode of confession: an examination of one's life to isolate the significant events as a means of defining a person's identity. Two chapters review key scenes and discuss Pip's relationships with figures who influence his concept of self. Notes Dickens is interested in explaining the importance of time in the process of growth and development. Argues Pip's view of time is positive: he looks forward to better circumstances for himself. Ironically, self-acceptance comes only when he confronts the past honestly and is able to transcend his earlier self.

Hard Times

Butt, John, and Kathleen Tillotson. "Hard Times: The Problems of a Weekly Serial." In their *Dickens at Work*. London: Methuen, 1957.
Careful analysis of Dickens' plans for the novel, including his choice of titles, to show how he was able to compress the action and description in this work to fit the requirements of weekly serialization. Offers some discussion of the way Dickens transforms his notes into specific scenes that make vivid the destructive qualities of Gradgrind's Benthamite philosophy.

Cazamian, Louis. *The Social Novel in England, 1830-1850: Dickens, Disraeli, Mrs. Gaskell, Kingsley*. Boston: Routledge & Kegan Paul, 1973.
Reads the novel as an example of the social novel in the tradition of writers

whose fiction examines specific social ills. Sees Dickens trying to point out the need for understanding of and sympathy for the workers; Dickens wants owners and manufacturers to have a change of heart and treat their workers charitably. Posits Dickens does not really understand the poor in northern England, though they are the subject of this novel.

Cockshut, A. O. J. *The Imagination of Charles Dickens.* New York: New York University Press, 1962.
Criticizes F. R. Leavis' claim that the work is Dickens' masterpiece. Argues that Dickens could never settle on the specific function of the work, vacillating between realistic social satire and moral fable; as a result, this novel fails to be fully convincing in its attack on specific social ills.

Collins, Philip, ed. *Dickens: The Critical Heritage.* Boston: Routledge & Kegan Paul, 1971.
Selections from five reviews of the novel by Dickens' contemporaries; represented are Dickens' close friend and biographer John Forster, John Ruskin, and American critic Edwin W. Whipple. Also includes an excerpt from a parody of the novel that appeared in *Our Miscellany*.

Davis, Earle. "The Social Microcosmic Pattern." In his *The Flint and the Flame: The Artistry of Charles Dickens.* Columbia: University of Missouri Press, 1963.
Cites the appeal of the novel to readers interested in social criticism. Outlines Dickens' three plot sequences: the stories of Gradgrind, Bounderby, and Stephen Blackpool. Shows how each is a variation on the central issues of the novel: the effects of the laissez-faire economy on England, the problems of the educational system, and the rigidity of the divorce laws. Notes Dickens' sympathy for the workers, but also points out his aversion to unionization.

Dyson, A. E. "*Hard Times*: The Robber Fancy." In his *The Inimitable Dickens: A Reading of the Novels.* London: Macmillan, 1970.
Views the novel as Dickens' most bitter work, in which good is impotent and evil seems to triumph. Argues that, throughout the work, Dickens shows the horror resulting when fancy and imagination are pushed out of people's lives. Also notes the extremes of characterization and the claustrophobic effect created by concentrating all the action in Coketown.

Fielding, Kenneth J. *Charles Dickens: A Critical Introduction.* London: Longman, 1958, enlarged ed. 1965.
Claims previous readings stressing the novel's function as social criticism are misleading; posits the work should be read as a moral fable, demonstrating Dickens' unswerving commitment to Christian principles as a means of bettering mankind. Detailed discussion of the novelist's attitudes toward religion.

Fowler, Roger. "Polyphony and Problematic in *Hard Times*." In *The Changing World of Charles Dickens*, edited by Robert Giddings. Totowa, N.J.: Barnes & Noble Books, 1983.

Uses Russian critic Mikhail Bahktin's theory of the polyphonic novel and A. K. Halliday's notion of linguistic registers to examine the speech patterns of several characters. Demonstrates that within the novel a variety of viewpoints clash without resolution, and there is no authorial voice to demand that the reader side with one position over others. Hence, the work's strength lies in the complexity of the problems presented to the reader, not in any single solution to the social or moral issues it presents.

Gomme, A. H. "Four Great Novels." In his *Dickens*. London: Evans Brothers, 1971.

Considers the novel a tragedy in which Mr. Gradgrind is the tragic figure: though a deeply loving father, his blindness to everything but the utilitarian system of education causes the ruination of his children and himself. Criticizes Dickens for including the overdrawn, sentimental character Stephen Blackpool in the work.

House, Humphry. "*Hard Times*." In *Dickens: Modern Judgments*, edited by A. E. Dyson. London: Macmillan, 1968.

Accounts for Dickens' decision to write the novel and explains his methods of collecting information for the plot. Posits Dickens' depiction of Gradgrind is motivated by his desire to explore the consequences of a man's attempt to live by any system. Acknowledges the novel's failure to portray the strikers and Stephen Blackpool effectively, but concludes the general effect which produces disquiet in the reader is intentional on Dickens' part.

Johnson, Edgar. "Critique of Materialism." In his *Charles Dickens: His Tragedy and Triumph*. Vol. 2. New York: Simon & Schuster, 1952.

Considers the novel a penetrating indictment of Victorian industrial society and its attendant materialism. Believes it has been ill received because Dickens writes without his usual dose of humor. He does so intentionally to stress the horror of a world where striving for economic advantage drives out all concern for human feelings. Notes how the world of the circus functions as an antidote to the world of Gradgrind and Bounderby.

Karl, Frederick R. *A Reader's Guide to the Nineteenth-Century Novel*. New York: Farrar, Straus & Giroux, 1964.

Provides background about the influence of Thomas Carlyle on Dickens' conception of the novel. Considers the work Dickens' attempt to deal artistically with the problems of the individual in an industrialized society, especially one in which ideologies such as utilitarianism have currency.

Leavis, F. R. *"Hard Times*: An Analytical Note." In his *The Great Tradition*. London: Chatto & Windus, 1948.

Praises the novel as one of Dickens' best; calls it a moral fable. Discusses key scenes in detail to show how Dickens mastered the conventions of the popular novel for moral purposes.

Shaw, George Bernard. *"Hard Times."* In *The Dickens Critics*, edited by George H. Ford and Lariat Lane, Jr. Westport, Conn.: Greenwood Press, 1972.

Praises the novel as Dickens' first to deal directly with the problems of a society in need of reform. Sees him shifting from a treatment of heroes and villains to a concern for victims and oppressors; believes he intends to make the reader uncomfortable with the circumstances he depicts. Faults Dickens for his portrait of Slackbridge and for some of his excessive rhetoric.

Spector, Stephen J. "Monsters of Metonymy: *Hard Times* and Knowing the Working Class." In *Charles Dickens*, edited by Harold Bloom. New York: Chelsea House, 1987.

Believes that a reason for Dickens' failure to create convincing working-class characters can be found in his adherence to principles of realistic writing, which relies on metonymy as its primary literary device. The novel vitiates the notion that people are exactly like the objects associated with them; rather, they are complex and individual. Briefly compares Dickens' attempts to understand the working classes with similar efforts by Friedrich Engels in *The Condition of the Working Class* in England.

Stoehr, Taylor. *Dickens: The Dreamer's Stance*. Ithaca, N.Y.: Cornell University Press, 1965.

In a brief discussion of the work, Stoehr explains how Dickens attempts to unify his double plot and explores the implications of such plotting. Such a technique allows Dickens to keep competing emotions (especially those associated with sexual and social conflicts) separate and allows him to displace the guilt characters feel over their actions from its real source.

Little Dorrit

Butt, John, and Kathleen Tillotson. "From 'Nobody's Fault' to *Little Dorrit*." In their *Dickens at Work*. London: Methuen, 1957.

Focuses on the political satire underlying Dickens' portrait of society. Shows how instances of mismanagement in the Crimean War prompted his indignation and led him to speak and write about governmental inefficiency in tones similar to those used in the novel. Sketches the genesis of the character of Amy

Dorrit, noting how closely she is affiliated with Little Nell of *The Old Curiosity Shop*—a conscious decision on Dickens' part to evoke recognition and sympathy.

Cockshut, A. O. J. *The Imagination of Charles Dickens*. New York: New York University Press, 1962.
Discusses several major characters in the novel to show the manner in which individuals of various social standings are affected by the merciless, impersonal machinations of government. Sees Dickens concerned with the moral implications rather than the social implications of the interactions of individuals and institutions.

Collins, Philip, ed. *Dickens: The Critical Heritage*. Boston: Routledge & Kegan Paul, 1971.
Four excerpts from reviews published shortly after the novel's appearance display the varying reactions the work evoked. A lengthy selection from James FitzJames Stephen's *Edinburgh Review* essay challenges Dickens' criticism of governmental agencies.

Davis, Earle. "The Social Microcosmic Pattern." In his *The Flint and the Flame: The Artistry of Charles Dickens*. Columbia: University of Missouri Press, 1963.
Considers the novel Dickens' darkest, and his most penetrating analysis of the evils of contemporary society. Outlines the six major plot sequences in the work, summarizes each, and shows how Dickens brings together characters from these separate stories to form a unified novel whose aim is to expose the many ways men are imprisoned within a society. Also discusses Dickens' use of various literary devices.

Dyson, A. E. "*Little Dorrit*: A Dickens First Chapter." In his *The Inimitable Dickens: A Reading of the Novels*. London: Macmillan, 1970.
Extensive analysis of the opening chapter of the novel shows how the pervasive image of the prison is used as a motif recurring throughout the story. Brief assessment of the role of Amy Dorrit as a virtuous person who is never rewarded for her virtue.

Fielding, Kenneth J. *Charles Dickens: A Critical Introduction*. London: Longman, 1958, enlarged ed. 1965.
Considers the novel Dickens' most important social satire; observes that the Marshalsea prison is used as a metaphor for society itself. Briefly discusses the novelist's failure to create a winsome heroine in Amy Dorrit. Also remarks on the criticism of the novel by those among Dickens' contemporaries who were upset with his attack on the government.

Gomme, A. H. *Dickens*. London: Evans Brothers, 1971.
Traces the psychological traumatization of one of the central characters, Mr. Dorrit, for whom imprisonment gradually comes to be an acceptable way to avoid the responsibilities of the world outside the Marshalsea prison. Careful analysis of key scenes demonstrates Dorrit's gradual decline.

Johnson, Edgar. "The Prison of Society." In his *Charles Dickens: His Tragedy and Triumph*. Vol. 2. New York: Simon & Schuster, 1952.
Argues that the novel shows Dickens' belief that all of society is a vast prison, where individuals of every social class are limited by strictures imposed from without and within. Analyzes the function of the Circumlocution Office as a symbol of governmental indifference and strangulation; discusses its real-life models. Brief but penetrating assessment of William Dorrit's failure to escape the prison of his past even when he leaves the physical confines of the Marshalsea prison.

Larson, Janet. "The Seer, the Preacher, and the Living Gospel: Vision and Revision in *Little Dorrit*." In her *Dickens and the Broken Scripture*. Athens: University of Georgia Press, 1985.
Monograph-length chapter provides a comprehensive review of the novel as an exemplar of the contradictory religious impulses expressed in the Book of Ecclesiastes and the Book of Revelation. Notes how this parallels Dickens' attempt to contrast the modes of the satirist and the mimetic novelist: the tension between presentation of types and documentary reporting. Stresses Dickens' prophetic stance in creating characters who portray the demise of society; also traces the apocalyptic nature of the narrative. Finds frequent parallels between the novel and Thomas Carlyle's writings.

Leavis, F. R. "Dickens and Blake: *Little Dorrit*." In F. R. Leavis and Q. D. Leavis' *Dickens the Novelist*. New Brunswick, N.J.: Rutgers University Press, 1979.
Treats the work as an example of Dickens' best writing, calling it one of the finest novels in the language. Sees Dickens' affinities with the Romantic poets in his outlook on the individual and society. Stresses the poetic qualities of Dickens' language in his evocation of character and scene. Extensive analysis of specific scenes demonstrates the complexity of characterization and reinforces Leavis' central thesis that the book presents a disinterested view of Victorian society; this quality sets *Little Dorrit* apart from other novels of the period.

Lucas, John. *The Melancholy Man: A Study of Dickens' Novels*. Reprint. Totowa, N.J.: Barnes & Noble Books, 1980.
Considers the novel Dickens' greatest, and one of the greatest in the language. Careful analysis of the complexity of characterization which separates this

work from Dickens' other novels that explore evils of society. Detailed critiques of Mr. Dorrit, Pancks, Clenham, Meagles, Doyce, and Amy. Shows how
the prison of self, man's willful effort to seal himself off from others, pervades
the novelist's handling of plot and characterization; concludes that Dickens
offers no routes for escape from self-made prisons.

Miller, J. Hillis. *Charles Dickens: The World of His Novels*. Cambridge, Mass.:
Harvard University Press, 1959.
Noting that this novel presents the darkest vision of society and human existence of any of Dickens' major works, Miller explores the way the novelist
employs two major images: the prison and the labyrinth. Displays the methods
used to dramatize the notion that imprisonment is as much a state of mind as it
is a condition imposed from outside.

Nunokawa, Jeff. "Getting and Having: Some Versions of Possession in *Little Dorrit*." In *Charles Dickens*, edited by Harold Bloom. New York: Chelsea House,
1987.
Focuses on the many references and allusions to acquisition and inheritance of
property as both the means by which Dickens conveys his social message and
as one of his subjects. Shows how human relationships in the novel are imaged
in the same terms that are used to describe wealth and inheritance.

Patten, Robert L. *Dickens and His Publishers*. Oxford, England: Clarendon Press,
1978.
Traces the sales of the monthly installments of the novel and reports Dickens'
profits. Claims that the novel had a strong following throughout its appearance
in serial form. A separate appendix gives details of the sales and publication
history during Dickens' lifetime.

Smith, Grahame. "The Years of Achievement." In his *Dickens, Money, and Society*.
Berkeley: University of California Press, 1968.
Views the novel as one dominated by feelings of loneliness; public isolation is
fused with private loneliness in the symbol of the prison. Examines characterization of Arthur Clenham, Amy Dorrit, and Merdle to show that only a few
can break free from the evils of a society in which the pursuit of wealth is a
national disease. Considers Dickens' portraits an advance over those in his
previous novels: the major figures in this work have a complexity that comes
much closer to realism than any of Dickens' earlier creations.

Stang, Richard. "*Little Dorrit*: A World in Reverse." In *Dickens the Craftsman:
Strategies of Presentation*, edited by Robert B. Partlow. Carbondale: Southern
Illinois University Press, 1970.
Taking his cue from a scene in the novel in which a rowdy crowd is com-

pared to the disarray visible on the wrong side of a patterned quilt, Stang argues the entire novel is an exposé of English society which has, in fact, turned human values inside out. Argues that Dickens' use of irony in dealing with Victorian conventions, and his constant reliance on reversals of fortune and situation, highlight this central theme.

Steig, Michael. "*Bleak House* and *Little Dorrit*: Iconography of Darkness." In his *Dickens and Phiz*. Bloomington: Indiana University Press, 1978.
Discusses Hablot K. Browne's illustrations for the novel. Detailed analysis of the title page, frontispiece, and several key drawings that highlight the major themes of the work; notes how Browne's handling of light and darkness in his drawings parallels Dickens' irony in dealing with the idea of imprisonment.

Stoehr, Taylor. *Dickens: The Dreamer's Stance*. Ithaca, N.Y.: Cornell University Press, 1965.
Detailed analysis of Dickens' use of the double plot, a device Stoehr associates with the dream method of experiencing and apprehending the world. Concentrates on Arthur Clenham's story, showing how he finally expiates his guilt. Considers the Amy Dorrit story line weaker, because Amy is too good to be a typical Dickens heroine: she has no secret in her past.

Trilling, Lionel. "*Little Dorrit*." In *Dickens: A Collection of Critical Essays*, edited by Martin Price. Englewood Cliffs, N.J.: Prentice-Hall, 1967.
Stresses the greatness of this novel, accounting for its success by citing the psychological depth of Dickens' portrait of society and his masterful use of symbolism, especially that of the prison. Discusses the character of Blandois as an example of the evil society can breed. Notes how Dickens personalizes the injustices of society by focusing on failed parents and unhappy children.

Martin Chuzzlewit

Collins, Philip. *Dickens and Crime*. Bloomington: Indiana University Press, 1962.
Brief discussion of Dickens' portrayal of Jonas Chuzzlewit, who is driven to murder by the circumstances in which he finds himself. Explains how Dickens rises above the level of melodrama in this portrait. Other comments about the novel are scattered throughout this study, explaining how Dickens' fascination with crime and criminals is transformed into fiction.

_____ , ed. *Dickens: The Critical Heritage*. Boston: Routledge & Kegan Paul, 1971.
Excerpts from reviews published shortly after the novel was issued, one by Dickens' friend and biographer John Forster; another excerpt, published in

1861 after the novel was reissued in the Library Edition of Dickens' works, provides a retrospective look at the book.

Davis, Earle. "From Alternation to Pattern: The Technique of Contrast." In his *The Flint and the Flame: The Artistry of Charles Dickens*. Columbia: University of Missouri Press, 1963.
Brief account of the novel as the best of Dickens' early works, because the novelist constructs three contrasting yet parallel plots around a central theme: the consequences of selfishness and hypocrisy. Explains how and why Dickens changed his original scheme when sales of the novel flagged. Criticizes Dickens for his overreliance on declamation to highlight his moral purposes.

Dyson, A. E. "*Martin Chuzzlewit*: Howls the Sublime." In his *The Inimitable Dickens: A Reading of the Novels*. London: Macmillan, 1970.
Describes the novel as the one in which Dickens best employs his comic vision to deal with dark subjects; through his power as a satirist he blunts the horrors that characters such as Pecksniff might inspire. Close analysis of Pecksniff, Sairey Gamp, and Tom Pinch shows Dickens' mastery at creating dialect, his ability to capture attitudes in his sketches of action, and his uneasiness at dealing with characters such as Tom who are largely agents of good.

Fielding, Kenneth J. *Charles Dickens: A Critical Introduction*. London: Longman, 1958, enlarged ed. 1965.
Criticizes the novel for its weak attempt at satire and for poor plotting. Notes Dickens' overriding purpose: to illustrate the evils of hypocrisy and selfishness. Introductory remarks in the chapter outline Dickens' experiences on his first trip to the United States and explain how these influenced the novelist's conception of the parts of *Martin Chuzzlewit* set in America.

Johnson, Edgar. "Selfishness and the Economic Man." In his *Charles Dickens: His Tragedy and Triumph*. Vol. 1. New York: Simon & Schuster, 1952.
Remarks on the vitality of Dickens' presentation, especially his characterization; focuses his analysis on Pecksniff and Sairey Gamp. Considers the novel a triumph its in structure and character portrayal, but faults Dickens for the invective he uses to deal with some of the evil characters, especially those in America.

Lucas, John. *The Melancholy Man: A Study of Dickens' Novels.* Reprint. Totowa, N.J.: Barnes & Noble Books, 1980.
Judges the novel to be almost great; claims Dickens' concept was to indict those who pursue self-interest at any expense, and to show that the entire society deserves this indictment. Pastoral values are contrasted with modern

urban ones, with the latter shown to be morally deficient. Unfortunately, Dickens' involvement with his characters caused him to blur distinctions between static moral types and individuals who grow as the story progresses, leaving readers confused about ways to understand the good and evil figures in the work.

Magnet, Myron. "*Martin Chuzzlewit* in Context." In his *Dickens and the Social Order*. Philadelphia: University of Pennsylvania Press, 1985.
Reads the novel as Dickens' portrait of the true nature of man: a creature whose humanity is defined by his efforts to become civilized. Lengthy explanation of the novelist's references to philosophers whose opinions about man's nature were current in his day. Detailed analysis of the American scenes, showing how Dickens sees the state of nature in America as being far from Edenic: America has no civilizing qualities because it overstresses individual license. Claims Todger's Boarding House stands in opposition to the American wilderness as a symbol of the good society, where each man has his place.

Marcus, Steven. "The Self and the World." In his *Dickens: From Pickwick to Dombey*. New York: Basic Books, 1965. Also in *Dickens: A Collection of Critical Essays*, edited by Martin Price. Englewood Cliffs, N.J.: Prentice-Hall, 1967.
Argues that the novel is the first of Dickens' works in which language is of great significance: characters define themselves by language, and rhetoric plays an important role in shaping both truth and illusion. Sees the novel as Dickens' indictment of the Edenic vision of Jean-Jacques Rousseau, using the American wilderness as an example of the horror of that vision.

Miller, J. Hillis. *Charles Dickens: The World of His Novels*. Cambridge, Mass.: Harvard University Press, 1959.
Detailed examination of Dickens' method of characterization. Notes that, while the novelist's professed aim is to display the evils of selfishness, the real focus is on the way all the major characters live autonomously or seek to establish their identity through association with something outside themselves. Excellent analysis of the psychological makeup and actions of Jonas Chuzzlewit and Sairey Gamp. Also discusses Dickens' attitude toward America and Americans.

Patten, Robert L. "Trouble in Eden: *American Notes* and *Martin Chuzzlewit*." In his *Charles Dickens and His Publishers*. Oxford, England: Clarendon Press, 1978.
Account of the genesis of the novel: its appearance was intentionally delayed to generate interest and anticipation. Discusses several reasons for the work's failure to sell widely, citing overall economic conditions in England and America as a significant cause.

Smith, Grahame. "The Mob and Society: America and *Martin Chuzzlewit*." In his *Dickens, Money, and Society*. Berkeley: University of California Press, 1968.
Sees this as a pivotal novel in Dickens' career: the last in which he uses the picaresque as an organizing principle, the first in which he attempts a comprehensive look at an entire society. Focuses on that portion of the book dealing with America; shows how Dickens' visit there, and his discussion of the American scene in *American Notes*, provides him with the overview needed to construct his scathing portrait of a land gone mad for money.

Steig, Michael. "From Caricature to Progress: *Master Humphrey's Clock* and *Martin Chuzzlewit*." In his *Dickens and Phiz*. Bloomington: Indiana University Press, 1978.
Lengthy analysis of the illustrations for the novel done by H. K. Browne. Shows how the frontispiece and the drawings for the monthly installments reflect an essential unity with the text; although the drawings are not always tied directly to specific scenes, they provide a visual complement to Dickens' attempt at exposing good and evil within respectable society.

Stone, Harry. "From *Pickwick* to *Chuzzlewit*: Fairy Tales and the Apprentice Novels." In his *Dickens and the Invisible World*. Bloomington: Indiana University Press, 1979.
Traces Dickens' use of fairy-tale characters and techniques. Extensive analysis of Old Martin as a kind of fairy godfather who manipulates events to insure a happy ending. Also discusses the relationship of other characters such as Sairey Gamp and Jonas Chuzzlewit to their counterparts in folk tales.

The Mystery of Edwin Drood

Collins, Philip. "The Mysteries of Edwin Drood." In his *Dickens and Crime*. Bloomington: Indiana University Press, 1962.
Detailed analysis of the extant portions of the novel. Believes Dickens intended Jaggers to be discovered as the murderer; argues the novelist's real interest is in the psychology of the murderer. Compares Jaggers to his predecessors in Dickens' fiction, pointing out the important differences include Jaggers' reliance on opium and on his hypnotic power over others. A good summary of previous critical responses to the work.

—————— , ed. *Dickens; The Critical Heritage*. Boston: Routledge & Kegan Paul, 1971.
Three excerpts from nineteenth century reviews provide a sense of the different reactions Dickens' contemporaries had toward his final, unfinished work. Two

reviews are highly critical; the third, published in the *Spectator* and attributed to noted critic R. H. Hutton, claims the characters, plotting, and flair for the dramatic evident in this novel all suggest Dickens still retained his literary powers.

Davis, Earle. "Dead or Alive?" In his *The Flint and the Flame: The Artistry of Charles Dickens*. Columbia: University of Missouri Press, 1963.
Primarily a review of attempts to determine how Dickens would have ended the novel. Identifies clues present in the work which suggest the possibilities Dickens had open to him for solving the mystery. Traces the novelist's sources in detective fiction. Offers a solution based on a reading of a Wilkie Collins play published in 1873, which Davis argues could have been based on discussions with Dickens about the Drood case.

Dyson, A. E. "*Edwin Drood*: A Horrible Wonder Apart." In his *The Inimitable Dickens: A Reading of the Novels*. London: Macmillan, 1970.
Penetrating analysis of John Jasper as a portrait of madness and of the modern consciousness. Dispels the notion that the novel is simply Dickens' contribution to the genre of mystery writing. Attacks Edmund Wilson's claim that Jasper can be seen as a hero.

Fielding, Kenneth J. *Charles Dickens: A Critical Introduction*. London: Longman, 1958, enlarged ed. 1965.
Offers suggestions regarding the way Dickens might have completed his novel; especially emphatic about the novel's being a mystery only in the broadest sense, in that Dickens lays bare clear evidence he intended John Jasper to be the villain. Speculates that Dickens may have been planning to have Jasper repent for his transgressions.

Johnson, Edgar. "The Dying and Undying Voice." In his *Charles Dickens: His Tragedy and Triumph*. Vol. 2. New York: Simon & Schuster, 1952.
Briefly reviews the plot of the surviving episodes and gives evidence available to show Dickens' intentions for completing the work. Careful analysis of the character of Jasper, noting important links to the Thugs, a Hindu sect which committed ritual murders; cites many clues to show the hero is a divided self. Also discusses Dickens' biting social criticism.

Patten, Robert L. *Charles Dickens and His Publishers*. Oxford, England: Clarendon Press, 1978.
Provides an account of the publishing arrangements for the novel, including Dickens' negotiations with his British and American publishers. Also relates the care with which Dickens composed those monthly installments he was able to complete before his death.

Peterson, Audrey. "Dickens and Detection." In her *Victorian Masters of Mystery*.
New York: Frederick Ungar, 1984.
Lengthy examination of the novel, offering a summary of various endings
which critics have proposed for this unfinished work. Detailed outline of
existing chapters and working notes, and of external evidence (for example,
Dickens' comments to John Forster), are offered as further evidence of Dickens' intentions for the novel.

Wright, James. *"The Mystery of Edwin Drood."* In *Dickens: Modern Judgments*,
edited by A. E. Dyson. London: Macmillan, 1968.
Analyzes the character of John Jasper as a representative of Victorian society, a
society divided against itself—respectable, yet having a dark underside it tries
to hide. Shows how Jasper's psychological complexities make him the fittest
candidate for the murderer of Drood, especially if Dickens intended to dramatize the divided nature of his own society.

Nicholas Nickleby

Collins, Philip, ed. *Dickens: The Critical Heritage*. Boston: Routledge & Kegan
Paul, 1971.
Comments on the novel are excerpted from various reviews in nineteenth
century periodicals, including the *Spectator* and *Fraser's*. Also includes an
excerpt from a review in the *Examiner* by Dickens' close friend John Forster.

Edgar, David. "Adapting *Nickleby*." In *The Changing World of Charles Dickens*,
edited by Robert Giddings. Totowa, N.J.: Barnes & Noble Books, 1983.
Conversational essay by the playwright who adapted the novel for the Royal
Shakespeare Company's stage production. Discusses the way scenes and
characters from the book were transformed for the stage. Highlights the condi-
tional nature of Dickens' world view: his stance for good is always taken with
an awareness that individuals must be willing to act morally if the world is to
be reformed.

Fielding, Kenneth J. *Charles Dickens: A Critical Introduction*. London, England:
Longman, 1958, enlarged ed. 1965.
Outlines Dickens' treatment of the major issues in the book: the necessity for
individuals to deal charitably with others and the importance of love in human
relationships. Relates the story of the novel's genesis, a trip Dickens took to
investigate conditions in Yorkshire schools.

Johnson, Edgar. "The Thieves' Den and the World." In his *Charles Dickens: His
Tragedy and Triumph*. Vol. 1. New York: Simon & Schuster, 1952.

Finds the strength of the novel in Dickens' portrayal of individual characters and scenes. Especially fulsome praise for scenes about Yorkshire schools. Provides character sketch of Ralph Nickleby. Notes the way Dickens combines expansiveness, joviality, and picaresque qualities reminiscent of *Pickwick Papers* with darker images and social criticism characteristic of *Oliver Twist*.

Lucas, John. *The Melancholy Man: A Study of Dickens' Novels*. Reprint. Totowa, N.J.: Barnes & Noble Books, 1980.
Considers the novel flawed, possibly because Dickens was overconfident in his powers. Examines faults in plotting and characterization, but notes that the novel foreshadows many important themes in Dickens' later works, especially the dire consequences of people's tendency to trade respectability and personal dignity for money and social status.

Magnet, Myron. "The Problem of Aggression." In his *Dickens and the Social Order*. Philadelphia: University of Pennsylvania Press, 1985.
Believes Dickens is obsessed with aggression as a passion that influences individual behavior. Concentrates on Squeers and Ralph Nickleby, two characters who exhibit consistently aggressive behavior, to examine the psychology of characters so motivated. Concludes that Dickens believes aggression is an integral part of human nature, a natural instinct influencing individual behavior with parallels in social activity.

Marcus, Steven. "The True Prudence." In his *Dickens: From Pickwick to Dombey*. New York: Basic Books, 1965.
Reads the novel as Dickens' exploration of the opposing concepts of prudence and improvidence as characteristics of human behavior. Groups characters according to their assimilation of one or the other of these traits; believes Dickens is seeking a middle ground between the two. Notes how characters in this novel are more fragmented than those in earlier works: for example, Nicholas and Smike represent the two possibilities that exist simultaneously in Oliver Twist. Also contains an extensive discussion of the function of the Cheerybles and the Crummles.

Miller, J. Hillis. *Charles Dickens: The World of His Novels*. Cambridge, Mass.: Harvard University Press, 1959.
Considers the special quality of the novel Dickens' ability to create a wide range of unique grotesque characters, without psychological depth but able to captivate and command readers' attention. Notes the importance of sentiment and melodrama; sees the scenes of the provincial theater as parallels to the larger action of the work. Illustrates the theatricality of the central characters and their lack of substance. Ranks this novel with the three preceding it as ones in which Dickens follows the familiar pattern of having his hero isolated from society and striving to find a place in it.

Patten, Robert L. *Charles Dickens and His Publishers*. Oxford, England: Clarendon Press, 1978.
Carefully detailed account of the creation and publication history of the work; notes how pressures from his other work in progress kept Dickens from completing installments on time, but observes that Dickens was pleased with the novel and gratified by its success. Separate appendixes chart Dickens' profits and list the serial printing history of the work.

Steig, Michael. "*Pickwick, Nickleby*, and the Emergence from Caricature." In his *Dickens and Phiz*. Bloomington: Indiana University Press, 1978.
Extensive analysis of the illustrations Hablot K. Browne ("Phiz") did for the novel, citing and explaining the unevenness of these sketches. Notes that not all of the monthly installment covers relate directly to the text, and some drawings focus on minor incidents, but generally the illustrations reinforce the narrative in depicting essential character traits.

The Old Curiosity Shop

Dyson, A. E. "*The Old Curiosity Shop*: Innocence and the Grotesque." In his *The Inimitable Dickens: A Reading of the Novels*. London: Macmillan, 1970.
Sees the novel as one of a group in which Dickens uses the grotesque as an organizing principle. Shows how Quilp, Dick Swiveller, and Kit Nibbles are exhibited more than analyzed, as Dickens presents a constant dramatic juxtaposition of good and evil. The novel displays a kind of realism different from Jane Austen or George Eliot, but no less convincing to readers who enter into the imaginative experience of the work.

Fielding, Kenneth J. *Charles Dickens: A Critical Introduction*. London: Longman, 1958, enlarged ed. 1965.
Brief review of the way the novel developed as a result of Dickens' failure to sustain his original idea of writing separate sketches for his magazine *Master Humphrey's Clock*. Discusses the immense success of Little Nell, noting the allegorical nature of events surrounding her life, and Dickens' insistent linking of his heroine with death. Also notes the novelist's success in creating other characters, especially Quilp.

Huxley, Aldous. "The Vulgarity of Little Nell." In *The Dickens Critics*, edited by George H. Ford and Lariat Lane, Jr. Westport, Conn.: Greenwood Press, 1972.
Highly critical analysis of Dickens' handling of the death of Little Nell. Points out the novelist's tendency to let himself be overcome by emotionalism and to lose artistic control over his materials.

Johnson, Edgar. "The Neglected and Misused." In his *Charles Dickens: His Tragedy and Triumph*. Vol. 1. New York: Simon & Schuster, 1952.
Outlines Dickens' success with the comic sections of the work. Acknowledges the sentimentalism of Nell's death, but says that twentieth century readers react more harshly than did Dickens' contemporaries. Traces the fairy-tale quality of the story—the pursuit of gold—noting how Dickens' treatment of Nell is an ironic comment on the fate of all Victorian innocents left to suffer from such mad pursuit.

Kincaid, James R. "Laughter and Pathos: *The Old Curiosity Shop*." In *Dickens the Craftsman: Strategies of Presentation*, edited by Robert B. Partlow. Carbondale: Southern Illinois University Press, 1970.
Careful critique of Dickens' use of laughter and evocation of pathos in the work, showing how he plays these emotions against each other to involve readers in the story. Explains how three groups of characters represent opposing forces: Nell, Quilp, and Dick Swiveller each stand at the center of a group. Intriguing comparison of Nell and Quilp to show how they are alike in many ways—two sides of the figure of the child.

Lucas, John. *The Melancholy Man: A Study of Dickens' Novels*. Reprint. Totowa, N.J.: Barnes & Noble Books, 1980.
Though noting the many flaws in the novel, Lucas argues that Dickens was using this story for two purposes: first, to account for the presence of death in the world (a subject of personal interest to Dickens because of the death of his sister-in-law, whom he adored); and second, to view death in a larger, metaphorical sense, as the death of the past and its ways. The more natural world of the past, represented by the country, is markedly better than the squalid present, identified with the city. Sees Quilp as an embodiment of modern corruption.

Marcus, Steven. "The Myth of Nell." In his *Dickens: From Pickwick to Dombey*. New York: Basic Books, 1965.
Considers the work Dickens' least successful, asserting the circumstance which gave rise to his imaginative creation of Nell—the death of his sister-in-law Mary Hogarth—led him to extremes of sentimentalism. Sees Nell and Quilp as polarities of human existence: purity and carnality. Shows how Dickens never overcomes his morbid fascination with death, a fault which leads him to produce some of his poorest prose.

Miller, J. Hillis. *Charles Dickens: The World of His Novels*. Cambridge, Mass.: Harvard University Press, 1959.
Links the novel with *Nicholas Nickleby* and *Barnaby Rudge* as ones in which

Dickens achieves great success in creating grotesques. Notes similarities among these works, and between them and *Oliver Twist*, in Dickens' exploration of the problems of the outcast who seeks a place within the community. Shows that, unlike the hero of *Oliver Twist*, characters in this novel cannot escape the city to find happiness in the country; Dickens argues instead that happiness must come through the actions of the community in caring for its members.

Patten, Robert L. " 'The Story-Weaver at His Loom': Dickens and the Beginning of *The Old Curiosity Shop*." In his *Charles Dickens and His Publishers*. Oxford, England: Clarendon Press, 1978.
Details the composition of the work, concentrating on Dickens' initial conception of the story and the changes he made to transform it from its place as an integrated tale in *Master Humphrey's Clock* into a separate novel. Uses manuscripts and letters to provide a corrective to earlier accounts of the composition process.

――――――― . *Charles Dickens and His Publishers*. Oxford, England: Clarendon Press, 1978.
Brief commentary on the genesis and composition of the novel. Emphasis is on the publication history of the work in monthly serialization; notes how sales grew as people both in England and in America became increasingly interested in Little Nell's fate. A separate appendix charts Dickens' profits from the sales of the work during his lifetime.

Poe, Edgar Allan. "*The Old Curiosity Shop*." In *The Dickens Critics*, edited by George H. Ford and Lariat Lane, Jr. Westport, Conn.: Greenwood Press, 1972.
Assessment by one of America's premier writers, praising the work for its ability to capture and hold readers' attention. Gives a long list of the novel's felicities and a shorter list of faults, including the death scene of Little Nell, which Poe considers too painful for readers (though exceptionally well drawn). Good example of the early nineteenth century reaction to Dickens' work.

Steig, Michael. *Dickens and Phiz*. Bloomington: Indiana University Press, 1978.
Brief account of Dickens' work with the two men who illustrated the monthly installments of the novel: Hablot K. Browne and George Cattermole. Details the way the illustrations, especially those of Quilp, reflect the action of the novel and reveal the dark side of life in London.

Stone, Harry. "From *Pickwick* to *Chuzzlewit*: Fairy Tales and the Apprentice Novels." In his *Dickens and the Invisible World*. Bloomington: Indiana University Press, 1979.

Sees the presence of fairy-tale elements dominating Dickens' portrayal of characters and incidents within an allegorical framework. Discusses Quilp as a storybook ogre bent on evil, and Nell and her grandfather as pilgrims on a journey toward the safe haven of death. Notes the presence of many other fairy-tale characters and scenes; also discusses ways Dickens' reliance on such stereotypes weakens the psychological depth of the novel.

Oliver Twist

Bagley, John. *"Oliver Twist*: Things as They Really Are." In *Dickens: A Collection of Critical Essays*, edited by Martin Price. Englewood Cliffs, N.J.: Prentice-Hall, 1967.
Examines the characters in the novel as examples of Dickens' attempt to portray a nightmare fantasy world which is actually only the obverse (not the antithesis) of the world represented by Mr. Brownlow and his circle. Extensive discussion of the Victorians' attitude toward crime and murder, showing how the two were viewed as essentially different.

Collins, Philip. *Dickens and Crime*. Bloomington: Indiana University Press, 1962.
Discusses the relationship of the work to the Newgate novels, explaining how Dickens' treatment of crime is more realistic and brutal, and less glamorous, than other novels of that genre. Focuses on the novelist's fascination with Bill Sikes, and on his obsession with the murder of Nancy—the frequent subject of his public readings in later years.

_____ , ed. *Dickens: The Critical Heritage*. Boston: Routledge & Kegan Paul, 1971.
Five excerpts of nineteenth century reviews of the novel and two selections from more general surveys of Dickens' early works. Includes comments from George Henry Lewes and William Makepeace Thackeray, and passages from Queen Victoria's diary that illuminate the strange love-hate relationship early Victorians had with novels.

Fielding, Kenneth J. *Charles Dickens: A Critical Introduction*. London: Longman, 1958, enlarged ed. 1965.
Focuses on the publication history of the novel and on Dickens' exceptional ability to portray the criminal underworld. Sketches the inconsistencies associated with Oliver, who has no active role in the work. Briefly discusses the book's social purpose: to reveal to contemporary readers a side of London usually unknown or ignored.

Hollingsworth, Keith. "The 'Real' World of *Oliver Twist*." In his *The Newgate Novel 1830-1847*. Detroit: Wayne State University Press, 1963.

Notes close links between Dickens' fictional portrayal of crime and the contemporary real-world situation in London. Traces some of the sources of Dickens' plot and characters, especially Fagin and Nancy. Brief discussion of Dickens' use of coincidence, and of his attempt to reproduce both the setting and language of the criminal world. Also discusses the stage versions of the novel.

Johnson, Edgar. "The Thieves' Den and the World." In his *Charles Dickens: His Tragedy and Triumph*. Vol. 1. New York: Simon & Schuster, 1952.
Extensive discussion of the historical background Dickens used to draw his portraits of the lives of those suppressed by the Poor Laws, and of the Victorian underworld which sprang up in part as a result of those laws. Some attention is paid to the many contrivances of the plot. Notes Dickens' hesitancy concerning problems of language and sexual relations among the criminal elements, but considers his portrait otherwise realistic.

Kettle, Arnold. "*Oliver Twist*." In *The Dickens Critics*, edited by George H. Ford and Lariat Lane, Jr. Westport, Conn.: Greenwood Press, 1972.
Sees the plot of the novel in conflict with the symbolic pattern Dickens creates. Judges the plot weak, but considers the novel a powerful symbolic representation of the plight of the poor in England. The appeal of the work comes from the contrast between the underworld and the respectable world of the Brownlows and Maylies. Shows how the novelist creates Oliver and others as type characters to elicit sympathy from readers.

Larson, Janet. "Early Biblical Boz: The Case of *Oliver Twist*." In her *Dickens and the Broken Scripture*. Athens: University of Georgia Press, 1985.
Traces the influence of biblical narratives on Dickens' idea for the novel. Illustrates parallels between this work and John Bunyan's *Pilgrim's Progress*, stressing the way Dickens modifies Bunyan's moralistic story to show how complex the struggle for goodness can be in modern society. Also displays Dickens' use and modification of the Parable of the Good Samaritan.

Lucas, John. *The Melancholy Man: A Study of Dickens' Novels*. Reprint. Totowa, N.J.: Barnes & Noble Books, 1980.
Considers the novel Dickens' first attempt at realism: a conscious effort to forego literary conventions in favor of a realistic portrait of the underworld, which the upperclass society (including Dickens' readers) refused to recognize. Stresses the importance of Oliver as a character whose wanderings force members of both the upper classes and the underworld to confront one another. Sees Oliver as a Rousseauesque child of nature. Discusses the major imagery that creates the sense of horror Dickens wished to achieve.

Marcus, Steven. "The Wise Child." In his *Dickens: From Pickwick to Dombey*. New York: Basic Books, 1965.

Analysis of the novel as Dickens' first attempt at social criticism: an attack on the methods proposed by Jeremy Bentham and his followers for dealing with the poor. Notes similarities between Oliver's story and that of Christian in John Bunyan's *Pilgrim's Progress*, but cites ways Oliver appears more secular. Considers Dickens' method of characterization akin to the satirist's, given to abstraction and laying stress on extremes to drive home his points. Also discusses the novelist's method of plotting and his reliance on coincidence.

Miller, J. Hillis. *Charles Dickens: The World of His Novels*. Cambridge, Mass.: Harvard University Press, 1959. Reprint. "The Dark World of *Oliver Twist*," in *Charles Dickens*, edited by Harold Bloom. New York: Chelsea House, 1987.

Convincing analysis of the two worlds portrayed in the novel: the criminal society of Fagin's London and the country society of Mr. Brownlow's estate. Shows how Oliver, an outcast from society from birth, searches for his place first in one, then in another of these alternative worlds; points out the many similarities, as well as the differences, between these environments. Sees Oliver becoming successful because he is so passive and adaptable.

Patten, Robert L. *Charles Dickens and His Publishers*. Oxford, England: Clarendon Press, 1978.

Provides details of the publication history of the novel, both in serialization and as a multi-volume hardback. Sketches Dickens' disgruntlement with his publisher over the work. A separate appendix gives information on sales figures for the novel during Dickens' lifetime.

Stone, Harry. "From *Pickwick* to *Chuzzlewit*: Fairy Tales and the Apprentice Novels." In his *Dickens and the Invisible World*. Bloomington: Indiana University Press, 1979.

Believes the preponderance of fairy-tale characteristics in the novel comes from Dickens' reliance on that mode of presentation to express his own profoundest fears and hopes. The novel is a struggle between elemental forces of good and evil. Fagin, at the center of the dark underworld, is given devil-like qualities; Brownlow, standing at the center of the world of the good, seems to possess powers beyond those which he could realistically be expected to have.

Westburg, Barry. *The Confessional Fictions of Charles Dickens*. DeKalb: Northern Illinois University Press, 1977.

Examines the novel as one of three written by Dickens in the mode of the confession: an exploration of a character's life to find significance and pattern in the fragmented experiences making up every person's existence. Explores

Dickens' handling of the process of Oliver's growth, finding the portrait static when compared with his other two great child-protagonists, David Copperfield and Pip. This novel is essentially picaresque, relying on changes in location to determine changes in character. An appendix points out parallels between characters in this work and real-life political figures from the seventeenth century, offering a way to read the novel as Dickens' attempt to infuse the tale with political significance.

Our Mutual Friend

Cockshut, A. O. J. *The Imagination of Charles Dickens*. New York: New York University Press, 1962.
Discusses Dickens' success in portraying two very different social worlds which exist side-by-side but seldom interact. Extensive examination of the major symbols of the novel, the river and the dust heaps, focusing on the way these are used to reveal character and theme. Notes how Dickens seems to suggest the upper classes are more simple than the lower, whose complexities fascinated him.

Collins, Philip. *Dickens and Crime*. Bloomington: Indiana University Press, 1962.
Noting that Dickens returns to the subject of murder as a central theme in the novel after twenty years, Collins explores the character of would-be murderer Bradley Headstone in detail. Demonstrates the psychological depth of characterization, an advance over murderers in earlier Dickens novels. Notes the way Dickens links murder and sexual relationships in his later novels, as murderers strive to eliminate rivals.

——————————— , ed. *Dickens: The Critical Heritage*. Boston: Routledge & Kegan Paul, 1971.
Excerpts from six nineteenth century reviews of the novel. Includes the caustic assessment by the young Henry James, who calls the work Dickens' poorest, praising the novelist for his humor but dismissing him as a philosopher. E. S. Dallas' laudatory remarks from his London *Times* review counterbalance James' criticisms.

Davis, Earle. "Inferno." In his *The Flint and the Flame: The Artistry of Charles Dickens*. Columbia: University of Missouri Press, 1963.
Compares the novel to Dante's *Inferno*, calling it Dickens' portrait of Victorian society as a kind of Hell. Stresses the importance of the dust heaps as an image of society as a whole. Traces the complex plotting and discusses some of the sources Dickens used as inspiration for characters such as Gaffer Hexam and Boffin. Also outlines the novelist's use of traditional literary devices such as caricature, melodrama, and gothic conventions.

Dyson, A. E. "*Our Mutual Friend*: Poetry comes Dearer." In his *The Inimitable Dickens: A Reading of the Novels*. London: Macmillan, 1970.

A highly personalized reading influenced by Dyson's association of the novel with his own childhood experiences. Explores Dickens' handling of humor in the work, suggesting that, although it has its sinister side, the novel is less dark than other critics have found it. Discusses the importance of chance occurrences and examines Dickens' treatment of his characters' moral development.

Fielding, Kenneth J. *Charles Dickens: A Critical Introduction*. London: Longman, 1958, enlarged ed. 1965.

Ranks the novel below Dickens' best, considering it too loosely constructed. Argues against critics who rate it highly. While conceding that the effective use of various symbols shows Dickens' attack on wealth and pretense, Fielding claims the central symbol, the dust heaps, is used ambiguously.

Johnson, Edgar. "The Great Dust Heap." In his *Charles Dickens: His Tragedy and Triumph*. Vol. 2. New York: Simon & Schuster, 1952.

Shows how the symbols Dickens uses in previous novels to highlight the failure of institutions reappear and coalesce in this, the novelist's most profound indictment of Victorian society. Examines the roles of several characters, especially the Veneerings, Podsnap, Boffin, Bella Wilfer, and Bradley Headstone, in highlighting the cauterizing effects the drive for wealth has on human values. Discusses the significance of the image of the dust heaps.

Knoepflmacher, U. C. "*Our Mutual Friend*: Fantasy as Affirmation." In his *Laughter and Despair: Readings in Ten Novels of the Victorian Era*. Berkeley: University of California Press, 1971.

Considers the novel Dickens' exposé of the demise of his society. Examines ways Dickens disorients readers by deliberately confusing the real with the unreal as a means of sharpening readers' perceptions and making them more acutely aware of the nature of a society which admires people like Podsnap.

Larson, Janet. "Dying unto Death: Biblical Ends and Endings in *Our Mutual Friend*." In her *Dickens and the Broken Scripture*. Athens: University of Georgia Press, 1985.

Stresses Dickens' use of allusions to the Bible as a means of driving home one of his main themes in the novel: conventional language itself is no longer life-giving or meaningful. Shows how scenes in the novel are consciously constructed to raise doubts in readers' minds concerning characters and values. Posits the novel is about "ends" and "endings"—and the inadequacy of pat solutions to human problems.

Lucas, John. *The Melancholy Man: A Study of Dickens' Novels*. Reprint. Totowa, N.J.: Barnes & Noble Books, 1980.

Attacks critics (including Henry James and George Eliot) who object that Dickens' fiction is not realistic; argues that Dickens is concerned with the problem of ascertaining a character's identity beneath the many masks worn in public. Believes Dickens considers it impossible to establish mutual friendships because men constantly strive to use others as means to some end. In light of these assertions, offers careful critiques of Bradley Headstone, Eugene Wrayburn, and the Boffins.

Miller, J. Hillis. *Charles Dickens: The World of His Novels*. Cambridge, Mass.: Harvard University Press, 1959. Reprint. *"Our Mutual Friend"* in *Dickens: A Collection of Critical Essays*, edited by Martin Price. Englewood Cliffs, N.J.: Prentice-Hall, 1967.

Points out the pervasiveness of money within the work: virtually every character, good or bad, is obsessed with acquiring it, and everyone defines himself or herself in terms associated with wealth. Points out that, through the objective narrator, Dickens demystifies these wrongheaded notions about money.

Morse, Robert. *"Our Mutual Friend."* In *Dickens: Modern Judgments*, edited by A. E. Dyson. London: Macmillan, 1968. Also in *The Dickens Critics*, edited by George Ford and Lariat Lane, Jr. Westport, Conn.: Greenwood Press, 1972.

The novel is used to illustrate the way Dickens is able to capture readers' attention and make them suspend disbelief. Explains how Dickens achieves his purpose through techniques of plotting, use of imagery (in this novel, the river and other water imagery, and the dust heaps), and reliance on doublings and pairings. An excellent summary of Dickens' craftsmanship.

Patten, Robert L. *Charles Dickens and His Publishers*. Oxford, England: Clarendon Press, 1978.

Discusses Dickens' involvement in the business aspects of the novel's production, including his work with a new illustrator, Marcus Stone. Notes the relative failure of the novel commercially, and the unusual step taken in issuing it in two rather than three volumes.

Phelps, Gilbert. *A Reader's Guide to Fifty British Novels, 1600-1900*. New York: Barnes & Noble Books, 1979.

Plot summary emphasizing the importance of John Harmon's various disguises. Complains Dickens is occasionally too strident in denouncing materialistic society, but notes his success in creating characters, especially his heroine, Bella Wilfer.

Sedgwick, Eva Kasofsky. "Homophobia, Misogyny, and Capital: The Example of *Our Mutual Friend*." In *Charles Dickens*, edited by Harold Bloom. New York: Chelsea House, 1987.

Uses Freudian and post-Freudian methods of psychological analysis to examine the novel's characters as reflecting unconsciously their accommodations of their own sexual preferences. Demonstrates how Dickens' imagery can be read in psychological terms to suggest this dimension of the novel. Also provides important background on the way Victorian men faced problems of sexual preference and orientation.

Smith, Grahame. "The Final Years: *Our Mutual Friend*." In his *Dickens, Money, and Society*. Berkeley: University of California Press, 1968.

Finds the novel disappointing for several reasons, including Dickens' seemingly contrived presentation of Boffin's greed as a sham and his strained use of the dust heaps as central images, maintaining that these have no human interest for readers (unlike the prison in *Little Dorrit*). Lengthy critical examination of Bradley Headstone as the central figure in the work, reflecting the changing nature and increasing complexity of society in Dickens' day.

Stewart, Garrett. "The Golden Bower of 'Our Mutual Friend.' " In his *Dickens and the Trials of Imagination*. Cambridge, Mass.: Harvard University Press, 1974.

Examines a variety of stylistic devices used to sketch the character of Jenny Wren, a type of heroine who has retreated from the world into her own realm of imagination, delineated by her art.

Stoehr, Taylor. *Dickens: The Dreamer's Stance*. Ithaca, N.Y.: Cornell University Press, 1965.

Considers the novel less typical of Dickens than most of his others because there is little sublimation of concerns about sexual or social status. Concentrates on an analysis of Eugene Wrayburn, especially his relationship with Lizzie Hexam, showing his continued unwillingness to act responsibly in dealing with others. Briefly discusses Bradley Headstone as the antithesis of Eugene.

Pickwick Papers

Butt, John, and Kathleen Tillotson. "From Sketches to Novel: *Pickwick Papers*." In their *Dickens at Work*. London: Methuen, 1957.

Sketches the background of Dickens' decision to embark on the monthly installments of this work, and his early comments distinguishing this effort from novel-writing. Carefully examines several early chapters as they appeared in installment form, showing how the novelist tied both the action and the season of year to actual events occurring in his readers' lives.

Chesterton, G. K. "*The Pickwick Papers*." In *The Dickens Critics*, edited by George Ford and Lariat Lane, Jr. Westport, Conn.: Greenwood Press, 1972.
Fulsome praise for what Chesterton considers Dickens' finest work. Claims it is not really a novel but a work of mythology, a romance celebrating life. Notes that the strength of all Dickens' works lies in his ability to create characters. Calls Dickens' creation of Mr. Pickwick as a middle-aged romantic hero a stroke of genius.

Collins, Philip, ed. *Dickens: The Critical Heritage*. Boston: Routledge & Kegan Paul, 1971.
Excerpts from nine sources, including reviews appearing shortly after the novel was published, a selection from William Makepeace Thackeray's *Paris Sketch Book* (1840), and essays published years after the novel first appeared that show its lasting power to sound a sympathetic chord in the Victorian reading public.

Davis, Earle. "Humor in Motion: The Farce-Caricature Technique." In his *The Flint and the Flame: The Artistry of Charles Dickens*. Columbia: University of Missouri Press, 1963.
Concentrates on Dickens' use of farce and caricature in creating scenes and characters for this picaresque work. Explains how the novelist follows his models, Henry Fielding and Tobias George Smollett, citing parallels between *Pickwick Papers* and the writings of these eighteenth century authors. Also discusses Dickens' use of irony. Complains that the interpolated tales are merely diversionary, a point refuted by many later critics.

Fielding, Kenneth J. *Charles Dickens: A Critical Introduction*. London: Longman, 1958, enlarged ed. 1965.
Decries attempts to measure the novel against artificial critical standards which invariably devalue it; argues its looseness of form does not disqualify it from being both entertaining and enlightening as a study of life. Examines the novelist's techniques for creating Mr. Pickwick, noting how even Dickens changed his attitude toward his hero as the story unfolded in serial form.

Johnson, Edgar. "The Knight of the Joyful Countenance." In his *Charles Dickens: His Tragedy and Triumph*. Vol. 1. New York: Simon & Schuster, 1952.
Delineates Dickens' ability to create human, individualized characters from stock models. These figures, especially Pickwick and Sam Weller, achieve genuine humanity and act as men of conscience. Discusses Dickens' reasons

for including the interpolated tales, most of which are not comic. Notes that beneath the comic strands lies a concern over the absence of justice in society.

Karl, Frederick R. "Charles Dickens: The Victorian Quixote." In his *A Reader's Guide to the Nineteenth-Century Novel*. New York: Farrar, Straus & Giroux, 1964.
Sees the novel as Dickens' attempt to define a utopian state, free of the distractions and difficulties of the contemporary world. Views Pickwick as a Quixotic figure striving to do good with his life and fortune. Examines the interpolated tales as grim counterpoints to the jovial story of Pickwick and his friends.

Lucas, John. *The Melancholy Man: A Study of Dickens' Novels*. Reprint. Totowa, N.J.: Barnes & Noble Books, 1980.
Highlights the conflict created by Dickens' vacillation between the idyllic and mimetic modes of writing. Notes that, while the overall comic tone suggests the author wishes the work viewed as a vision of what might be, traces of sordid realism undermine the idyllic narrative of Pickwick's adventures.

Marcus, Steven. "The Blest Dawn." In his *Dickens: From Pickwick to Dombey*. New York: Basic Books, 1965.
Claims that the novel is a genuine classic, having influenced generations of readers because it posits a Christian vision of the possibility of salvation and of goodness in the world; believes that its optimism springs from sources not normally examined by modern critics. Lengthy examination of the work as an advance over the tradition within which Dickens worked. Demonstrates how virtually all the subjects of Dickens' subsequent novels are hinted at in this work.

_____ . "Language into Structure: Pickwick Revisited." In *Charles Dickens*, edited by Harold Bloom. New York: Chelsea House, 1987.
Detailed examination of Dickens' use of language in the novel. Through careful analysis of the various prefaces and key scenes, demonstrates Dickens' mastery over his medium and his penchant for a poet's free play with language; the play of language even dictates action and characterization. Shows how Sam Weller, the master of language within the work, is an alter ego for Dickens.

Miller, J. Hillis. *Charles Dickens: The World of His Novels*. Cambridge, Mass.: Harvard University Press, 1959.
Examines characterization in the novel, especially Mr. Pickwick. Excellent discussion of the structure, demonstrating how the novel is essentially a collection of disparate scenes. Both characterization and structure reveal Dickens'

ties to the picaresque tradition and his growing awareness that goodness such as Pickwick's is endangered by an indifferent and sometimes dark world. Shows the importance of the novelist's persona in the work, which gives it a comic tone.

Patten, Robert L. *Charles Dickens and His Publishers*. Oxford, England: Clarendon Press, 1978.
Informative discussion of the serial publication of the sketches Dickens wrote for the publishing firm of Chapman and Hall. Offers illuminating information about the history of serial publication and of British publishing practices. A separate appendix provides data on sales of the novel during Dickens' lifetime.

Phelps, Gilbert. *A Readers Guide to Fifty English Novels, 1600-1900*. New York: Barnes & Noble Books, 1979.
Sketches Dickens' boyhood and early life; outlines the novel's major action. Brief critical assessment shows Dickens' method of composition, concentrating on ways he vivifies episodes and uses dozens of characters in a sweeping exploration of society in this comic adventure story.

Steig, Michael. "*Pickwick, Nickleby* and the Emergence from Caricature." In his *Dickens and Phiz*. Bloomington: Indiana University Press, 1978.
Discusses the way Hablot K. Browne ("Phiz") created sketches to accompany the monthly installments of *Pickwick Papers* and the changes made in these drawings in subsequent editions. Notes how Browne's changes reflect his own interpretation of the novel as well as Dickens' influence on the creation of the illustrations.

Stewart, Garrett. *Dickens and the Trials of Imagination*. Cambridge, Mass.: Harvard University Press, 1974.
Devotes three chapters to an extended examination of the style of Dickens' first novel; shows how the novelist uses various literary devices to expose the rhetorical and stylistic ills of the literature of his day and to probe the emotional makeup of the hero. Also explores the characterization of Sam and Tony Weller in detail.

Stone, Harry. "From *Pickwick* to *Chuzzlewit*: Fairy Tales and the Apprentice Novels." In his *Dickens and the Invisible World*. Bloomington: Indiana University Press, 1979.
Though noting that in this novel Dickens relies less on fairy tales as sources of his inspiration than in any other of his works, Stone traces the importance of fantasy literature in the interpolated tales. Also shows how Mr. Pickwick takes on qualities of a fairy godfather toward the end of the story.

A Tale of Two Cities

Alter, Robert. "The Demons of History in Dickens' *Tale*." In *Charles Dickens*, edited by Harold Bloom. New York: Chelsea House, 1987.
Explains Dickens' method in the novel as being essentially allegorical: the writer uses history as a means of discussing the conflict between anarchy and order. Hence, both imagery and character are employed in illustrating mob psychology. Sees Dickens using coincidence to reinforce the notion of instability; notes the sober realism that comes through the surface tone of the attempted happy ending.

Beckwith, Charles E., ed. *Twentieth Century Interpretations of "A Tale of Two Cities."* Englewood Cliffs, N.J.: Prentice-Hall, 1972.
Collection of eleven previously published articles and excerpts from longer works discussing the novel from various perspectives. Includes comments by George Bernard Shaw, George Orwell, and filmmaker Sergei Eisenstein.

Collins, Philip, ed. *Dickens; The Critical Heritage*. Boston: Routledge & Kegan Paul, 1971.
Selections from several of Dickens' letters to John Forster and Wilkie Collins regarding his intent for the novel. Also contains an excerpt from Forster's unsigned review in the *Examiner*. In a headnote, the editor discusses the relative indifference with which the British public greeted the work.

Davis, Earle. "Recalled to Life." In his *The Flint and the Flame: The Artistry of Charles Dickens*. Columbia: University of Missouri Press, 1963.
Reviews the way Dickens handled his sources for this novel: Wilkie Collins' *The Frozen Deep*, a play which provided the idea for the love triangle and the sacrifice of Carton for Darnay; Edward Bulwer-Lytton's novel *Zanoni* and Collins' short stories about the French Revolution, which suggested setting and subject; and the writings of Thomas Carlyle (as well as other books Carlyle loaned Dickens), which provided many specific incidents Dickens used for characterization, plotting, and theme. Sketches the reasons for some of the weaknesses in the novel, caused in part by weekly serialization.

Dyson, A. E. "*A Tale of Two Cities*: Recalled to Life." In his *The Inimitable Dickens: A Reading of the Novels*. London: Macmillan, 1970.
Believes the novel was inspired by Dickens' conservative radicalism, which bred in him a horror of revolutions such as the one France had witnessed. Discusses in detail the characterizations of Darnay, Carton, and Manette, to show the possibilities Dickens offers for reacting to a nation in chaos.

Fielding, Kenneth J. *Charles Dickens: A Critical Introduction*. London: Longman, 1958, enlarged ed. 1965.

Explains difficulties Dickens had in plotting and development as a result of his decision to publish in weekly installments. Highlights the novelist's debt to Thomas Carlyle, and notes that the underlying element of determinism is derived from him. Points out that, despite the horror suggested by the anarchy of the Revolution, Dickens still manages to infuse the story with a note of Christian optimism.

Gross, John. "*A Tale of Two Cities.*" In *Dickens: Modern Judgments*, edited by A. E. Dyson. London: Macmillan, 1968.
Provides insight into the way the novel reflects concerns important to Dickens throughout his career. Notes the importance of references to ghosts, suggesting a sense of unreality; sees this reinforced by Dickens' reticence to provide details about character and setting. Examines Sidney Carton in some detail. Cites the particular irony of the work: events are grim, but the reader senses hope in individual characters who believe redemption for themselves and for society is still possible.

Johnson, Edgar. "The Tempest and the Ruined Garden." In his *Charles Dickens: His Tragedy and Triumph*. Vol. 2. New York: Simon & Schuster, 1952.
Explains how events in Dickens' life, specifically his affection for Ellen Ternan, affected the emotional content of the novel. Highlights the energy with which Dickens informs scenes of the Revolution. Accounts for the many differences between this work and others considered more typical of Dickens, noting the absence of humor, thinness of character development, and confusion of themes caused by Dickens' attempt to deal with both the social phenomenon of revolution and the moral issue of redemption through love.

Monod, Sylvere. "Some Stylistic Devices in *A Tale of Two Cities.*" In *Dickens the Craftsman: Strategies of Presentation*, edited by Robert B. Partlow. Carbondale: Southern Illinois University Press, 1970.
Careful study of the text, focusing on four stylistic devices: repetition, cumulative effect, imagery, and hyperbole. Notes Dickens' reliance on William Shakespeare and Thomas Carlyle for many elements of style in the work. Highlights ways the novelist demonstrates control over his materials; traces the effects stylistic devices have on creating characters with psychological depth, giving resonance to scenes, and offering insight into Dickens' views on the nature of revolution as a social phenomenon.

Patten, Robert L. *Charles Dickens and His Publishers*. Oxford, England: Clarendon Press, 1978.
Sketches the serial publication of the novel in *All the Year Round*, the magazine Dickens edited. Notes how the financial losses Dickens suffered from publishing in his own magazine caused him difficulties. Outlines the popularity of the work in both Britain and America.

Stephen, Sir James FitzJames. "*A Tale of Two Cities*." In *The Dickens Critics*, edited by George Ford and Lariat Lane, Jr. Westport, Conn.: Greenwood Press, 1972.

Scathing review by a contemporary of Dickens, attacking the novelist for his overuse of pathos and the grotesque. Accuses Dickens of unfamiliarity with French history, heavy reliance on Thomas Carlyle's philosophy, and weak construction. Discusses Darnay's role as the hero of the novel; explains the significance of the many hidden strands and mysteries associated with him. Also notes the importance of Dickens' attempt to make Darnay's tale an overtly Christian story of sacrifice and redemption. Explores the way the novelist dramatizes the social forces driving the people of Paris to revolution.

BENJAMIN DISRAELI

General Studies

Bloomfield, Paul. *Disraeli*. London: Longmans, Green, 1961.
 A general sketch of Disraeli's work as a novelist, providing brief commentaries on individual books, especially the three important social novels (*Coningsby*, *Sybil*, and *Tancred*). Explains Disraeli's growing involvement in politics and the effect this involvement had on his career as a writer.

Cazamian, Louis. *The Social Novel in England, 1830-1850: Dickens, Disraeli, Mrs. Gaskell, Kingsley*. Boston: Routledge & Kegan Paul, 1973.
 Excellent brief sketch, showing how Disraeli came to accept the principles of the Young England movement as a reaction against traditional Toryism. Discusses the influence of biography on the novels, especially *Vivian Grey*. Critical analyses of *Coningsby*, *Sybil*, and *Tancred*.

Chandler, Alice. "Medievalism in Action: Young England and Disraeli." In her *A Dream of Order: The Medieval Idea in Nineteenth-Century English Literature*. Lincoln: University of Nebraska Press, 1970.
 A particularly good background essay on the activities of the group (with which Disraeli associated himself) that adopted principles of medievalism as a means of reforming modern England. Shows how ideals of a nobility acting much like feudal lords, committed to the populace, struck Disraeli as apt and became the basis for both his political and literary positions. Sees both *Coningsby* and *Sybil* as Disraeli's attempts to illustrate his version of this new feudalism.

Collins, Norman. *The Facts of Fiction*. London: Victor Gollancz, 1932.
 Offers brief comments on Disraeli's talents. Ranks him among the second-best novelists of the period. Faults him for his inability to portray realistic characters, but acknowledges the importance of his political trilogy in highlighting social conditions in England. Collins' views are colored, however, by his anti-Semitic attitudes.

Dahl, Curtis. "Benjamin Disraeli; Edward Bulwer-Lytton." In *Victorian Fiction: A Guide to Research*, edited by Lionel Stevenson. Cambridge, Mass.: Harvard University Press, 1964.
 A bibliographical essay providing information on editions of Disraeli's works and collections of his correspondence; summarizes important works of general criticism and critical commentaries of individual novels. Good reference source for scholarship on Disraeli published before 1962.

Frietzsche, Arthur H. *The Monstrous Clever Young Man: The Novelist Disraeli and His Heroes*. Logan: Utah State University Press, 1959.
A study of Disraeli's major novels focusing on the central male figure in each. Notes the essential similarities among these heroes: each is ambitious, charming, and young, yet none is in control of his own fate. Shows how, despite these similarities, Disraeli demonstrates some subtle differences among these characters. As the novelist matures, so do his fictional creations; they gradually show greater concern for the welfare of others.

Holloway, John. *The Victorian Sage*. New York: W. W. Norton, 1968.
Reviews Disraeli's fiction to prove he is one of the writers who examines contemporary society and attempts to provide moral guidance to his readers. Characters in his novels confront the uncertainties of the age, and in solving their problems offer models for nineteenth century readers who had lost faith in traditional religion as a guide for living.

Hoyt, Charles A. *Minor British Novelists*. Carbondale: Southern Illinois University Press, 1961.
Excellent summary of Disraeli's career as a novelist. Characterizes early novels as representative of the Silver Fork School, focusing on manners and activities of the upper classes. Brief analysis of the important trilogy Disraeli wrote to illustrate the condition of England and to offer a solution to the country's social problems.

Karl, Frederick R. "Five Victorian Novelists." In his *A Reader's Guide to the Nineteenth-Century Novel*. New York: Farrar, Straus & Giroux, 1964.
Faults Disraeli's novels for being political tracts rather than works of art; sees the three Young England novels as attempts to explain the pitfalls of democracy while arguing for reform of the moribund political system in the country.

Levine, Richard A. *Benjamin Disraeli*. New York: Twayne, 1968.
Monograph assessing Disraeli's merits and accomplishments as a novelist. Focuses on the Young England trilogy in which Disraeli makes his most significant statements about the condition of England. Provides important details about the political and social climate out of which these novels grew. Includes separate chapters on the early and later novels, and a selected bibliography.

Moers, Ellen. *The Dandy: Brummell to Beerbohm*. New York: Viking Press, 1960.
Concentrates on Disraeli's upbringing and heritage, and on his early efforts as a novelist. Good discussion of *Vivian Grey*, his first novel, and briefer commentary on *The Young Duke*. Specific focus is on Disraeli's attitude toward the life-style now referred to as Dandyism.

Quiller-Couch, Sir Arthur. "Disraeli." In his *Charles Dickens and Other Victorians*. New York: G. P. Putnam's Sons, 1925.
Survey of Disraeli's political qualities and his literary accomplishments, showing how his work as a novelist hampered his progress in political spheres. Comments on Disraeli's highly rhetorical style, which Quiller-Couch calls "eastern," believing it is linked to Disraeli's heritage. Brief but insightful commentary on the creation of the novelist's serious social novels, calling *Coningsby* the first political novel in English.

Rosa, Matthew Whiting. *The Silver Fork School*. New York: Kennikat Press, 1964.
Concentrates on Disraeli's early work, examining his first novels as exemplars of the Silver Fork School. Traces the publication history of *Vivian Grey* and discusses the expectations of readers who made such works successes. Shows how Disraeli's social novels grew out of the earlier books, and how elements of these fashionable novels remain in the more serious works.

Sherman, Stuart P. *Points of View*. New York: Charles Scribner's Sons, 1924.
Assessment of Disraeli's career by an influential American critic of the early twentieth century. Explains how Disraeli's personal ambitions motivated both his political activity and his novel-writing. A good review of Disraeli's literary efforts, which in Sherman's view exemplify both his personality and his political platforms.

Speare, Morris E. *The Political Novel: Its Development in England and in America*. Reprint. New York: Russell & Russell, 1966.
Devotes five chapters (approximately half of his study) to an analysis of Disraeli's contribution to the literary genre which he initiated with the publication of *Coningsby*. Extensive analysis of the novelist's experiments with political subjects in his early works. Explores his development of a distinct political philosophy; his ability to transform that philosophical outlook into fiction; and his impact on, and legacy to, British literature.

Stephen, Leslie. *Hours in a Library*. Vol. 2. Reprint. Grosse Point, Mich.: Scholarly Press, 1968.
Comments from a younger contemporary of the novelist who was himself a dominant critic of the nineteenth century. Gives high marks to Disraeli's efforts at fiction, considering his contributions to literature as valuable as his work in politics. Discusses the author's political trilogy in detail to show how these works exhibit Disraeli's unflagging love for the Jewish people and his unshakable commitment to the power of intellect. Offers comments on his style, citing faults and particular strengths.

Stewart, R. W., ed. *Disraeli's Novels Reviewed, 1926-1968*. Metuchen, N.J.: Scarecrow Press, 1975.

Collection of excerpts from reviews and critical studies of all of Disraeli's major works of fiction. Includes a lengthy section of general criticism and a second section providing information about specific works. Most of the selections are from essays published during Disraeli's lifetime, providing excellent sources for readers interested in the contemporary reaction to the novels.

Coningsby

Cazamian, Louis. *The Social Novel in England, 1830-1850: Dickens, Disraeli, Mrs. Gaskell, Kingsley*. Boston: Routledge & Kegan Paul, 1973.
Discusses the political background, concentrating on Disraeli's efforts to transform his particular view of conservatism into fiction. While noting that the novel articulates the writer's hope for England in his plan to have an aristocracy active in social reform, Cazamian judges the work only marginally successful as fiction: the plot is disjointed and the dialogue contrived. Points out its success with Disraeli's contemporaries, who enjoyed identifying real-life figures thinly disguised in the fiction.

Chandler, Alice. "Medievalism in Action: Young England and Disraeli." In her *A Dream of Order: The Medieval Idea in Nineteenth-Century English Literature*. Lincoln: University of Nebraska Press, 1970.
Brief analysis of the novel as an example of Disraeli's political philosophy. Through the character of Coningsby, Disraeli is able to illustrate the shortcomings of a political system in which the upper class denies its responsibilities to the poor; Chandler describes Disraeli's alternative system as medievalism in action. Coningsby's wedding symbolizes the union of the Norman and Saxon elements still existing side by side in modern England and which, united, offer hope for the future.

Frietzsche, Arthur H. *The Monstrous Clever Young Man: The Novelist Disraeli and His Heroes*. Logan: Utah State University Press, 1959.
Acknowledges this is the first political novel; briefly summarizes the action, focusing on events directly affecting the hero. Points out essential similarities between Coningsby and other Disraeli heroes. Posits the hero's major quality is his political awareness, yet notes his reticence to act on his convictions; considers him less active than other characters in Disraeli's works. Like other Disraeli heroes, Coningsby's fate is not in his own hands, but is subject to chance occurrences.

Levine, Richard A. *Benjamin Disraeli*. New York: Twayne, 1968.
Traces the political background which led Disraeli to create this novel as an explanation of the way political parties are created and how they change.

Outlines the novelist's development of his hero as a representative of the Young England movement, bent on reforming the Tory party; argues that the novel vivifies Disraeli's belief that the aristocracy must take responsibility for initiating social reforms. Also discusses the importance of religion as Disraeli portrays it in the work.

Speare, Morris E. *The Political Novel: Its Development in England and America.* Reprint. New York: Russell & Russell, 1966.
Concentrates on Disraeli's ability to create vivid sketches of realistic political characters and striking scenes of political activity and social injustice. Coningsby is influenced by three characters: the Jew Sidonia, the clergyman Edward Lyle, and the energetic aristocrat Millbank. Considers Disraeli's depiction of the dissolute Lord Monmouth especially convincing. Believes Sidonia is an idealized portrait of Disraeli himself.

Stewart, R. W., ed. *Disraeli's Novels Reviewed, 1926-1968.* Metuchen, N.J.: Scarecrow Press, 1975.
Provides excerpts from fourteen reviews and critical notices of Disraeli's first political novel. Ten appeared in periodicals shortly after the novel was published; among these are pieces by Richard Monckton Milnes, Lord Houghton, and novelist William Makepeace Thackeray. Also includes a critical assessment by Arthur H. Frietzsche (from 1960) of Sidonia, Disraeli's wise Jewish character who appears in both *Coningsby* and *Tancred.*

Sybil

Cazamian, Louis. *The Social Novel in England, 1830-1850: Dickens, Disraeli, Mrs. Gaskell, Kingsley.* Boston: Routledge & Kegan Paul, 1973.
Considers the novel one of the first works of social fiction in England. In it Disraeli argues that the best chance for England to improve its social climate lies not in existing forms of conservatism or liberalism, but rather in a political system with a privileged aristocracy taking responsibility for improving the conditions of the workers. Praises Disraeli's descriptions of the conditions of working classes; notes the importance he attaches to the Church, especially as it was being influenced by the Oxford Movement, as a vehicle for aiding the lot of the poor.

Chandler, Alice. "Medievalism in Action: Young England and Disraeli." In her *A Dream of Order: The Medieval Idea in Nineteenth-Century English Literature.* Lincoln: University of Nebraska Press, 1970.
Notes the advance in dramatic structure of this novel over its predecessor, *Coningsby.* Shows how Disraeli illustrates his central idea, the contrast be-

tween the lives of the rich and the poor, through the adventures of his central character, Charles Egremont. Sees the harsh lot of the workers in the town of Wogate as evidence that democracy does not work; instead, a return to pre-Reformation ideology, expounded in the novel by Walter Gerard, is seen as the best hope for improving the condition of the working classes.

Frietzsche, Arthur H. *The Monstrous Clever Young Man: The Novelist Disraeli and His Heroes*. Logan: Utah State University Press, 1959.
Brief assessment of the novel's hero, Charles Egremont, noting the importance of chance in determining his success or failure. Considers Egremont the least characteristic Disraeli hero; argues that the real heroic interest of the novel centers on the masses. Describes the central action of the novel, focusing on the destructive qualities of the Chartist movement.

Levine, Richard A. *Benjamin Disraeli*. New York: Twayne, 1968.
Reads the novel as Disraeli's attempt to dramatize the condition of the populace living under the rules of an outmoded political system. Traces the development of the hero, Charles Egremont, who grows to realize that the aristocracy has the responsibility to effect social change. Also discusses the importance of the Church in bringing about reforms to improve the living conditions of the lower classes.

Lucas, John. "Mrs. Gaskell and Brotherhood." In *Tradition and Tolerance in Nineteenth Century Fiction*, edited by David Howard, John Lucas, and John Goode. London: Routledge & Kegan Paul, 1966.
Indicts Disraeli for failing to create real working-class characters and for betraying his stated thesis that social progress can come only when the two nations, rich and poor, are united. Notes that all the good characters are really aristocrats; Sybil is a working-class heroine only because of circumstance: She is descended from, and her affinities are with, the aristocracy.

Phelps, Gilbert. *Fifty British Novels, 1600-1900*. New York: Barnes & Noble Books, 1979.
Summary of Disraeli's early career as a novelist and politician, followed by synopsis of the plot of *Sybil*. Critical analysis focuses on the novel's subtitle, "The Two Nations," showing why the work deserves notice as the first political novel.

Speare, Morris E. *The Political Novel: Its Development in England and in America*. Reprint. New York: Russell & Russell, 1966.
Sees the novel as an advance over *Coningsby*: Disraeli displays a more panoramic vision of English society, and his attack focuses not on individuals but on the conditions causing social unrest. Further, he is able to present his

central theme, the need for the aristocracy and the Church to take the lead in reform, through a series of contrasts: rich versus poor, indolent upper class versus those members of the aristocracy willing to accept their responsibilities as leaders. Speare also provides samples of nineteenth century critical reaction to the novel.

Stewart, R. W., ed. *Disraeli's Novels Reviewed, 1926-1968*. Metuchen, N.J.: Scarecrow Press, 1975.
   Provides six excerpts of reviews and critical essays offering varying perspectives on the work. Notices by William Makepeace Thackeray and W. W. Greg appearing shortly after the novel was published give a sense of the reactions of Disraeli's initial critics. Reprints of letters by two of Disraeli's female readers show the impact of the work on the novelist's contemporaries. A 1967 review by a Soviet scholar points out the tensions between Disraeli's concern for the workers and his insistence on the need for an aristrocracy.

Williams, Raymond. *Culture and Society, 1780-1950*. London: Chatto & Windus, 1954.
   Brief account of the novel, highlighting its role as a political polemic. Notes Disraeli's tendency to offer generalizations appealing to a wide readership; likens him to Dickens in this respect. Notes that the marriage of Egremont and Sybil at the end of the novel is intended to symbolize the union of the two nations (rich and poor) Disraeli describes as existing side by side in England.

Tancred

Cazamian, Louis. *The Social Novel in England 1830-1850: Dickens, Disraeli, Mrs. Gaskell, Kingsley*. Boston: Routledge & Kegan Paul, 1973.
   Brief account of the plot and a discussion of its symbolic and implausible nature. Notes Disraeli's attempts to justify the Jewish culture and its outlook in the work. Judges the novel less effective than either *Coningsby* or *Sybil*.

Frietzsche, Arthur H. *The Monstrous Clever Young Man: The Novelist Disraeli and His Heroes*. Logan: Utah State University Press, 1959.
   Traces the many elements of Disraeli's earlier fiction present in this work. Briefly summarizes the major action, focusing on the way Disraeli develops his central character, who is similar in upbringing, social status, and temperament to many of the novelist's heroes from previous works, especially in his religious zeal and his egotism.

Levine, Richard A. *Benjamin Disraeli*. New York: Twayne, 1968.
   Lengthy analysis of the novel, focusing on Disraeli's religious theme. Argues

that in the work Disraeli pleads for the necessity of returning to Judeo-Christian religious principles, especially those practiced by the early Christian church; these should form the moral basis for the political and social reformation of England. Explores Disraeli's development of Tancred as a Carlylean hero figure who penetrates the sham institutions of society in search of more lasting structures on which human relationships can be built.

Speare, Morris E. *The Political Novel: Its Development in England and in America.* Reprint. New York: Russell & Russell, 1966.

Sees Disraeli's purpose as a call for a spiritual renaissance in England: The novelist wants to see a coalition formed by the Crown, the people, and the Church. Traces Disraeli's adventure-filled plot as his hero travels to the East to gain an understanding of the strength and significance of the Jewish heritage on which Christianity is based. Considers the novel especially important because Disraeli expresses in it virtually every idea about foreign policy he was to implement when he became Prime Minister nearly three decades after the work was published.

Stewart, R. W., ed. *Disraeli's Novels Reviewed, 1926-1968.* Metuchen, N.J.: Scarecrow Press, 1975.

Nine excerpts from reviews and criticism offer an idea of the reaction the novel inspired in Disraeli's contemporaries. Includes comments by James Russell Lowell, offering an American perspective on a novel whose primary focus is the British social hierarchy. Also reprints an excerpt from Richard Levine's 1967 *Nineteenth Century Fiction* essay on "The Great Asian Mystery," a central issue in the novel.

GEORGE ELIOT
(Marian Evans)

General Studies

Beer, Gillian. *George Eliot*. Bloomington: Indiana University Press, 1986.
A feminist analysis of George Eliot's life and writings. Introductory chapters review the novelist's reaction to the problem of women's place in Victorian society and her developing consciousness of her own attitude as it evolved from her reading of other women writers. Detailed discussions of the major novels, continually focusing on the works as products of a woman writer.

Beer, Patricia. *Reader, I Married Him: A Study of the Women Characters of Jane Austen, Charlotte Brontë, Elizabeth Gaskell, and George Eliot*. London: Macmillan, 1974.
Shows how George Eliot's novels, like those of other important female authors of the period, deal with understanding and frankness about the unequal status of women in Victorian society during a time when "the woman question" was becoming an important issue in England. Believes George Eliot had great faith in women's potential, but little hope of its being realized.

Bloom, Harold, ed. *George Eliot*. Modern Critical Views Series. New York: Chelsea House, 1986.
Collection of seventeen essays originally published between 1953 and 1986. At least one selection on each of the major novels, as well as several discussing themes common to George Eliot's fiction. Bloom's introductory essay provides an assessment of George Eliot's achievement as a novelist.

Carroll, David, ed. *George Eliot: The Critical Heritage*. New York: Barnes & Noble Books, 1971.
A collection of excerpts from almost seventy reviews and essays published during George Eliot's lifetime or immediately after her death provides a record of the reactions of the first readers of her novels. The editor attempts a balance between encomiums and harsh critiques. Also includes comments on George Eliot's achievements as a novelist by critics such as Leslie Stephen and Henry James.

Cooper, Lettice. *George Eliot*. London: Longman, 1951, rev. ed. 1970.
Brief monograph sketches major events in George Eliot's life and provides key details of her relationship with other important Victorian figures, especially George Henry Lewes. Short but useful critical assessments of each of the major novels highlight the importance of the author's treatment of moral issues.

Haight, Gordon. *George Eliot: A Biography*. New York: Oxford University Press, 1968.

A detailed scholarly study of Marian Evans' life based on extensive use of manuscripts, letters, unpublished documents, and memoirs. Investigates the novelist's relationship with important figures in her life, especially John Chapman and George Henry Lewes. Explains the genesis and biographical significance of her major works. Considered the standard twentieth century biography.

_____ , ed. *A Century of George Eliot Criticism*. Boston: Houghton Mifflin, 1965.

Useful collection of reviews and critical studies (some excerpted) of George Eliot's life and works. Includes commentary on every major novel. Arranged chronologically, these selections cover the period from 1858, when George Eliot's first novel appeared, to 1962. Contains selections from several important twentieth century critics such as F. R. Leavis, Basil Willey, John Holloway, and Dorothy Van Ghent. Haight's introduction sketches the novelist's critical reputation from the publication of *Adam Bede* (1859) to the early 1960's.

Hanson, Lawrence, and Elizabeth Hanson. *Marian Evans and George Eliot: A Biography*. New York: Oxford University Press, 1952.

Scholarly life of Marian Evans, intended to correct distorted impressions of the novelist created by the biography written by her husband, John Cross. Provides a detailed account of her childhood, her decision to move in with George Henry Lewes, and the importance of that relationship both personally and professionally. Comments on George Eliot's major works are interspersed throughout the biographical narrative; individual chapters are devoted to each work.

Hardy, Barbara. *The Novels of George Eliot: A Study in Form*. New York: Oxford University Press, 1959.

Concentrates on George Eliot's ability to give formal structure to her works and to present her characters and situations in patterns that reinforce her meaning. Special notice is paid to the importance of the tragic form her best works take; hence, careful attention is given to characters who possess tragic qualities in varying degrees. An introductory chapter describes what Hardy calls George Eliot's development of the "unheroic tragedy." Other chapters discuss the function of plotting, imagery, and characterization in achieving artistic effect.

_____ . *Particularities: Readings in George Eliot*. Athens: Ohio University Press, 1983.

Collection of essays by a prominent critic of George Eliot's work. Half deal with specific issues arising from a reading of *Middlemarch*. Also includes lengthy essays on *The Mill on the Floss* and chapters on general themes and techniques of narration, such as "Rituals and Feeling," "The Reticent Narrator," "George Eliot on Imagination."

Harvey, W. J. "George Eliot." In *Victorian Fiction: A Guide to Research*, edited by Lionel Stevenson. Cambridge, Mass: Harvard University Press, 1964.
A bibliographical essay surveying criticism written before 1962. Divided into sections focusing on bibliographies of George Eliot's work and collections of her correspondence; biographical studies; the intellectual and cultural milieu in which she wrote, and its effect on her fiction; general criticism of her achievement as a novelist; studies of specific topics such as social reform, religion, and historical events; and criticism of individual novels.

Holloway, John. *The Victorian Sage*. New York: W. W. Norton, 1965.
Part of a study of Victorian figures whose writings were overtly prophetic and intended to provide moral guidance to readers. Presents a sweeping review of George Eliot's novels to show her constant concerns and recurrent trends in developing characters and scenes. These distinguish her novels as significant attempts to show how humans can live happily and ethically within an increasingly deterministic universe.

Karl, Frederick R. *A Reader's Guide to the Nineteenth-Century Novel*. New York: Farrar, Straus & Giroux, 1964.
Extensive analysis of the major works, explaining why George Eliot deserves her reputation as one of the greatest novelists of the period despite her occasional overemphasis on morality at the expense of artistry.

Knoepflmacher, U. C. "Unwilling Men: Power and Masculinity in George Eliot's Fiction." In *Men by Women*, edited by Janet Todd. New York: Holmes & Meier, 1981.
Explains George Eliot's relatively sympathetic handling of male characters and her concurrent harshness in treating her women figures as the novelist's attempt to assert her own power over both sexes, and to demonstrate the power of female novelists to move beyond the limits set for women writers of her time.

Leavis, F. R. *The Great Tradition*. London: Chatto & Windus, 1948.
Places George Eliot among the truly great novelists in English, alongside Jane Austen, Henry James, Joseph Conrad, and D. H. Lawrence. Considers her works important because she advances the craft of novel-writing and offers a well developed moral vision of her society.

Levine, George. *The Realistic Imagination: English Fiction from Frankenstein to Lady Chatterly*. Chicago: University of Chicago Press, 1981.
In two chapters, George Eliot is contrasted with Joseph Conrad to show how the nineteenth century's movement toward realism, prevalent in her works and perhaps best exemplified there, gave way to modernist notions of both human nature and the external world, and to novelists' new methods of dealing with both. Stresses the importance of the growth of science as the catalyst for causing the shift in the way novelists viewed their subjects and their art.

Martin, Hazel T. *Petticoat Rebels: A Study of the Novels of Social Protest of George Eliot, Elizabeth Gaskell, and Charlotte Brontë*. New York: Helios Books, 1968.
Sees George Eliot as a rebel unwilling to conform to society's expectations for the woman novelist, who was expected to support conventional notions of marriage, motherhood, and morality. Examines George Eliot's sympathetic treatment of women who sought fulfillment in other ways.

Praz, Mario. *The Hero in Eclipse in Victorian Fiction*. Translated by Angus Davidson. New York: Oxford University Press, 1956.
Sees George Eliot's works consistently celebrating the commonplace over the heroic. Notes the novelist's debts to Auguste Comte's theories of positivism and to William Wordsworth's portrayals of rustic scenes and characters. Believes both her subjects and her methods opened the way for future novelists to deal even more carefully with internal human concerns rather than with larger social and political problems.

Qualls, Barry V. "Speaking Through Parables: George Eliot." In his *The Secular Pilgrims of Victorian Fiction*. Cambridge, England: Cambridge University Press, 1982.
Sees George Eliot relying heavily on the structural patterns of earlier religious writers to shape her fiction because she has adopted the role of moral teacher within her works; finds her novels a kind of secular scripture for readers who no longer turn immediately to biblical passages for inspiration and guidance.

Redinger, Ruby V. *George Eliot: The Emergent Self*. New York: Alfred A. Knopf, 1975.
Detailed psychological study of Marian Evans' early life and the influence of her religious upbringing on the development of her self-image. Traces her relationships with several individuals to show her need for love and acceptance, her growing disillusionment with religion, and her emergence as an intellectual with strong ethical principles. Explores the relationship between Evans' life and her works.

Sprague, Rosemary. *George Eliot: A Biography*. Philadelphia: Chilton, 1968.
A detailed biography exploring Marian Evans' childhood amid a loving family, her intellectual growth, her relationship with George Henry Lewes, and her achievement as a writer. Commentary on individual novels is interspersed throughout the biographical narrative, giving readers a sense of the relationship between the novels and Evans' life.

Williams, Merryn. *Women in the English Novel, 1800-1900*. New York: St. Martin's Press, 1984.
Explores George Eliot's treatment of women characters in her major works; notes that the novelist is more concerned with women's responsibilities to make and uphold choices about important personal relationships than with the mere conventions of courtship. Observes that as she grew in her profession, George Eliot became more concerned with the problems of doomed marriages.

Adam Bede

Carroll, David, ed. *George Eliot: The Critical Heritage*. New York: Barnes & Noble Books, 1971.
Five excerpts from reviews of the work and letters by George Eliot's contemporaries recording their reactions to her first full-scale novel. Included are remarks from letters by Jane Welsh Carlyle and Charles Dickens, and Anne Mozley's lengthy analysis of the work from the July, 1859, issue of *Bentley's Quarterly Review*. In his introductory essay, the editor assesses the impact of this novel on the Victorian reading public.

Goode, John. "*Adam Bede*." In *Critical Essays on George Eliot*, edited by Barbara Hardy. New York: Barnes & Noble Books, 1970.
Argues that the novel is actually an example of social realism; shows why George Eliot uses the period of the 1790's to provide a stable backdrop not already modernized—to develop her thesis that social conventions are extensions of natural law. Discusses the structure of the novel in some detail and provides analysis of Hetty, Adam, and Dinah to demonstrate the varying attitudes of individuals within society.

Haight, Gordon. *George Eliot: A Biography*. New York: Oxford University Press, 1968.
Details the composition process and publication arrangements, with comments regarding Marian Evans' desire to remain unknown behind her pseudonym. Reprints a long letter of praise for the novel from Jane Welsh Carlyle and notes the many favorable reviews. Discusses the controversy stirred by pseudonymous publication.

Haight, Gordon, ed. *A Century of George Eliot Criticism*. Boston: Houghton Mifflin, 1965.
Several selections in this collection of reprints provide useful commentary on the work: E. S. Dallas' 1859 review offers insight from one of George Eliot's contemporaries; W. A. E. Axon remarks on her use of dialect in the novel; excerpts from Dorothy Van Ghent's essay on the work and from W. J. Harvey's article on the treatment of time in the novel are complemented by remarks from several essays dealing with George Eliot's achievement and stature as a writer.

Halperin, John, and Janet Kunert. *Plots and Characters in the Fiction of Jane Austen, the Brontës, and George Eliot*. Hamden, Conn.: Archon Books, 1976.
Extensive plot outline is interspersed with critical commentary on George Eliot's method of composition and characterization. Also contains brief sketches of major and minor characters, highlighting the traits George Eliot wishes to emphasize.

Hanson, Lawrence, and Elizabeth Hanson. *Marian Evans and George Eliot: A Biography*. New York: Oxford University Press, 1952.
Rates the novel only a moderate success artistically, even though it was immensely popular with the Victorian reading public. Brief sketch of the major characters shows Hetty and Arthur to be well drawn, but Adam and Dinah much less so. Praises George Eliot's depiction of the Warwickshire countryside and her realistic portrait of peasant life.

Hardy, Barbara. "The Tragic Process in Adam Bede." In her *The Novels of George Eliot: A Study in Form*. New York: Oxford University Press, 1959.
Focuses on Adam Bede as a tragic hero typical of those George Eliot was to create throughtout her fiction. His heroism is muted, and his tragic awareness comes through a gradual change in his outlook on life as he becomes conscious of the illusory nature of his ideals. Emphasizes George Eliot's ability to reflect real, gradual changes in Adam's character, fulfilling the novelist's belief that character is molded by actions and is not a constant property. Arthur Donnithorne is treated in a separate chapter on egoists in George Eliot's fiction.

Holmstrom, John, and Laurence Lerner, eds. *George Eliot and her Readers: A Selection of Contemporary Reviews*. New York: Barnes & Noble Books, 1966.
Contains six entries excerpted from writings by George Eliot's contemporaries. Four reviews offer varying perspectives on the work, including E. S. Dallas' laudatory analysis. Includes a note from one admirer asking George Eliot to issue a cheaper edition of her work, and comments from a biography of Prince Albert noting the Prince Consort's high regard for the book.

Karl, Frederick R. *A Reader's Guide to the Nineteenth-Century Novel*. New York: Farrar, Straus & Giroux, 1964.
Highlights George Eliot's commitment to celebrating the lives of common people in the novel. Discusses the work as a prose version of William Wordsworth's poetry—a tribute to rustic values. Shows how George Eliot achieves structural symmetry; provides analysis of characters, including several of the minor figures.

Martin, Hazel T. *Petticoat Rebels: A Study of the Novels of Social Protest of George Eliot, Elizabeth Gaskell, and Charlotte Brontë*. New York: Helios Books, 1968.
Posits the novel is aimed primarily at exploring religious issues, especially the Church's tolerance of the double standard applied to men and women in matters of sexual morality. Notes George Eliot's concern with intolerance, both religious and moral.

Redinger, Ruby V. *George Eliot: The Emergent Self*. New York: Alfred A. Knopf, 1975.
Records the genesis and composition of the novel, noting the rather difficult circumstances under which it was written. Compares it with "Amos Barton," an earlier story by George Eliot, to show how closely the novelist relies on her own experiences for material. Notes the positive public reaction to the work, and the mixed response of the novelist to this acclaim; she wanted to revel in the success but could not, because she had published the work pseudonymously.

Sprague, Rosemary. *George Eliot: A Biography*. Philadelphia: Chilton, 1968.
Traces the origins of the novel in George Eliot's imagination. Brief plot summary, followed by analysis of four major characters: Adam, Hetty, Arthur, and Dinah. Believes the strength of the novel lies in George Eliot's ability to show events evolving as a result of the interaction of strong characters with their surroundings. Considers Dinah Morris one of the novelist's greatest creations.

Van Ghent, Dorothy. "*Adam Bede*." In *George Eliot*, edited by Harold Bloom. New York: Chelsea House, 1986.
Discusses George Eliot's techniques for achieving the slow pace of the novel, focusing on her handling of descriptive details. Quotes extensively from the text to illustrate passages creating this effect; key among them is the recurrent image of Mrs. Poyser's clock.

Daniel Deronda

Beer, Gillian. *George Eliot*. Bloomington: Indiana University Press, 1986.
Reads the novel as George Eliot's investigation of the difficulties encountered by exceptional women in society. Considers it highly experimental both in technique and subject. Believes that through her story George Eliot attempts to explore individual expressions of kinship among people, cutting across lines of gender and race. Special attention is given to Gwendolyn Harleth's struggle to become free of conventional bonds.

Carroll, David, ed. *George Eliot: The Critical Heritage*. New York: Barnes & Noble Books, 1971.
Collects thirteen documents to give a sense of the public response to the novel. Included are reviews by R. H. Hutton, George Saintsbury, A. C. Dicey, Henry James, and Edward Dowden; extracts from George Eliot's journal, in which she records her reaction to the novel's reception; and a letter from George Eliot to Harriet Beecher Stowe on the Jewish element in the work. In his introduction, the editor summarizes the checkered critical reception of the novel.

Haight, Gordon. *George Eliot: A Biography*. New York: Oxford University Press, 1968.
Details George Eliot's extensive preparations for writing this book, especially her investigation of Jewish history. Outlines her friendship with Emanuel Deutsch, an early proponent of Jewish nationalism. Chronicles her struggles to get the novel finished. Sketches the business arrangements for publication and reviews the speculation by George Eliot's Victorian contemporaries on the real-life models for her fictional characters.

——————, ed. *A Century of George Eliot Criticism*. Boston: Houghton Mifflin, 1965.
Reprints of three reviews, two by Henry James, give an indication of the reaction to the novel by George Eliot's contemporaries. Excerpts from studies by Edward Dowden and F. R. Leavis compare the novel to George Eliot's *Middlemarch* and Henry James' *Portrait of a Lady* respectively. Also includes comments by Oliver Elton on George Eliot's strengths and weaknesses in the work; by Vernon Rednall on her use of classical literature; by Joan Bennett on her handling of humor and comedy; and by Barbara Hardy on the coincidences and unrealized possibilities in the work, especially in the relationship between Gwendolyn Harleth and Daniel Deronda.

Halperin, John, and Janet Kunert. *Plots and Characters in the Fiction of Jane Austen, the Brontës, and George Eliot*. Hamden, Conn.: Archon Books, 1976.

Exceptionally comprehensive synopsis of the novel, covering every scene in this intricately plotted work; useful in aiding readers to keep clear the details of the action. Also contains character sketches of more than seventy figures.

Hanson, Lawrence, and Elizabeth Hanson. *Marian Evans and George Eliot: A Biography*. New York: Oxford University Press, 1952.
Provides details on George Eliot's developing interest in the problems of the Jews in England and western Europe, which gave impetus to this book. Considers the book a failure as a novel, largely because Daniel Deronda is simply an intellectual creation without life, as are the other Jews in the story. Gwendolyn, on the other hand, is a masterful creation, and her relationship with Grandcourt is handled with great understanding of the psychological makeup of men and women.

Hardy, Barbara. *The Novels of George Eliot: A Study in Form*. New York: Oxford University Press, 1959.
Detailed comments on various aspects of the novel are presented throughout this broad study of George Eliot's work. Discusses Gwendolyn Harleth as a tragic heroine and comments on Daniel Deronda's function in the work; considers George Eliot's portrait of Daniel flawed. Extensive commentary on the plotting; briefer remarks on George Eliot's use of coincidence. Also provides analysis of the novelist's use of imagery to create pathos and to give readers a sense of the irony of her characters' fates.

Holmstrom, John, and Laurence Lerner, eds. *George Eliot and her Readers: A Selection of Contemporary Reviews*. New York: Barnes & Noble Books, 1966.
The editors devote substantial space to reprinting nineteenth century materials about the novel. Included are excerpts from twelve reviews; three letters to George Eliot from her publisher, John Blackwood; three letters from George Eliot to various correspondents; and an extract from the author's journal. Documents prove that, while the novel was praised, many critics strongly objected to the part of the book dealing with the Jewish culture. The editors show that Jews themselves were pleased with George Eliot's treatment of their heritage.

Martin, Graham. "*Daniel Deronda*: George Eliot and Political Change." In *Critical Essays on George Eliot*, edited by Barbara Hardy. New York: Barnes & Noble Books, 1970.
Examines the novel as an example of George Eliot's efforts to involve herself in political and social reform in her country. Notes her affinities with the ideas of Ludwig Feuerbach and Karl Marx, and cites the novelist's methods of transforming political and social ideology into art. Contains an extensive examination of the two major characters, who represent two different social

images: one expansive (Daniel), the other (Gwendolyn) caught in a claustrophobic society that stymies possibilities for human development.

Qualls, Barry V. "Speaking Through Parables: *Daniel Deronda*." In *George Eliot*, edited by Harold Bloom. New York: Chelsea House, 1986.
Provocative analysis of the novel as an epic-historical document which relies on Torquato Tasso's *Jerusalem Liberated* for its structure. Gives substantial evidence of the novelist's use of conventions of the epic and romance. Traces Daniel's and Gwendolyn's stories as alternative paths to a realization that the acceptance of the values associated with Judaism is necessary to achieve personal and social salvation. Heavy emphasis on the importance of religion and myth to George Eliot's concept of the function of art.

Raider, Ruth. " 'The Flash of Fervour': *Daniel Deronda*." In *Reading the Victorian Novel: Detail into Form*, edited by Ian Gregor. New York: Barnes & Noble Books, 1980.
Contends George Eliot intended to evoke violent and unsettling reactions in her readers by uniting the conventional story of Gwendolyn Harleth with the overtly political and inflammatory account of Zionism at the heart of Daniel Deronda's search for a Jewish utopia. Sees the novel as George Eliot's commentary on the futility of seeking such utopias; at the same time it highlights the notion of heroism associated with such searches—a form of behavior George Eliot admired.

Redinger, Ruby V. *George Eliot: The Emergent Self*. New York: Alfred A. Knopf, 1975.
Abbreviated discussion of George Eliot's single intention for this double-plotted novel: to view the consequences of human behavior emanating from egoism or its absence. Highlights the brief interactions between Daniel and Gwendolyn in the work. Also notes the importance of the figure of the mother—this is the only time George Eliot focuses on that member of the family, after writing for so long about brothers and fathers.

Sprague, Rosemary. *George Eliot: A Biography*. Philadelphia: Chilton, 1968.
Considers the work experimental. Discusses George Eliot's sympathetic (and prophetic) treatment of the Jewish culture and provides background on the status of Jews in nineteenth century England. Sees George Eliot emphasizing the potential for tragedy for characters who live by illusions. In that light, Sprague argues Gwendolyn is George Eliot's greatest creation, a character exemplifying the author's long-held belief that individuals determine their destiny and that all people must eventually suffer the consequences of their own decisions.

Felix Holt, the Radical

Beer, Gillian. *George Eliot*. Bloomington: Indiana University Press, 1986.
    Concentrates on the character of Mrs. Transome as an antithesis to the pseudo-
    radical attitudes of many other characters in the novel; believes the conflicts
    Mrs. Transome faces in dealing with conventional Victorian morality are actu-
    ally more dramatic than Felix's political radicalism. Sees the essential tension
    in the book between the private world of society and family, dominated by
    women, and the public world of politics, dominated by men.

Caserio, Robert. "*Felix Holt* and *Bleak House*." In *George Eliot*, edited by Harold
    Bloom. New York: Chelsea House, 1986.
    Compares scenes from these two novels to show the radical differences be-
    tween Dickens' and George Eliot's notions of plotting and their understanding
    of the relationship between external action and the internal nature of individ-
    uals engaged in these actions. Sees George Eliot undermining conventional
    notions of plotting because she is more concerned with her characters' internal
    motivations. Stresses the novelist's belief in the indeterminacy of action, con-
    stantly noting the accidental nature of most events.

Carroll, David, ed. *George Eliot: The Critical Heritage*. New York: Barnes & Noble
    Books, 1971.
    Reprints reviews of the novel by four important Victorian men of letters:
    R. H. Hutton, John Morley, E. S. Dallas, and G. S. Venables, as well as one by
    the young Henry James, in which he faults George Eliot's skills in plotting but
    praises her ability at characterization. Also includes an excerpt from a letter by
    George Eliot's friend, the Positivist Frederic Harrison. In the introduction to
    the volume, the editor surveys the critical reaction the novel engendered upon
    its publication.

Emery, Laura Comer. *George Eliot's Creative Conflict: The Other Side of Silence*.
    Berkeley: University of California Press, 1976.
    Psychoanalytic assessment focuses on George Eliot's characterization of Esther
    Lyon, whose development shows similarities to that of Maggie Tulliver in *The
    Mill on the Floss*, but with differences that suggest ways George Eliot was
    maturing as a novelist. Separate sections outline the novelist's initial character-
    ization of her heroine; discuss the two male characters who impel Esther to
    change in the course of the tale, Felix Holt and Rufus Lyon; and analyze the
    mother-daughter relationship between Mrs. Transome and Esther.

Haight, Gordon. *George Eliot: A Biography*. New York: Oxford University Press, 1968.
    Brief comments regarding George Eliot's painstaking research for this book
    and her enlistment of Frederic Harrison to assist her in guaranteeing the

accuracy of the legal aspects. Sketches the highly favorable public reception, noting the praise given the novel by several contemporary reviewers.

—————— , ed. *A Century of George Eliot Criticism*. Boston: Houghton Mifflin, 1965.
Contains reviews by three of George Eliot's influential contemporaries: E. S. Dallas, John Morley, and Henry James. Scattered comments about the novel are presented in several other wide-ranging essays about George Eliot's career and achievements.

Halperin, John, and Janet Kunert. *Plots and Characters in the Fiction of Jane Austen, the Brontës, and George Eliot*. Hamden, Conn.: Archon Books, 1976.
Synopsis of the action of the novel, offering a clear summary of George Eliot's intricate plotting. Also contains character sketches of the major and minor figures in the work.

Hanson, Lawrence, and Elizabeth Hanson. *Marian Evans and George Eliot: A Biography*. New York: Oxford University Press, 1952.
Abbreviated discussion pointing out the novel's defects in plotting and its focus on a historical period for which George Eliot provides well-researched details, but no life. Considers the two major characters, Esther and Felix, weakly drawn and too ideological. Sees some strength in the subplot involving the relationship between Mrs. Transome and her son Harold.

Hardy, Barbara. *The Novels of George Eliot: A Study in Form*. New York: Oxford University Press, 1959.
Discusses the novel within this larger study of George Eliot's ability to achieve success through manipulation of structural devices. Brief analyses of Esther Lyon and of George Eliot's use of parallel structure to present several pairs of characters whose stories finally converge for a single climax. Also includes a discussion of the novelist's use of coincidence and an analysis of several scenes having symbolic significance.

Holmstrom, John, and Laurence Lerner, eds. *George Eliot and her Readers: A Selection of Contemporary Reviews*. New York: Barnes & Noble Books, 1966.
A reprinting of excerpts from several nineteenth century reviews, showing the wide range of critical opinions which the work generated among initial readers: some thought the work highly successful, while others (including Henry James) saw major faults in characterization. The editors add a critical assessment of the general reaction, noting the strengths and weaknesses pointed out by the reviewers.

Kettle, Arnold. "*Felix Holt, the Radical*." In *Critical Essays on George Eliot*, edited by Barbara Hardy. New York: Barnes & Noble Books, 1970.

Claims George Eliot fails to fulfill her major purpose for the novel: to show the two kinds of radicalism that emerged as a response to deteriorating conditions for the poor in England. Especially critical of George Eliot's plotting, which Kettle says detracts from the purpose of the work. Believes the novelist never gave her major figure, Felix Holt, a chance to lead the commoners, and hence to exhibit the possibilities of his brand of radicalism. Claims George Eliot's knowledge of the common people's problems was only theoretical, preventing her from creating convincing portraits.

Meckier, Jerome. "Hidden Rivalries in Victorian Fiction: The Case of the Two Esthers." In *The Changing World of Charles Dickens*, edited by Robert Giddings. Totowa, N.J.: Barnes & Noble Books, 1983.
Reads the novel as George Eliot's attempt to rewrite Dickens' *Bleak House*; points out numerous parallels of character and incident, highlighting George Eliot's parodies of Dickens' sentimentalism and his insistence in achieving reform by cataclysmic means. George Eliot, on the other hand, sees true reform coming gradually, through moral improvement of individuals. Meckier considers this novel only one example of the tendency of Victorian novelists to write in direct response to the work of their contemporaries.

Redinger, Ruby V. *George Eliot: The Emergent Self*. New York: Alfred A. Knopf, 1975.
Brief commentary on the composition of the novel and on George Eliot's return to William Blackwood as her publisher. Discusses the critical reaction, noting the diversity of opinion about the work; among unfavorable comments were ones attacking the unseemliness of Mrs. Transome's story. Notes the majority of the reviewers saw the work as an improvement over *Romola*, its immediately predecessor.

Speare, Morris E. "George Eliot and Radicalism." In his *The Political Novel: Its Development in England and America*. Reprint. New York: Russell & Russell, 1966.
Detailed examination of George Eliot's concern for political issues that led her to select her subject for this work. Brief plot summary focusing on the novelist's exploration of the concept of Radicalism; suggests George Eliot saw true reform of government as possible only after men achieved moral reforms. Sees the working class as the real heroes of the work. Believes that Felix Holt is a Carlylean hero figure who sees the possibilities for reform available through enfranchisement of the working classes; he strives to make these people effective in their new role.

Sprague, Rosemary. *George Eliot: A Biography*. Philadelphia: Chilton, 1968.
Noting the dated nature of some of the material in the novel, Sprague

nevertheless believes it shows advances in George Eliot's career in several ways, especially as it is the first of her works with two distinct plots. Traces the stories of Felix Holt and of the Transome family in some detail. Claims Felix represents an idea held in esteem by the novelist: education will improve the lot of the poor. Points out the excellence of George Eliot's psychological portraits of Mrs. Transome and her son.

Williams, Raymond. "The Industrial Novels." In his *Culture and Society, 1780-1950*. London: Chatto & Windus, 1954.
Considers the novel one of several which examine problems inherent in the growing industrialism of England. Compares it with works by Disraeli, Gaskell, and Kingsley, judging it superior largely because George Eliot brings a finer intelligence and capacity for discrimination to bear. Notes that George Eliot, like her contemporaries, feared the possibilities of mob violence and was skeptical of democracy; her solution for improvement, however, begins with moral and educational reform for workers. Williams argues that George Eliot shows special skill at depicting human relationships.

Middlemarch

Armstrong, Isobel. "*Middlemarch*: A Note on George Eliot's 'Wisdom.' " In *Critical Essays on George Eliot*, edited by Barbara Hardy. New York: Barnes & Noble Books, 1970.
Focuses on the generalizations and aphorisms in the novel, showing how these examples of George Eliot's "wisdom" appeal to readers and lead them to assent to the author's moral stance toward her characters. Compares her use of these sayings with William Makepeace Thackeray's use of the same technique to show George Eliot is better at integrating these generalizations into her tale. Demonstrates that, through skillful manipulation of tone and careful placement of these observations, George Eliot is able to gain readers' acceptance of her viewpoint on the relationship between individuals and society.

Beer, Gillian. *George Eliot*. Bloomington: Indiana University Press, 1986.
Lengthy analysis of the novel traces the influence of the women's movement on George Eliot's conception of her story; demonstrates how the story reflects key issues of that movement, especially the importance of education, money, and independence for women trying to break free from male dominance. Traces George Eliot's relationship with many influential figures in the women's movement in her century. Compares *Middlemarch* to other proto-feminist works, especially Elizabeth Barrett Browning's *Aurora Leigh*.

Beer, Patricia. *Reader, I Married Him: A Study of the Women Characters of Jane Austen, Charlotte Brontë, Elizabeth Gaskell, and George Eliot*. London: Macmillan, 1974.

Reads the novel as an example of George Eliot's ability to depict heroines who arc unable to avoid the necessity of renouncing dreams of personal fulfillment in favor of conventional social roles; George Eliot shows great compassion for Dorothea, who can do nothing without the approval or assistance of men.

Carroll, David, ed. *George Eliot: The Critical Heritage*. New York: Barnes & Noble Books, 1971.

Collects seven reviews (some excerpted) from important nineteenth century British and American periodicals. Contributors include R. H. Hutton, Edward Dowden, A. V. Dicey, and Henry James. These reviews show how strongly the novel affected its first readers, who recognized it as a masterpiece. The editor's commentary in the introduction to this collection sheds further light on the impact the work had on the Victorian reading public.

Ellmann, Richard. "Dorothea's Husbands." In *George Eliot*, edited by Harold Bloom. New York: Chelsea House, 1986.

Reviews available evidence for identifying real-life models for Casaubon; argues intriguingly that the old scholar is actually based on elements of George Eliot's own personality she wished to exorcise. Also contends Will Ladislaw is based on John Cross, whom George Eliot met when she was writing *Middlemarch*, and who ironically became the novelist's husband some years later.

Emery, Laura Comer. *George Eliot's Creative Conflict: The Other Side of Silence*. Berkeley: University of California Press, 1976.

Extensive psychoanalytic reading of the novel, using Freudian terminology to explain the significance of the actions and motivations of the various characters. Concentrates on the relationship between George Eliot and the major figures she creates for this story, showing how the characters reflect her inner equilibrium. Separate sections examine Dorothea and, to a lesser extent, Casaubon; discuss the relationship between Dorothea and Will Ladislaw; and an analyze Lydgate, whose development parallels Dorothea's. Includes a discussion of Rosamond Vincy and Bulstrode.

Haight, Gordon. *George Eliot: A Biography*. New York: Oxford University Press, 1968.

Traces the history of the novel's composition and its unusual form of publication: eight half-volume installments. Details the way George Eliot united two separate stories into what became a comprehensive view of English provincial life. Sketches the critical reception of the work by George Eliot's contemporaries, citing the many laudatory reviews and the favorable comments from important personages in British and American literary circles. Reviews the controversy accompanying speculation over the real-life models for George Eliot's fictional portraits.

—————— , ed. *A Century of George Eliot Criticism*. Boston: Houghton Mifflin, 1965.
Reprints two reviews by George Eliot's contemporaries and excerpts from essays by Jerome Beatty and Quentin Anderson. Also contains excerpts from essays of a more general nature. These include Oliver Elton's brief comments on the major characters, V. S. Pritchett's remarks on structure, Mark Shorer's assessment of the novel's metaphoric qualities, and Martin J. Svaglic's discussion of George Eliot's religious attitudes as exhibited in this work.

Halperin, John, and Janet Kunert. *Plots and Characters in the Fiction of Jane Austen, the Brontës, and George Eliot*. Hamden, Conn.: Archon Books, 1976.
Especially detailed summary of this complex, densely plotted work; very helpful in clarifying the intricate relationships among the dozens of characters George Eliot has included. An appendix provides useful sketches of the more than ninety men and women mentioned in the book.

Hanson, Lawrence, and Elizabeth Hanson. *Marian Evans and George Eliot: A Biography*. New York: Oxford University Press, 1952.
Considers the novel a masterpiece in which George Eliot's prose matches her conception. Points out strengths of characterization; however, the authors note some tendency on George Eliot's part to idealize Dorothea. Quotes extensively from the text to illustrate George Eliot's felicitudes in handling character and theme.

Hardy, Barbara. *The Novels of George Eliot: A Study in Form*. New York: Oxford University Press, 1959.
Extensive discussion of the novel in a general study of George Eliot's fictional techniques. Includes an analysis of Dorothea as a tragic heroine, and of Casaubon as a failed egoist. Examines plotting and key scenes having symbolic import, remarks on George Eliot's use of chance and coincidence, and offers observations on her use of irony in the work.

Hertz, Neil. "Recognizing Casaubon." In *George Eliot*, edited by Harold Bloom. New York: Chelsea House, 1986.
Uses the theory of semiotics to discuss the nature and function of Casaubon as a representative of the written word, with certain indeterminacies which stand in the way of perceiving reality. Hence, both reader and writer (in this case, George Eliot) must come to terms with the problems writing poses in

obscuring as well as illuminating reality. Detailed analysis of specific passages from the text, as well as ones from George Eliot's letters and other writings, which are introduced to support Hertz's thesis.

Holmstrom, John, and Laurence Lerner, eds. *George Eliot and her Readers: A Selection of Contemporary Reviews*. New York: Barnes & Noble Books, 1966.
A lengthy section of this anthology is devoted to materials on the novel, including excerpts from fifteen reviews and from four letters between George Eliot and various correspondents. Many of the reviews were written while the novel was being released in parts; hence, one can follow the development of the public's attitude toward the work as George Eliot brought her tale to completion. Commentary by the editors discusses the responses of George Eliot's contemporaries, showing Victorian readers found much to praise and little to blame in this work.

Karl, Frederick R. *A Reader's Guide to the Nineteenth Century Novel*. New York: Farrar, Straus & Giroux, 1964.
Outlines the intellectual background of the novel, especially the influence of religious writings on George Eliot. Extensive analysis of Dorothea Brooke and other characters within the social setting of the town of Middlemarch. Shows how the novelist handles the complexities of human relationships, especially those involving love and marriage.

Knoepflmacher, U. C. "*Middlemarch*: Affirmation through Compromise." In his *Laughter and Despair: Readings in Ten Novels of the Victorian Era*. Berkeley: University of California Press, 1971.
A penetrating analysis of the novel, comparing it to William Makepeace Thackeray's and Charles Dickens' works to show how George Eliot reaches a compromise between cynicism and idealism in her vision of society. Discusses in detail the function of the narrator. Traces the four concentric circles within which the novel's individuals operate: the large historical world in which comparisons to a heroic past show the unheroic nature of the modern world; the specific historical events of the early nineteenth century; the more restricted events of the mythical Middlemarch community; and a character's immediate social sphere. Also discusses the function of imagery in the work.

Levine, George. "The Hero as Dilettante: *Middlemarch* and *Nostromo*." In his *The Realistic Imagination: English Fiction from Frankenstein to Lady Chatterly*. Chicago: University of Chicago Press, 1981.
Contrasts George Eliot's novel with Joseph Conrad's to show how both deal with the ways new perspectives on human nature and society afforded by scientific discoveries yield insight into the human condition and offer hope for man. Both novels concentrate on the figure of the outsider (in *Middlemarch*,

Will Ladislaw) to show the follies of "common sense" and convention. George Eliot, however, is not as pessimistic as Conrad in her views of society; she still hopes for man's eventual social and moral redemption.

_____ . "The Scientific Texture of *Middlemarch*." In *George Eliot*, edited by Harold Bloom. New York: Chelsea House, 1986.
A careful analysis of the novel as George Eliot's attempt to humanize theories of science that provided a new view of the world for the Victorians. Traces the scientific background informing the novel. Shows how George Eliot humanizes the scientific vision, a perspective that forces people to stand outside themselves and seek a comprehensive view of the world.

Miller, J. Hillis. "Optic and Semiotic in *Middlemarch*." In *George Eliot*, edited by Harold Bloom. New York: Chelsea House, 1986.
Detailed discussion of three central metaphors: the web, the stream, and the double-lens microscope. Intriguing analysis shows how metaphors come into conflict, and how no universal perspective can be achieved, even by the omniscient narrator. Every perspective is egocentric and every description of reality expressed in metaphor is bounded by the terms of relation between the metaphor and the object it describes.

Phelps, Gilbert. *A Reader's Guide to Fifty British Novels, 1600-1900*. New York: Barnes & Noble Books, 1979.
Outlines the genesis of the novel and summarizes its major plots. Critical comments focus on the way George Eliot re-creates an entire provincial society and explores with great insight the relationships between the men and women in her work.

Redinger, Ruby V. *George Eliot: The Emergent Self*. New York: Alfred A. Knopf, 1975.
Brief assessment of the novel pointing out parallels between various characters in the work and people in George Eliot's life; notes similarities between the novelist and Dorothea. Argues that, despite these similarities, George Eliot is in full control of her narrative and does not let the autobiographical impulse dictate the action. Thought-provoking description of the parallels between Casaubon and David Friedrich Strauss, whose *Das Leben Jesu* influenced George Eliot's concept of religion and myth.

Sprague, Rosemary. *George Eliot: A Biography*. Philadelphia: Chilton, 1968.
Some discussion of the conception and composition of the novel and of the method of publication. Detailed analysis of the four major plots, each of which interacts with others at key points in the narrative. Notes the pathos evoked by Dorothea and Casaubon's ill-matched union, paralleled by the marriage of

Lydgate and Rosamond Vincy, and set in relief by Fred Vincy's marriage to Mary Garth. Shows how Nicholas Bulstrode serves as a means of binding the three other narratives together in what is clearly George Eliot's finest portrait of an entire society.

The Mill on the Floss

Allen, Walter. "*The Mill on the Floss*." In *George Eliot*, edited by Harold Bloom. New York: Chelsea House, 1986.
  Noting parallels between Maggie and her creator, Allen argues that the heroine meets a tragic fate because she is a creative spirit in a materialistic society. Sees George Eliot condemning that society throughout the novel. Justifies the novelist's use of the cliché ending because she was forced to bring her heroine to some end, rather than leave the action unresolved, as later novelists have been free to do.

Beer, Gillian. *George Eliot*. Bloomington: Indiana University Press, 1986.
  Provides a feminist reading of the novel, focusing on George Eliot's development of Maggie as a woman who refuses to be bound by the conventions of her society. Emphasis is on the sexual implications of the narrative and on the novelist's boldness in depicting both female and male sensations in human relationships.

Carroll, David, ed. *George Eliot: The Critical Heritage*. New York: Barnes & Noble Books, 1971.
  Thirteen selections from reviews and letters provide a summary of contemporary reactions to the novel. In addition to several reviews originally appearing in influential journals, the editor reprints correspondence from Edward Bulwer-Lytton and from George Eliot herself, showing some of the objections raised to the work and the novelist's reaction to these criticisms. Also includes commentary written some years later by A. C. Swinburne and John Ruskin. In his introduction, the editor summarizes the reaction of George Eliot's contemporaries to the work.

Daleski, H. M. "*The Mill on the Floss*: The Dividing of the Seasons." In his *The Divided Heroine: A Recurrent Pattern in Six English Novels*. New York: Holmes & Meier, 1984.
  Argues that central qualities of Maggie Tulliver are her divided sensibility and her need to love and be loved. In childhood no division of sensibility exists and she shares love reciprocally with her family; as she grows, however, her sensual nature conflicts with her intellectual leanings, eventually leading to tragedy. Extensive discussion of Maggie's relationships with Philip Waken and Stephen Guest.

Emery, Laura Comer. *George Eliot's Creative Conflict: The Other Side of Silence*. Berkeley: University of California Press, 1976.
Psychoanalytic reading of the novel; considers the work George Eliot's attempt to work out internal conflicts by externalizing them in the character of Maggie Tulliver. Focuses on the changes Maggie undergoes, seeing them as expressions of Freudian oral, anal, and sadistic needs. Sees her conflict in psychological terms as a struggle between id and superego—her failure to reconcile these competing forces leads to her death. Relates Maggie's predicament to George Eliot's life as an artist.

Haight, Gordon. *George Eliot: A Biography*. New York: Oxford University Press, 1968.
Sketches the genesis and history of the novel's composition, giving careful attention to George Eliot's determination to be accurate in factual detail. Comments on the appearance of the novel and its highly favorable reception by the British reading public.

——————— , ed. *A Century of George Eliot Criticism*. Boston: Houghton Mifflin, 1965.
Several articles and excerpts in this collection of reprinted materials give useful information on George Eliot's techniques and highlight her themes in this novel. Included are E. S. Dallas' 1860 review in the London *Times*; Gordon Haight's introduction to the Riverside edition; and comments on the work appearing in essays such as Virginia Woolf's observations in her centenary review of George Eliot's achievement, Vernon Rednall's catalog of classical allusions in the novel, and F. R. Leavis' character analysis of Maggie Tulliver.

Halperin, John, and Janet Kunert. *Plots and Characters in the Fiction of Jane Austen, the Brontës, and George Eliot*. Hamden, Conn.: Archon Books, 1976.
Useful plot summary that can help readers understand the family and community relationships George Eliot develops in the novel. More than forty characters who appear in the novel are described briefly in a separate section of the study.

Hanson, Lawrence, and Elizabeth Hanson. *Marian Evans and George Eliot: A Biography*. New York: Oxford University Press, 1952.
Brief discussion of the novel focuses on parallels between Maggie Tulliver and her creator; sees the book as George Eliot's attempt to write about her own spiritual struggles and her relationship with her brother. Faults the novelist for weak characterization and didacticism; praises her for creating believable background, thus making the actions of her characters seem credible.

Hardy, Barbara. *The Novels of George Eliot: A Study in Form*. New York: Oxford University Press, 1959.

Commentary on individual aspects of the novel is included in this study of
George Eliot's techniques. Contains a discussion of Maggie as a tragic heroine,
brief comments on George Eliot's contrasting of Tom and Maggie, remarks on
the novelist's plotting and her use of authorial voice in the text, and an analysis
of key scenes with symbolic significance.

Hardy, Barbara. "*The Mill on the Floss*." In *Critical Essays on George Eliot*, edited
by Barbara Hardy. New York: Barnes & Noble Books, 1970.
Believes the novel is a great work of realism until its end, when George
Eliot succumbs to fantasy to extricate her heroine from her harsh fate. Notes
the close parallels between this novel and George Eliot's life. Extensive discussion of Maggie's progress toward self-knowledge, focusing on the crises she
undergoes and showing the limited options she has in making choices. Outlines the ways George Eliot uses Maggie to make a statement about moral
issues.

Holmstrom, John, and Laurence Lerner, eds. *George Eliot and her Readers: A
Selection of Contemporary Reviews*. New York: Barnes & Noble Books, 1966.
Reprints excerpts from ten reviews that appeared in influential nineteenth
century periodicals shortly after the novel was published, showing the reactions of George Eliot's contemporaries to the novel. Also includes comments
by the editors on the general response of George Eliot's initial readers and
excerpts from three of the novelist's letters, expressing her reaction to the
criticisms.

Knoepflmacher, U. C. "The Intrusion of Tragedy: *The Ordeal of Richard Feverel*
and *The Mill on the Floss*." In his *Laughter and Despair: Readings in Ten
Novels of the Victorian Era*. Berkeley: University of California Press, 1971.
Compares George Eliot's work with George Meredith's novel to demonstrate similarities of theme and characterization. Discusses George Eliot's
handling of family relationships in a world in which old values fail to be
effective. Faults her for refusing to follow through with the harsh criticism she
displays through the character of Maggie. Considers the ending weak because
the novelist cannot seem to let Maggie come to the bitter end the course of
events dictates; sees the heroine's death on the river as an escape from that
fate.

Lee, A. Robert. "*The Mill on the Floss*: 'Memory' and the Reading Experience." In
Reading the Victorian Novel: Detail into Form, edited by Ian Gregor. New
York: Barnes & Noble Books, 1980.
Argues that the novel, far from being flawed, as earlier critics contend, is
successful in that George Eliot uses autobiography well and manages to tran-

scend its limitations. Claims the novel affects sympathetic readers and helps them overcome reservations about the cliché nature of the later chapters.

Martin, Hazel T. *Petticoat Rebels: A Study of the Novels of Social Protest of George Eliot, Elizabeth Gaskell, and Charlotte Brontë*. New York: Helios Books, 1968.
Brief analysis of the novel focuses on George Eliot's growing distaste for hypocrisy, including for her contemporaries' double standard of morality whereby women alone were blamed for all incidences of sexual transgression. Also cites her dislike for the growing intolerance of the middle class for those who stray from strict conventional moral codes. Claims that the novelist foreshadows existentialism by championing the notion that people are really products of their free choices.

Phelps, Gilbert. *A Reader's Guide to Fifty British Novels, 1600-1900*. New York: Barnes & Noble Books, 1979.
Outlines George Eliot's upbringing and intellectual development. A plot summary sketching major events of the novel is followed by critical commentary pointing out its faults, especially George Eliot's reliance on sentimentality and her lack of control over her heroine. Also notes the way the novelist's interest in philosophical issues informs her fiction.

Redinger, Ruby V. *George Eliot: The Emergent Self*. New York: Alfred A. Knopf, 1975.
Traces the composition of the novel, noting the parallels between the fiction and George Eliot's life, especially her continuing emotional attachment to her brother Isaac, on whom the fictional Tom Tulliver is based. Sees the third part of the novel paralleling George Eliot's situation at the time the novel was written, as she had been forced by her relationship with George Henry Lewes to choose between her personal feelings and the moral conventions of her society. Also discusses the novel's public reception and George Eliot's reaction to the comments of her contemporaries. Believes that by writing this novel George Eliot purged herself of several destructive emotional tendencies.

Sprague, Rosemary. *George Eliot: A Biography*. Philadelphia: Chilton, 1968.
Notes the autobiographical impulses in George Eliot's conception of the work; sees *The Mill on the Floss* as a justification of George Eliot's own conduct in agreeing to live with George Henry Lewes. Traces Maggie Tulliver's fortunes, focusing on her relationships with Philip Wakem and Stephen Guest to show how Maggie adheres to a strict moral code which, though not conventional, is nevertheless admirable.

Weed, Elizabeth. "The Liquidation of Maggie Tulliver." In *George Eliot*, edited by Harold Bloom. New York: Chelsea House, 1986.

A reading of the novel that applies theories of narratology, feminist criticism, and deconstruction to account for George Eliot's failure to create a convincing and satisfying heroine in Maggie Tulliver. Sees underlying tendencies of male domination in the society George Eliot creates and notes tendencies of indeterminacy in the language used to describe both characters and scenes; both contribute to the failure of characterization.

Romola

Beer, Gillian. *George Eliot*. Bloomington: Indiana University Press, 1986.
Examines George Eliot's ability to deal with the problems and possibilities of marriage, focusing on Romola and Tito's relationship. Claims the decision to set the novel far back in history allows George Eliot to explore male-female relationships more freely than she could if the work were set in modern times. Explains how the figure of the Madonna plays an important role in George Eliot's imagination: the novelist refused to contrast the Virgin Mother with the whore, a typical Victorian technique.

Carroll, David, ed. *George Eliot: The Critical Heritage*. New York: Barnes & Noble Books, 1971.
Excerpts from four reviews that appeared in important Victorian periodicals shortly after the novel was published. One is R. H. Hutton's commentary from the July, 1863, *Spectator*; George Eliot's letter to Hutton praising his understanding of her intentions is also reprinted. Includes a note of fulsome praise from fellow novelist Anthony Trollope. The editor offers a brief critical comment on the reception of the novel.

Emery, Laura Comer. *George Eliot's Creative Conflict: The Other Side of Silence*. Berkeley: University of California Press, 1976.
Psychoanalytic reading of the novel, using Freudian terminology to explain George Eliot's reasons for writing the story and to discuss the actions and motivations of principal characters. Reads the novel as a reflection of George Eliot's state of mind: she uses writing as a means of psychological defense against her deep-seated fears and as a means of gaining control over repressed feelings. Extensive analysis of Romola as a projection of the novelist herself. Also includes an analysis of various characters as dramatizations of psychological complexes.

Haight, Gordon. *George Eliot: A Biography*. New York: Oxford University Press, 1968.
Extensive review of George Eliot's reading and study in preparation for writing this historical novel; gives a good sense of the wide range of her investigation

into the background for the book. Traces sources for the major fictional characters, Romola and Tito. Also discusses the novelist's decision to publish the work serially and the impact this decision had on its composition.

Halperin, John, and Janet Kunert. *Plots and Characters in the Fiction of Jane Austen, the Brontës, and George Eliot*. Hamden, Conn.: Archon Books, 1976.
A scene-by-scene synopsis of this intricately plotted historical novel. Helpful in establishing the identity of the various historical and fictional personages. Characters are also identified and described briefly in an alphabetical listing in another section of this text.

Hanson, Lawrence, and Elizabeth Hanson. *Marian Evans and George Eliot: A Biography*. New York: Oxford University Press, 1952.
Details George Eliot's efforts to collect materials for the novel and outlines the role George Henry Lewes played in assisting her with this and other works. Brief assessment judges the novel a failure, lacking the spark of life George Eliot's works have when she writes about the area she knows best, the English midlands.

Hardy, Barbara. *The Novels of George Eliot: A Study in Form*. New York: Oxford University Press, 1959.
Comments on the novel are provided throughout this general study of George Eliot's artistry. Includes a discussion of Romola as a tragic heroine and an analysis of Tito's egoism; comments on the moral triangle of Romola, Tito, and Savanarola. Brief analysis of the novelist's techniques for plotting and her use of authorial commentary within the text; also examines some of the key scenes symbolic of George Eliot's larger concerns.

Holmstrom, John, and Laurence Lerner, eds. *George Eliot and her Readers: A Selection of Contemporary Reviews*. New York: Barnes & Noble Books, 1966.
Reprints R. H. Hutton's 1863 review from the *Spectator*, in which Hutton outlines the novel's central conflict, the struggle between classical Greek and Christian cultures as they clashed in the Renaissance; also discusses George Eliot's portrait of Savanarola. In a brief commentary, the editors of the volume add their assessment of nineteenth century attitudes toward the work, noting most readers were disappointed with George Eliot's venture into historical fiction.

Levine, George. "*Romola* as Fable." In *Critical Essays on George Eliot*, edited by Barbara Hardy. New York: Barnes & Noble Books, 1970.
Noting that most critics consider the work a failure, Levine suggests that George Eliot is actually working with parallel traditions, realism and romance. Romola's story belongs to the realm of romance, whereas Tito's fall into evil is

more novelistic. The strong emphasis on pattern, especially in Romola's story, highlights the relationship of the work to the tradition of the fable, a genre with a clear moral purpose. Levine also argues that the novel looks forward to several of George Eliot's other works, including *Middlemarch* and *Daniel Deronda*.

Redinger, Ruby V. *George Eliot: The Emergent Self*. New York: Alfred A. Knopf, 1975.
Includes substantial details about George Eliot's decision to switch publishers for this novel to allow the work to be published in monthly installments. Notes the difficulties she had in composing the work. Though acknowledging the lukewarm contemporary reaction, Redinger believes George Eliot's decision to cast the novel in the fifteenth century was liberating because she was able to create characters who would not have been accepted if placed in English society. Considers Romola, however, as yet another alter ego for her creator, who treats her harshly as a means of projected self-abasement.

Sprague, Rosemary. *George Eliot: A Biography*. Philadelphia: Chilton, 1968.
Good discussion of George Eliot's trials in getting the book written. Stresses her desire to be historically accurate, a demand that causes her writing to appear clotted at some points. Admires her attempt to create an entire society, but sees her real strength being characterization. Explains why George Eliot made Romola so idealized and presents a detailed analysis of Tito, whom Sprague considers the most interesting and best drawn character in the novel.

Silas Marner

Beer, Gillian. *George Eliot*. Bloomington: Indiana University Press, 1986.
Brief analysis of the novel focuses on George Eliot's use of chance and coincidence. Considers a central issue of the work to be the nature of parenting and the importance of nurturing as a function of parenting that transcends gender.

Carroll, David, ed. *George Eliot: The Critical Heritage*. New York: Barnes & Noble Books, 1971.
Five contemporary reviews from influential Victorian publications indicate the critical reaction to this novel when it first appeared. Includes R. H. Hutton's perceptive comments from his April, 1861, *Economist* review. Also presents two excerpts from letters between George Eliot and her publisher, John Blackwood, concerning the concept of the story and outlining details of publication. In the introduction, the editor offers a synopsis of the general critical reception of the work.

Emery, Laura Comer. *George Eliot's Creative Conflict: The Other Side of Silence*. Berkeley: University of California Press, 1976.

Psychoanalytic examination of the novel using Freudian techniques of character analysis to explain the significance of both Silas' and Godfrey's stories. Believes the novel dramatizes man's primitive desire for wish-fulfillment. Points out the importance of parent-child relationships to show that Silas' crisis is patterned on the basic Oedipal complex: he is aggressive toward his absent parents, regresses into a kind of childhood, and emerges only when he can take on the role of parent himself. Sees Godfrey's story paralleling Silas', although Godfrey is a failed parent.

Haddakin, Lilian. "*Silas Marner*." In *Critical Essays on George Eliot*, edited by Barbara Hardy. New York: Barnes & Noble Books, 1970.

Calls the work a minor masterpiece. Outlines its genesis in George Eliot's recollections and notebook entries. Discusses William Wordsworth's influence on the work in the novelist's use of rustic scenes, memory, and the functions of the child. Also traces George Eliot's development of the psychological dimension of Silas; discusses the functions of other characters such as Godfrey, Nancy, and Dolly in creating a unified portrait of the way human feelings operate in the world.

Haight, Gordon, ed. *A Century of George Eliot Criticism*. Boston: Houghton Mifflin, 1965.

Contains two reviews of the novel published shortly after its appearance in 1861, including E. S. Dallas' assessment in the London *Times*. Other selections in this miscellany contain brief comments, including a pithy evaluation by F. R. Leavis in a passage excerpted from his important study *The Great Tradition* (1948).

Halperin, John, and Janet Kunert. *Plots and Characters in the Fiction of Jane Austen, the Brontës, and George Eliot*. Hamden, Conn.: Archon Books, 1976.

Synopsis of the plot presented scene by scene, emphasizing the hero's goodness and his isolation from the community. In a separate section of the text, three dozen characters who appear in the work are described briefly.

Hanson, Lawrence, and Elizabeth Hanson. *Marian Evans and George Eliot: A Biography*. New York: Oxford University Press, 1952.

Brief chapter points out George Eliot's initial dilemma over the form of this story, noting that she contemplated writing the tale as a poem. Discusses the poetic qualities of the story, giving special praise to George Eliot's prose style.

Holloway, John. *The Victorian Sage*. New York: W. W. Norton, 1965.

Examines the novel as a striking example of the way George Eliot constructs her fiction to illustrate her overriding moral purposes. Stresses the ethical basis upon which the novelist develops specific scenes and creates characters, showing the universality of the incidents and emotions exhibited by the men and women in this rustic setting.

Holmstrom, John, and Laurence Lerner, eds. *George Eliot and her Readers: A Selection of Contemporary Reviews*. New York: Barnes & Noble Books, 1966.
Reprints a highly favorable review from the *Saturday Review* of April, 1861, which considers the novel an advance in characterization and plotting over *The Mill on the Floss*. The editors' commentary summarizes the Victorian public's reaction to the work, which was generally favorable, and notes that George Eliot's contemporaries found little in the novel to arouse their fears about spiritual conflicts—a characteristic of George Eliot's other novels.

Redinger, Ruby V. *George Eliot: The Emergent Self*. New York: Alfred A. Knopf, 1975.
Reads the novel as George Eliot's personal myth: sees Silas' fictional saga paralleling the novelist's. He is first ostracized unfairly (as George Eliot thought she had been), then becomes withdrawn, but is finally rejoined to society through his care for the child Eppie, a humane action (paralleling George Eliot's reunion through her socially responsible novels, which received wide acclaim).

Sprague, Rosemary. *George Eliot: A Biography*. Philadelphia: Chilton, 1968.
Brief review of the work, judging it George Eliot's most perfect in terms of form. Notes that the success of the novel is due to the author's skillful portrayal of Silas, whose fall away from humanity and his redemption achieved through the love he shows for Eppie is seen as an allegory. Believes secular rather than religious activity forms the basis for judgment of the protagonist: Silas is finally revered by his fellow men because he puts the welfare of others ahead of his own self-interest.

ELIZABETH GASKELL

General Studies

Allott, Miriam. *Elizabeth Gaskell*. New York: Longmans, Green, 1960.
Abbreviated overview of Gaskell's work. An introductory chapter provides a brief biographical sketch. The novels are discussed briefly, as is Gaskell's *The Life of Charlotte Brontë*. Contains a bibliography listing the novelist's published works.

Barry, James D. "Elizabeth Cleghorn Gaskell; Charles Kingsley." In *Victorian Fiction: A Guide to Research*, edited by Lionel Stevenson. Cambridge, Mass.: Harvard University Press, 1964.
Useful bibliographical essay summarizing scholarship written before 1962. Separate sections outline information on bibliographies of Gaskell's writings, summarize biographical studies of the novelist, give details of editions and collections of letters, and offer evaluations of criticism of her major works.

Beer, Patricia. *Reader, I Married Him: A Study of the Women Characters of Jane Austen, Charlotte Brontë, Elizabeth Gaskell, and George Eliot*. London: Macmillan, 1974.
Examines the novels and stories as examples of Gaskell's willingness to deal frankly with sexual relationships and with the inequities and horrors created for women by Victorian social mores.

Cazamian, Louis. "Mrs. Gaskell and Christian Intervention." In his *The Social Novel in England, 1830-1850: Dickens, Disraeli, Mrs. Gaskell, Kingsley*. Boston: Routledge & Kegan Paul, 1973.
Brief account of Gaskell's life, focusing on her social work and her precepts as a reformist who turned her talents to fiction. Notes the close link between her attitudes toward industrialism's ills and her strong belief in Christian principles. Contains detailed analyses of *Mary Barton* and *North and South*.

Faber, Richard. *Proper Stations: Class in Victorian Fiction*. London: Faber & Faber, 1971.
Discussion of Gaskell's use of setting, especially the regions of Knutsford and Manchester, to ground her novels. Argues that the contrast between the agricultural and industrial areas with which she was familiar is expanded in her works to include contrasts of social class. Believes that Gaskell was in sympathy with all classes, seeing value in humanity at every social level.

Ffrench, Yvonne. "Elizabeth Cleghorn Gaskell." In *From Jane Austen to Joseph Conrad*, edited by R. L. Rathburn and Martin Steinmann. Minneapolis: Uni-

versity of Minnesota Press, 1958.
General overview of Gaskell's career as a writer, summarizing each of her works and providing an assessment of her technical skills. Includes a more detailed analysis of *Cranford*, which Ffrench considers Gaskell's finest novel.

Ganz, Margaret. *Elizabeth Gaskell: The Artist in Conflict*. New York: Twayne, 1969.
Attempts a comprehensive assessment of Gaskell's achievement as a writer, examining all of her published works (novels, short stories, essays, and her biography of Charlotte Brontë). Ganz organizes her discussion thematically, grouping together works concerning social issues, those displaying Gaskell's talents as a humorist, ones illustrating the novelist's moralizing and melodrama, and those portraying Gaskell's sense of tragedy.

Lansbury, Coral. *Elizabeth Gaskell: The Novel of Social Crisis*. New York: Barnes & Noble Books, 1975.
Critical readings aimed at showing how Gaskell's mastery of technique and subtle understanding of human nature complement her keen knowledge of social conditions in her country. Believes that her strengths as a craftsman, coupled with her vision of life, should merit her a place among England's finest novelists. Separate chapters examine Gaskell's major fiction and her biography of Charlotte Brontë.

Lucas, John. *The Literature of Change: Studies in the Nineteenth Century Provincial Novel*. New York: Barnes & Noble, 1977.
In two chapters of this study, Lucas examines Gaskell's treatment of provincial life. Concentrates on three works: *A Dark Night's Work*, *Cousin Phyllis*, and *Sylvia's Lovers*. Compares Gaskell's descriptions of conditions in Manchester with those of Friedrich Engels. Also contains an analysis of *Mary Barton*.

Martin, Hazel T. *Petticoat Rebels: A Study of the Novels of Social Protest of George Eliot, Elizabeth Gaskell, and Charlotte Brontë*. New York: Helios Books, 1968.
Examines Gaskell's works as examples of her willingness to break from conventions imposed by society on women novelists of the period. Argues that Gaskell's strength lies in her ability to discuss openly the unequal treatment of women and of the laboring classes.

Masefield, Muriel. *Women Novelists from Fanny Burney to George Eliot*. Reprint. Freeport, N.Y.: Books for Libraries Press, 1967.
Contains a biographical chapter and a chapter outlining the major themes of Gaskell's chief novels. Also includes a bibliography of criticism, largely focused on scholarship produced during the first quarter of the twentieth century.

McVeagh, John. *Elizabeth Gaskell*. New York: Humanities Press, 1970.
  Brief, helpful review of Gaskell's accomplishments as a writer. Relies heavily on excerpts from her works to illustrate the critical commentary. Separate sections sketch her aims as a social critic, her achievement as a biographer, her skill at portraying country life, and her philosophical outlook on the human condition and possibilities for its betterment. Also assesses her narrative methods.

Pollard, Arthur. *Mrs. Gaskell: Novelist and Biographer*. Cambridge, Mass.: Harvard University Press, 1966.
  Critical assessment of Gaskell's career by the coeditor of her letters. An introductory chapter summarizes critical responses to her works, covering the period from her death to 1965. A brief biographical chapter is followed by individual sections on the major writings and one on the minor fiction. Also includes a general critique of the novelist's particular strengths, focusing on her techniques of presentation and her vision of society.

Quiller-Couch, Sir Arthur. *Charles Dickens and Other Victorians*. New York: G. P. Putnam's Sons, 1925.
  Praises the novelist for her ability to render realistic portraits of the poor and of the working classes. Singles out *Mary Barton*, *Cranford*, and *Cousin Phyllis* for special praise. Quotes extensively from the texts of these works to illustrate Gaskell's ability at creating character and scene.

Sanders, Gerald DeWitt. *Elizabeth Gaskell*. Reprint. New Haven, Conn.: Yale University Press, 1971.
  Useful early twentieth century biographical and critical study, giving special attention to the major novels. Includes a chronology of important events in Gaskell's life, a note on her use of dialect, and a detailed bibliography (organized chronologically) documenting criticism from the nineteenth and early twentieth centuries.

Shapiro, Charles. "Mrs. Gaskell and 'The Severe Truth.' " In *Minor British Novelists*, edited by Charles A. Hoyt. Carbondale: Southern Illinois Press, 1967.
  Contrasts *Mary Barton* and *Cransford* to show Mrs. Gaskell at her worst and at her best. Finds her pleading and her strident social criticism in *Mary Barton* produces poor writing and a bad novel. In *Cransford*, on the other hand, Gaskell is more observer than reformist, offering insight into her characters and treating them evenhandedly; the result is a novel presenting a believable portrait of Victorian life.

Welch, Jeffrey. *Elizabeth Gaskell: An Annotated Bibliography, 1929-1975*. New York: Garland, 1977.

Surveys critical essays and monographs devoted to study of Gaskell's works; provides useful summaries of these secondary sources. Also contains listings of editions of Gaskell's publications and a chronology noting important events in her life.

Wheeler, Michael. *English Fiction of the Victorian Period, 1830-1890*. New York: Longman, 1985.
Abbreviated review of Gaskell's literary accomplishments, highlighting her techniques of plotting and the importance of setting. Pays special attention to *North and South* as an example of Gaskell's mature fiction, focusing on Margaret Hale's role in the work.

Williams, Merryn. *Women in the English Novel, 1800-1900*. New York: St. Martin's Press, 1984.
Studies Gaskell's treatment of various types of women: working class, old maids, and fallen women. Notes that in her later novels Gaskell insisted that women, like men, must learn to do what is right regardless of the consequences.

Wright, Edgar. *Mrs. Gaskell: The Basis for Reassessment*. London: Oxford University Press, 1965.
Critical monograph examining Gaskell's major concerns, giving special emphasis to her use of the urban setting of Manchester and the country environment of Knutsford. Gives important details of biography, particularly the influence of Unitarianism on her moral outlook; discusses Gaskell's attitudes toward social problems. Analyzes several novels in detail and explores the novelist's narrative techniques, especially as they affect her style and structure.

Mary Barton

Allott, Miriam. *Elizabeth Gaskell*. New York: Longmans, Green, 1960.
Brief sketch of the plot, followed by assessments of Gaskell's technical skills in plotting and in creating believable dialect. Connects the novel with those by Disraeli, Kingsley, and others who were interested in social problems in England.

Beer, Patricia. *Reader, I Married Him: A Study of the Women Characters of Jane Austen, Charlotte Brontë, Elizabeth Gaskell, and George Eliot*. London: Macmillan, 1974.
Discusses the novel as an example of a woman novelist's willingness to deal frankly and directly with important issues between the sexes, including the problem of prostitution. Sees Gaskell working to expose Victorian hypocrisies attendant to sexual relationships.

Cazamian, Louis. "Mrs. Gaskell and Christian Intervention." In his *The Social Novel in England,1830-1850: Dickens, Disraeli, Mrs. Gaskell, Kingsley*. Boston: Routledge & Kegan Paul, 1973.
Calls the novel a graphic representation of the plight of the poor in an industrial community; argues Gaskell is promoting intervention by government to alleviate distress because manufacturers cannot or will not change their ways. Rather than preaching her social message, Gaskell illustrates her point through details of plot and setting. Offers analyses of John Barton and Carson as representatives of the working class and manufacturing bosses, respectively.

Ganz, Margaret. *Elizabeth Gaskell: The Artist in Conflict*. New York: Twayne, 1969.
Extensive analysis of the novel's characters, especially John Barton and Mary Barton. Praises Gaskell's portrait of the former, noting his growing alienation from his fellow workers. Faults the novelist for her inability to make Mary sufficiently complex, and for failing to deal realistically with solutions for workers living in oppressive conditions. Cites Gaskell's powers of description and narration. In the course of her critique, Ganz summarizes judgments of earlier critics.

Lansbury, Coral. "*Mary Barton*: The Conditions of the Working Class in Manchester." In her *Elizabeth Gaskell: The Novel of Social Crisis*. New York: Barnes & Noble Books, 1975.
Detailed examination of Gaskell's transformation of the plight of contemporary rural and industrial commoners into a powerful social novel that remains true to factual details. Notes the complexity of characterization in Gaskell's working class men and women; praises the novelist for her realism in treating issues such as sexual relations, death, and the role of women in working class society. Argues that the novel is an accurate history of working class people in Victorian England.

Lucas, John. "Mrs. Gaskell and Brotherhood." In *Tradition and Tolerance in Nineteenth-Century Fiction*, edited by David Howard, John Lucas, and John Goode. London: Routledge & Kegan Paul, 1966.
Considers this novel an advance over similar works of social criticism by Kingsley and Disraeli. Discusses the significance of John Barton as a representative of the poor class affected by growing industrialism. Attention is given to the reaction the novel generated from contemporary reviewers, who felt the power of the work but were troubled by its implications.

_____ . *The Literature of Change: Studies in the Nineteenth Century Provincial Novel*. New York: Barnes & Noble, 1977.
Compares Gaskell's depiction of the Manchester working classes with

Friedrich Engels' portrait of those same people in his *The Condition of the Working Classes in England*. Notes how much more sensitive and varied Gaskell is in showing the variegated responses of working class men and women to the conditions in which they are forced to live.

Martin, Hazel T. *Petticoat Rebels: A Study of the Novels of Social Protest of George Eliot, Elizabeth Gaskell, and Charlotte Brontë*. New York: Helios Books, 1968.
Notes the importance of labor injustice and the treatment of women as background for the novel; provides some details regarding the reaction of Gaskell's contemporaries to her treatment of these social ills.

McVeagh, John. *Elizabeth Gaskell*. New York: Humanities Press, 1970.
Briefly sketches Gaskell's skill in presenting realistic portraits of the new urban working classes; cites her inability to handle her twin aims of portraying problems in manufacturing towns and relating the personal narratives of her principal characters. In a separate section, McVeagh uses *Mary Barton* as an illustration of Gaskell's ability to organize her novels as a series of key scenes, thereby keeping authorial intrusion to a minimum.

Pollard, Arthur. *Mrs. Gaskell: Novelist and Biographer*. Cambridge, Mass.: Harvard University Press, 1966.
Outlines the background of the social problem novel. Insists Gaskell's main purpose is to explore the lives of people existing under the harsh conditions of the industrial world. Sees broad social issues counterpointed and reinforced by the stories of individuals in whom the reader's central interest lies. Finds Gaskell's portrait of John Barton as a suffering hero convincing; believes Mary is less so. Posits Gaskell's theme is the need for human kindness amid tragic circumstances.

Sanders, Gerald DeWitt. *Elizabeth Gaskell*. Reprint. New Haven, Conn.: Yale University Press, 1971.
Sketches the genesis of the novel and notes Gaskell's difficulties in finding a publisher. Outlines conditions in England that led to the rise of the social novel; argues that Gaskell's solution for social unrest lay in application of the Golden Rule. Believes the real strength of her work lies in her depiction of characters, especially John Barton.

Tillotson, Kathleen. *Novels of the Eighteen Forties*. Oxford: Clarendon Press, 1954.
Discusses Gaskell's success in creating a novel tied closely to a specific social issue (the "condition of England" question, hotly debated in the 1830's and 1840's), while transcending the limitations of its social focus. Much of the discussion is centered on Gaskell's achievements in characterization.

Williams, Raymond. "The Industrial Novels." In his *Culture and Society, 1780-1950*. London: Chatto & Windus, 1954.

Considers the novel among the best of those describing the plight of the people who suffer from oppression in England's industrial regions. Judges the work flawed, however, because Gaskell was forced to change her original concept for the story: she had intended to center the narrative around John Barton, but was persuaded to shift the focus to Mary, eventually making John a murderer. Gaskell seems repulsed by the notion, Williams maintains, and her writing at the end of the novel appears forced.

Wright, Edgar. *Mrs. Gaskell: The Basis for Reassessment*. London: Oxford University Press, 1965.

Discusses the importance of the religious underpinnings of the novel. Notes that, throughout the story, Gaskell displays her belief in simple faith as a means of helping man overcome most social difficulties and of providing a cure for the evils of industrialism. In a separate section, Wright discusses the structure of the novel, citing its growth from Gaskell's initial conception to its published form.

North and South

Allott, Miriam. *Elizabeth Gaskell*. New York: Longmans, Green, 1960.

Links the novel to *Mary Barton*, pointing out parallels in subject but noting Gaskell's change of focus: from the poor Manchester workers to the owners of the mills. Believes Gaskell's major concern to be the hindrance to social progress caused by the rift between capital and labor. Considers the strong point of the novel is Gaskell's creation of a forceful hero and heroine.

Cazamian, Louis. "Mrs. Gaskell and Christian Intervention." In his *The Social Novel in England, 1830-1850: Dickens, Disraeli, Mrs. Gaskell, Kingsley*. Boston: Routledge & Kegan Paul, 1973.

Believes Gaskell takes a more cautious approach to social reform in this novel than in *Mary Barton*. Focusing on the employers rather than the workers, Gaskell dramatizes the opposition between old and new forms of civilizations; the marriage at the end of the book symbolizes a reconciliation of these conflicting life-styles. Provides extensive plot summary to illustrate Gaskell's handling of the characters through whom she portrays the central conflicts of the work.

David, Deirdre. *Fictions of Resolution in Three Victorian Novels: North and South, Our Mutual Friend, and Daniel Deronda*. New York: Columbia University Press, 1981.

Extensive analysis of Gaskell's attempt to transform into fiction her observations about social conditions and their impact on individuals. While acknowledging the tendency to read such novels as tracts about real ills, David focuses
on Gaskell's novelistic aims: to examine estrangements among the classes, to
effect a reconciliation among individuals, and to highlight the need to return to
ethical and religious principles as a means of combatting the evils of growing
commercialism. Two chapters examine Gaskell's portraits of individuals and
family groups.

Ganz, Margaret. *Elizabeth Gaskell: The Artist in Conflict*. New York: Twayne, 1969.
Sees the novel as an advance over *Mary Barton* in its treatment of social
problems, but notes Gaskell's detachment from the emotional impact of these
issues on individuals. Extensive discussion of Margaret Hale's role in the work;
Ganz cites the novelist's heightened interest in the romantic elements of her
tale, an interest sometimes overshadowing concerns for social issues. Believes
Gaskell offers no real solution to the social problems she catalogs because she
is ultimately hesitant to challenge the established order.

Lansbury, Coral. "*North and South*: Civilising Capitalism." In her *Elizabeth Gaskell: The Novel of Social Crisis*. New York: Barnes & Noble Books, 1975.
Extensive analysis of Gaskell's handling of personal and social issues. Sees the
novel as an extension of the novelist's continuing interest in the relationship
between the working and middle classes, and her ongoing concern for the
problems of sexuality and gender. Detailed critique of Margaret Hale, with
briefer sketches of Thornton and Higgins. Concludes Gaskell's only solutions
to problems of social injustice lie in individual understanding and compromise.

Lucas, John. "Mrs. Gaskell and Brotherhood." In *Tradition and Tolerance in
Nineteenth-Century Fiction*, edited by David Howard, John Lucas, and John
Goode. London: Routledge & Kegan Paul, 1966.
Reads the novel as Gaskell's defense of northern English society. Lengthy
analysis of Dickens' *Hard Times* shows the excesses of social criticism Gaskell
tries to avoid in her work. Shows how Gaskell praises the many good qualities
of northern society, while acknowledging the need for the humanizing influence of culture, normally associated with the south. Also notes several weaknesses of conception and plotting which detract from the artistic merit of the
novel.

Martin, Hazel T. *Petticoat Rebels: A Study of the Novels of Social Protest of George
Eliot, Elizabeth Gaskell, and Charlotte Brontë*. New York: Helios Books, 1968.
Brief commentary on a novel Martin considers less controversial than others
by Gaskell. Notes the main lines of Gaskell's argument in dealing with re-

ligious controversy, class conflict, and the difficulties members of the labor force had in relating with those who possessed the capital to support industry.

McVeagh, John. *Elizabeth Gaskell*. New York: Humanities Press, 1970.
Brief critical remarks and several excerpts from the text give evidence of Gaskell's growing ability to unite concern for social ills with her interest in her fictional creations. Argues that the novel presents a more balanced view of workers and their employers than does *Mary Barton*.

Phelps, Gilbert. *A Reader's Guide to Fifty British Novels, 1600-1900*. New York: Barnes & Noble Books, 1979.
Biographical information explains how Gaskell turned to novel writing. Plot synopsis includes comments about the novelist's mastery of plotting and characterization. Critical comments highlight the political focus of the work, but also remark on Gaskell's ability to add a sociological and psychological dimension to her fiction.

Pollard, Arthur. *Mrs. Gaskell: Novelist and Biographer*. Cambridge, Mass.: Harvard University Press, 1966.
Brief review of the circumstances surrounding the composition and publication of the work. Notes parallels to *Mary Barton*. Sketches the major action to show the book's unity and to display Gaskell's control over her materials. Extensive discussion of the function of characters in the story, especially Thornton, Margaret Hale, and her father. Considers this novel Gaskell's best effort at integrating public and private matters into an artistic whole.

Sanders, Gerald DeWitt. *Elizabeth Gaskell*. Reprint. New Haven, Conn.: Yale University Press, 1971.
Notes parallels to *Mary Barton*, but cites several ways this novel is more complex in plotting and in its treatment of a variety of themes extending beyond Gaskell's concern with growing industrialism. Outlines the background behind her portrayal of manufacturers and workers, citing real-life changes that had occurred since the publication of *Mary Barton*. Argues that Gaskell's portrait of Margaret Hale is particularly strong.

Williams, Raymond. "The Industrial Novels." In his *Culture and Society, 1780-1950*. London: Chatto & Windus, 1954.
A notice of the work as one of several important industrial novels of the Victorian era. Considers Gaskell a sympathetic observer of the plight of those oppressed by the growing industrial complex. Traces the relationship between Margaret and Thornton to show its symbolism as a unification of the energy of the manufacturing northern England and the sensibility of southern English society.

Wright, Edgar. "The Attempt at Reconciliation: *North and South*." In his *Mrs. Gaskell: The Basis for Reassessment*. London: Oxford University Press, 1965.

Sketches the impact of serial publication on the structure of the work. Considers Gaskell's major aim the restoration of a balanced view of masters and workers in the industrial north, a theme overshadowing secondary concerns with the contrasts between the manufacturing districts of the north and the agricultural areas of the south. Believes that Gaskell is always more interested in people than in issues.

THOMAS HARDY

General Studies

Beach, Joseph Warren. *The Techniques of Thomas Hardy*. Reprint. New York: Russell & Russell, 1962.
Explores Hardy's craftsmanship in great detail. Separate sections examine each of the fourteen novels, showing how Hardy's concern for characterization and plot dominates his artistry. Sees Hardy's career reaching an early apex with *Return of the Native*, falling off in his middle years, and rising to a final climax with his two best novels, *Tess of the D'Urbervilles* and *Jude the Obscure*.

Bloom, Harold, ed. *Thomas Hardy*. New York: Chelsea House, 1987.
Collection of essays reprinted from monographs and literary journals, all originally published between 1965 and 1987. Includes at least one selection on each of the major novels and several essays on Hardy's poetry. Bloom's introductory essay provides an assessment of Hardy's literary achievement.

Boumelha, Penny. *Thomas Hardy and Women: Sexual Ideology and Narrative Form*. Totowa, N.J.: Barnes & Noble Books, 1982.
A study of Hardy's attitudes toward women and his treatment of female figures, focusing on the novelist's understanding of the nature of sexuality. Boumelha is heavily influenced by feminist theory and theories of narratology, and by assessments of the function of ideology in literature developed by philosopher Louis Althusser and Marxist literary critic Terry Eagleton. Contains a good bibliography of secondary sources, both those focusing on Hardy and those dealing with feminist issues.

Brooks, Jean R. *Thomas Hardy: The Poetic Structure*. Ithaca, N.Y.: Cornell University Press, 1971.
Comprehensive assessment of Hardy's work as a writer, giving equal weight to the poetry and the fiction. Individual chapters are devoted to each of the major novels. Concentrates on the essentially poetic nature of Hardy's vision, showing how this approach influences the production of his fiction as well as his verse.

Butler, Lance St. John. *Thomas Hardy After Fifty Years*. London: Macmillan, 1977.
Twelve essays provide a wide-ranging look at Hardy's achievements and his legacy to the twentieth century. Selections examine such topics as the form of Hardy's fiction, his attitudes toward religion, the relationship between Hardy and D. H. Lawrence, and a review of textual scholarship of the novelist's works. Provides a useful overview of Hardy's artistry and ideology.

Carpenter, Richard. *Thomas Hardy*. New York: Twayne, 1964.
Analysis of Hardy's fiction and poetry, concentrating on his use of imagery, especially mythic imagery. An introductory chapter sketches the major concerns of Hardy's fiction. Also includes a chronology and a selected bibliography of secondary sources.

Cox, R. G., ed. *Thomas Hardy: The Critical Heritage*. New York: Barnes & Noble Books, 1970.
Collection of excerpts from reviews by Hardy's contemporaries of all of his novels and volumes of poetry. Includes general assessments of Hardy's achievement published at various stages of his career. Excellent source for determining Victorian readers' reactions to Hardy's intentionally controversial treatment of sensitive subjects.

Fayen, George S., Jr. "Thomas Hardy." In *Victorian Fiction: A Guide to Research*, edited by Lionel Stevenson. Cambridge, Mass.: Harvard University Press, 1964.
Bibliographical essay reviewing scholarship published before 1962. Separate sections discuss bibliographies of Hardy's work; editions of the novels and textual studies; biographical essays and monographs; general evaluations of Hardy's achievement as a novelist, his major themes, and his methodology; and criticism of individual novels.

Guerard, Albert. *Thomas Hardy: The Novels and Stories*. Cambridge, Mass.: Harvard University Press, 1949.
Study of Hardy's works as part of a larger examination of the development of the modern novel; makes frequent comparisons to the work of Joseph Conrad and Andre Gide, the other subjects of this critical examination. Concentrates on Hardy's artistry, pointing out how critical preconceptions have affected later readers' attitudes toward Hardy's works. A lengthy chapter discusses Hardy's heroes and heroines in great detail.

_____ , ed. *Hardy: A Collection of Critical Essays*. Englewood Cliffs, N.J.: Prentice-Hall, Inc., 1963.
Thirteen excerpts from previously published studies of Hardy's fiction and poetry provide a broad assessment of his achievements in both genres. Guerard's introduction is a particularly good summary of the major issues affecting Hardy's work, offering a succinct statement of the writer's place in English literary history.

Hawkins, Desmond. *Hardy: Novelist and Poet*. New York: Barnes & Noble Books, 1976.
Cast as a critical biography, this study of Hardy's major fiction and poetry pays special attention to the way events in the writer's life influenced the

production of individual works. Separate appendixes provide plot synopses and list dramatizations of Hardy's works in Britain and America. Also includes a brief bibliography of secondary sources.

Holloway, John. *The Victorian Sage*. New York: W. W. Norton, 1965.

Views Hardy as a serious novelist with a consistent moral purpose: to offer a realistic view of man's ethical nature, though not necessarily with the aim of making his readers religious. Reviews Hardy's techniques of characterization and scenic construction to show how he accomplishes his aim; traces the importance of improbability and of natural forces in Hardy's novels. Insists that *Jude the Obscure* is not representative of Hardy's world view.

——————. "Hardy's Major Fiction." In *From Jane Austen to Joseph Conrad*, edited by R. L. Rathburn and Martin Steinmann. Minneapolis: University of Minnesota Press, 1958.

Focuses on plot as the most important element in Hardy's fiction, through which he illuminates his central ideas. Notes the recurrent conflict between the rural environment and the intrusion of modern ways upon the country folk; believes Hardy finds the old ways are inadequate for surviving in the modern world. Argues that all of Hardy's major fiction centers on the gradual degradation of a protagonist committed to the old order. Traces this pattern in *The Mayor of Casterbridge* and *Tess of the D'Urbervilles*.

Hornback, Bert G. *The Metaphor of Chance: Vision and Technique in the Works of Thomas Hardy*. Athens: Ohio University Press, 1971.

Analyzes the major novels and *The Dynasts*, concentrating on the setting common to most of them, Hardy's Wessex, to show how place and time influence the action. Also examines the concepts of fatalism and coincidence, and the significance of history in shaping Hardy's ideas about his characters and about life. Believes Hardy's view of the world was iconoclastic, as he rejected Victorian conventions about progress, goodness, and success.

Hyman, Virginia. *Ethical Perspectives in the Novels of Thomas Hardy*. Port Washington, N.Y.: Kennikat Press, 1975.

Concentrates on Hardy's understanding of the influence of historical forces on individuals and his belief in the dichotomy between egotism and altruism— concepts that provide the philosophical underpinning for all of his works. Insists that to appreciate the novels fully, readers must understand Hardy's own view of these issues, rather than applying modern definitions of these notions to Hardy's fiction. Individual chapters offer readings of the major novels, demonstrating how Hardy's concern for the evolutionary process in ethical development informs his portraits of characters.

Kramer, Dale. *Thomas Hardy: The Forms of Tragedy*. Detroit: Wayne State University Press, 1975.
Investigates ways Hardy consciously manipulates the materials of fiction to create his tragedies. Pays special attention to Hardy's handling of structure as a means of developing and controlling his tragic vision. Separate chapters discuss each of Hardy's major novels; throughout, Kramer notes how the novelist moves from mechanical handling of formal devices to a more organic development of plot and theme.

————————— , ed. *Critical Approaches to the Fiction of Thomas Hardy*. New York: Barnes & Noble Books, 1979.
Twelve original essays on Hardy's fiction. In addition to selections devoted to individual novels, several essays offer insight into Hardy's narrative techniques and his use of regional settings. The introduction provides a valuable assessment of the novelist's impact on English fiction and reviews the varying critical responses his works have provoked.

Meisel, Perry. *Thomas Hardy: The Return of the Repressed*. New Haven, Conn.: Yale University Press, 1972.
A review of Hardy's fiction, focusing on the tensions between religion and evolution, topics of great significance in the novelist's own day. An introductory chapter sketches Hardy's life and outlines parallels between his development of an understanding of evolution and Darwin's development of the concept in his scientific writings.

Miller, J. Hillis. *Thomas Hardy: Distance and Desire*. Cambridge, Mass.: Belknap Press, 1970.
Examines the corpus of Hardy's creative work to show the significance of a single pattern that permeates his writing: the relationship between desire (sometimes manifested as love) and distance (a form of separation, either temporal or spatial), with the latter often serving as the impetus for the former. Concentrates on close reading of texts, rather than on extraliterary matters. An especially good analysis of the way a common theme gives shape to Hardy's creative genius.

Millgate, Michael. *Thomas Hardy: A Biography*. New York: Random House, 1982.
Scholarly biography offering critical judgments of Hardy's fiction and poetry by a leading twentieth century critic, who is the editor of Hardy's letters. Includes detailed analysis of Hardy's character and of the impact events in the writer's life had on the creation of his work. Special attention is paid to *Far from the Madding Crowd*, *The Woodlanders*, *Tess of the D'Urbervilles*, and *Jude the Obscure*.

Page, Norman. *Thomas Hardy*. Boston: Routledge & Kegan Paul, 1977.
Monograph assessing Hardy's career as a writer. Separate chapters give a brief biographical sketch, discuss the major and minor novels, analyze Hardy's verse, and remark on the short stories and nonfiction prose.

——————— , ed. *Thomas Hardy: The Writer and His Background*. New York: St. Martin's Press, 1980.
Collection of essays that place Hardy in historical and ideological context. Separate selections cover topics such as Hardy's reading, his affinity for the region he transformed into the fictional area of Wessex, and his attitudes toward Darwinism and education. Also provides a useful chronology, placing events of Hardy's life in the context of literary and political events.

Paris, Bernard J. "Experiences of Thomas Hardy." In *The Victorian Experience: The Novelists*, edited by Richard Levine. Athens: Ohio University Press, 1976.
Using *Tess of the D'Urbervilles* as his primary example but ranging through Hardy's other works as well, Paris examines ways various critical approaches have helped him understand the significance of Hardy's achievement. Explores the novelist's philosophical outlook; provides a detailed character analysis of Tess, using tools of psychological criticism. Discusses Hardy's authorial voice in the fiction.

Scott-James, R. A., and C. Day Lewis. *Thomas Hardy*. London: Longman, 1970.
Brief but useful introduction to Hardy's life and career. Separate chapters provide assessments of the major fiction, examine Hardy's epic poem, *The Dynasts*, and offer critical comments on Hardy's other poetry. Also contains a selected bibliography of primary and secondary works.

Williams, Merryn. *Thomas Hardy and Rural England*. New York: Columbia University Press, 1972.
Argues that most critics misunderstand the nature of the rural society Hardy depicts in his novels; hence they misread the works. Separate sections outline the historical background which provided Hardy with materials for his fiction and examine Hardy's Wessex novels, paying special attention to the novelist's portrayal of rural life in seven of his works.

Far from the Madding Crowd

Beach, Joseph Warren. *The Techniques of Thomas Hardy*. Reprint. New York: Russell & Russell, 1962.
Considers the novel an early masterpiece in Hardy's career. Sketches the plot in some detail; examines the way Hardy uses the setting, focusing on the

rural countryside and its inhabitants, to create a pastoral idyll. Notes Hardy's constant allusions to the Bible and William Shakespeare, adding depth to his tale. Also remarks on Hardy's characterization of Bathsheba and Gabriel.

Beegel, Susan. "Bathsheba's Lovers: Male Sexuality in *Far from the Madding Crowd.*" In *Thomas Hardy*, edited by Harold Bloom. New York: Chelsea House, 1987.
Revising the discussion of earlier critics, Beegel sees the novel not as a tragedy, but as a study of male-female relationships with a truly happy ending. Notes both the overt and subtle references to sexuality in the work; examines several chapters and scenes in detail to show that Gabriel is the only man worthy of Bathsheba's love, and that their union at the end of the novel is appropriate.

Brooks, Jean R. "*Far From the Madding Crowd*: A Pastoral Novel." In her *Thomas Hardy: The Poetic Structure*. Ithaca, N.Y.: Cornell University Press, 1971.
Discusses the many poetic qualities of the work. Notes ways the structure parallels the ballad form. Details how each of the five major characters reacts to—and adjusts within—the natural environment. Also discusses Hardy's use of metaphoric language in the novel.

Carpenter, Richard. "Fiction: The Major Chord." In his *Thomas Hardy*. New York: Twayne, 1964.
Considers the work Hardy's first major novel. Discusses the function of the peasantry and the community's activities; these provide a sense of the constancy of rural life, suggesting the insignificance of any individual's activities. Analyzes Bathsheba's actions, calling her a strong woman whose vanity blinds her to the solid figure of Gabriel Oak. Discusses the sexual symbolism Hardy uses to make clear the nature of Bathsheba's relationship with Sergeant Troy.

Casagrande, Peter J. "A New View of Bathsheba Everdene." In *Critical Approaches to the Fiction of Thomas Hardy*, edited by Dale Kramer. New York: Barnes & Noble Books, 1979.
Revises the conventional critical opinion that Bathsheba grows from foolishness to wisdom; claims Hardy considers her thwarted by fate from achieving any real growth. Some attempt at psychological analysis; finds little evidence in the text to support any notion that psychological factors influence Bathsheba. Rather, Hardy adheres to a theme common throughout his work: woman is infirm and at the mercy of chance and circumstance, and not fully responsible for her folly.

Cox, R. G., ed. *Thomas Hardy: The Critical Heritage*. New York: Barnes & Noble Books, 1970.
Excerpts from six reviews by Hardy's contemporaries, appearing in influen-

tial British and American periodicals shortly after the novel was published. Critics represented include R. H. Hutton, Henry James, and Andrew Lang. Several reviewers compare Hardy's work with George Eliot's.

Gatrell, Simon. "Hardy the Creator: *Far from the Madding Crowd*." In *Critical Approaches to the Fiction of Thomas Hardy*, edited by Dale Kramer. New York: Barnes & Noble Books, 1979.
A careful examination of the manuscript of the novel and its publication in various forms, from serialization to the definitive Wessex edition of Hardy's works. Shows how the novelist's creative genius shaped and reshaped sections of the story to achieve his final portrait of characters such as Gabriel Oak and Bathsheba. Argues that Hardy's changing attitudes toward his characters can be seen in the progressive versions of the text.

Hawkins, Desmond. *Hardy: Novelist and Poet*. New York: Barnes & Noble Books, 1976.
Brief discussion of the book, highlighting its importance to Hardy's career: it was the first to bring him serious attention from literary critics, and it solidified his commitment to Wessex as the fictional setting for his major works. Provides analysis of Bathsheba and Troy. Considers the happy ending contrived, but notes that, throughout the work, Hardy is intent on showing how even trivial actions can bring about dire consequences.

Hornback, Bert G. "The Minor Novels: Discovery of Technique." In his *The Metaphor of Chance: Vision and Technique in the Works of Thomas Hardy*. Athens: Ohio University Press, 1971.
Brief analysis of Hardy's use of the Wessex terrain as the setting for this novel; argues that Hardy fails to emphasize the importance of setting in determining character and action in this work (an emphasis present in later novels). Discusses the essentially comic nature of the novel, despite Hardy's serious treatment of such scenes as Fanny's death and Boldwood's ruination.

Hyman, Virginia. *Ethical Perspectives in the Novels of Thomas Hardy*. Port Washington, N.Y.: Kennikat Press, 1975.
Brief account of the way the novel illustrates Hyman's thesis that all of Hardy's greatest fiction deals in some way with the conflict of egotism vs. altruism. Concentrates on Bathsheba's transformation from an egotist to someone willing to sacrifice herself for others. Notes the ethical emphasis throughout the book; Hardy contrasts what characters ought to do with what they actually do.

Kramer, Dale. "*Far from the Madding Crowd*: The Non-Tragic Predecessor." In his *Thomas Hardy: The Forms of Tragedy*. Detroit: Wayne State University Press, 1975.

In a book tracing Hardy's development of a tragic vision, Kramer shows how the novel, though not a tragedy, displays many of the technical devices Hardy will use in later works to achieve tragic effect; especially important are schematic patterning for the story and the use of dichotomy in defining characters. Provides extensive analysis of the opposing forces at work in Bathsheba. Includes a discussion of Hardy's treatment of the status of man in relationship to the natural world.

Meisel, Perry. "The Early Novels: *Under the Greenwood Tree*, *A Pair of Blue Eyes*, and *Far from the Madding Crowd*." In his *Thomas Hardy: The Return of the Repressed*. New Haven, Conn.: Yale University Press, 1972.
Examines the novel as a portrait of the Wessex community about which Hardy wrote with great insight. Notes how various characters, especially Bathsheba, define themselves in relationship to their community. Briefly traces the central conflict between man and the natural world appearing in this and other Hardy novels.

Page, Norman. *Thomas Hardy*. Boston: Routledge & Kegan Paul, 1977.
Scattered comments throughout this study discuss the novel's publication and reception by readers, and notes how this work shows an advance in Hardy's skill in dealing with sexual relationships. Ranks the novel among Hardy's major works.

Williams, Merryn. *Thomas Hardy and Rural England*. New York: Columbia University Press, 1972.
Brief examination of the major characters' relationship to the rural community in which they work. Notes each is defined and judged by that relationship; every individual is depicted as a positive or negative force in preserving the community's productivity and wealth. From this perspective, Gabriel Oaks is seen as a strong yet complex figure, able to endure by adapting to changes and subordinating self to community.

Jude the Obscure

Alvarez, A. "*Jude the Obscure*." In *Hardy: A Collection of Critical Essays*, edited by Albert Guerard. Englewood Cliffs, N.J.: Prentice-Hall, Inc., 1963.
Analyzes the novel as a tragedy of frustration and missed fulfillment. Sees Jude as the only hero in the work; neither female figure achieves heroic stature. Believes Hardy's central interest is Jude's frustrating relationship with Sue; the hero's failure to get into Christminster is a minor parallel tale. Argues that Jude fails not because of outside circumstances but because of inner

tensions. Considers the awkward dialogue appropriate for emphasizing the failure of characters to communicate; it highlights Jude's loneliness.

Beach, Joseph Warren. *The Techniques of Thomas Hardy*. Reprint. New York: Russell & Russell, 1962.
Ranks the work with *Tess of the D'Urbervilles* and *Return of the Native* as one of Hardy's greatest. Sees the novelist's central concern being the exploration of truth beneath the illusions of individuals and society; hence, Hardy portrays vividly the misery and squalor Jude encounters as he pursues his ideals. Marriage is seen as the great antagonist, because social conventions prevent individuals from achieving true marital happiness. Distinguishes fatalism from determinism, considering Hardy a believer in the latter.

Boumelha, Penny. *Thomas Hardy and Women: Sexual Ideology and Narrative Form*. Totowa, N.J.: Barnes & Noble Books, 1982.
Concentrates on the characterization of Sue Bridehead as a representative of the "new woman," a figure coming into prominence in the late nineteenth century and causing significant controversy. Believes Sue's tragedy involves her idealism in believing she can escape social conventions. Boumelha argues that Sue must learn to come to grips with her own sexuality, something she denies; in that denial she appears open to charges of frigidity and unresponsiveness.

Brooks, Jean R. "*Jude the Obscure*: A Novel of Affirmation." In her *Thomas Hardy: The Poetic Structure*. Ithaca, N.Y.: Cornell University Press, 1971.
Finds parallels to the epic in Hardy's conception of Jude's quest for meaning and self-definition. Notes ironic parallels between the novel's characters and biblical figures. Discusses several scenes to show how Hardy uses poetic techniques to illuminate character traits and reinforce the central theme of Jude's quest and his failure. Considers the work a precursor of the modern psychological novel and of twentieth century existentialist works.

Carpenter, Richard. *Thomas Hardy*. New York: Twayne, 1964.
A careful examination of the novel as Hardy's dark vision of men and women caught by social and cosmic forces which frustrate their desires. Notes Hardy's direct attack on various social institutions that limit individuals. Extensive analysis of Jude, whom Carpenter sees torn between idealism and the natural desires of the flesh; also discusses Arabella as an earth-mother figure and Sue as a parallel to Jude's idealistic impulses.

Collins, Philip. "Hardy and Education." In *Thomas Hardy: The Writer and His Background*, edited by Norman Page. New York: St. Martin's Press, 1980.
In an essay dealing with Hardy's attitude toward education, Collins exam-

ines *Jude the Obscure* as a novel exploring the possibilities for a poor man in Victorian England to receive a university education. Notes parallels between Jude and Hardy, who was never able to pursue a university degree. Notes the idealized portrait of Christminster, which makes Jude's failure in getting into the university and his subsequent disillusionment appear more tragic.

Cox, R. G., ed. *Thomas Hardy: The Critical Heritage*. New York: Barnes & Noble Books, 1970.
Eleven excerpts from British and American periodicals offer an enlightening portrait of the extreme reactions this novel provoked in Hardy's contemporaries. Some discuss it as Hardy's worst work, citing the unrelieved pessimism and mechanistic contrivances of plot as grounds for harsh judgment. Others, including William Dean Howells, find great power in Hardy's tragic vision of life, despite some infelicities of composition.

Hawkins, Desmond. *Hardy: Novelist and Poet*. New York: Barnes & Noble Books, 1976.
Views the work as another of Hardy's attempts to explore the true nature of love and marriage. Carefully reviews the major action of the novel; provides extensive discussion of the complex relationship between Jude and Sue, whose love exemplifies the dilemma and tragedy Hardy saw in the conventional restrictions governing relationships between men and women in his day.

Hornback, Bert G. *The Metaphor of Chance: Vision and Technique in the Works of Thomas Hardy*. Athens: Ohio University Press, 1971.
Considers the novel Hardy's bleakest, a tragedy featuring Jude as a representative of all men, in the Hardyean tradition of Michael Henchard (*The Mayor of Casterbridge*) and Clym Yeobright (*Return of the Native*). Discusses Jude's marriage to Arabella as his tragic fault in a novel constructed along the lines of a Sophoclean drama. Also details the importance of setting and the significance of history in highlighting Jude's tragedy.

Hyman, Virginia. *Ethical Perspectives in the Novels of Thomas Hardy*. Port Washington, N.Y.: Kennikat Press, 1975.
Two chapters are devoted to analysis of the major figures in the novel. The first is an extensive discussion of Jude's change and development from an egotist interested in selfish intellectual pursuits to an altruist whose first concerns are ethical. In the second chapter, Hyman argues that Sue's progress in the novel runs counter to Jude's, as she is hidebound by her intellectualism and by her egotism.

Kramer, Dale. "*Jude the Obscure*: Doctrine or Distanced Narrator?" In his *Thomas Hardy: The Forms of Tragedy*. Detroit: Wayne State University Press, 1975.

Concentrates on Hardy's handling of point of view, claiming that the omniscient narrator is neither the voice of Hardy nor totally knowledgeable or reliable as an interpreter of character or theme. Reviews several scenes to show how the narrator functions in the work; suggests that no viewpoint, neither the narrator's nor any one of the character's, is definitive. Argues that this technique reinforces Hardy's belief in relativism.

Lawrence, D. H. "Sue Bridehead." In *Hardy: A Collection of Critical Essays*, edited by Albert Guerard. Englewood Cliffs, N.J.: Prentice-Hall, Inc., 1963.
Psychoanalytic study of Sue by one of the twentieth century's greatest novelists. Lawrence sees her as completely lacking in what he calls the female principle, but nevertheless emotionally charged with the desire for knowledge and spiritual camaraderie. Sees Jude turning from Arabella to Sue because the latter is attractive as an object representing knowledge. Finds Sue's marriage to Phillotson appropriate because the scholar represents no sexual threat to her.

Lodge, David. "*Jude the Obscure*: Pessimism and Fictional Form." In *Critical Approaches to the Fiction of Thomas Hardy*, edited by Dale Kramer. New York: Barnes & Noble Books, 1979.
Explores ways Hardy creates scenes and uses reinforcing patterns of metaphor and symbolism to give the effect of unrelieved pessimism throughout the work. Provides a careful analysis of the use of references to pigs (and the squalor associated with them); also highlights Hardy's use of parallels between Jude and Christ for ironic purposes.

Meisel, Perry. *Thomas Hardy: The Return of the Repressed*. New Haven, Conn.: Yale University Press, 1972.
Considers this Hardy's finest novel, one in which the novelist highlights the isolation characterizing the life of every man. Sees Jude's tragedy arising from the elemental conflict between spirit and flesh within him: the two women in his life represent these two opposing forces. Discusses the function of Sue Bridehead as the catalyst who initiates Jude's full tragedy, as she causes him to experience genuine frustration.

Page, Norman. *Thomas Hardy*. Boston: Routledge & Kegan Paul, 1977.
Demonstrates the pictorial qualities of the novel. Analyzes the way Hardy uses images of seeing and sight to explain the differences between illusion and reality; traces Jude's growth from naïve idealist to one who comes to understand and accept the tragedy of his life.

Phelps, Gilbert. *A Reader's Guide to Fifty British Novels, 1600-1900*. New York: Barnes & Noble, 1979.
Analytic remarks incorporated into a detailed plot summary show how

Hardy manipulates character and scene to present this tragedy of unfulfilled dreams. Critical commentary explains why this novel is appropriately Hardy's last, because in it he comes to realize the intolerable nature of his vision of modern society.

Saldivar, Ramon. "*Jude the Obscure*: Reading and the Spirit of the Law." In *Thomas Hardy*, edited by Harold Bloom. New York: Chelsea House, 1987.
Applies the theory of deconstruction to account for the problems of misreading by Hardy's contemporaries and to show the novel actually undercuts the possibilities of simple, clear, meaningful readings. Argues that Jude's insistence on finding a single reference or system of references upon which to discover truth is doomed to failure. Claims natural and civil law are simply competing systems of signs to be interpreted; neither is absolute.

Williams, Merryn. *Thomas Hardy and Rural England*. New York: Columbia University Press, 1972.
Believes the novel is Hardy's greatest; notes how early critics devalued it, in part because of its explicit treatment of what Victorians considered objectionable subjects. Devotes significant attention to Jude's attitudes toward Christminster and the reaction of those in the city to Jude's plight. Explores the multifaceted view of the city in the novel, and notes the irony arising from these competing and often contradictory views.

Wing, George. "Hardy and Regionalism." In *Thomas Hardy: The Writer and His Background*, edited by Norman Page. New York: St. Martin's Press, 1980.
In an essay on Hardy's use of the region in which he grew up as a backdrop for his work, Wing discusses the vehemence with which the novelist portrays the city of Christminster as a destroyer of Jude's dreams.

The Mayor of Casterbridge

Beach, Joseph Warren. *The Techniques of Thomas Hardy*. Reprint. New York: Russell & Russell, 1962.
Considers the novel an uneven performance; acknowledges the strength of Hardy's characterization of Michael Henchard, but faults the novelist for overuse of coincidence, violence, melodrama, and other tricks to maintain readers' interest. Compares the development of scenes in the work to those in cinema, seeing the techniques Hardy uses to create his most powerful episodes as closely paralleling methods used by early moviemakers.

Brooks, Jean R. "*The Mayor of Casterbridge*: A Novel of Character and Environment." In her *Thomas Hardy: The Poetic Structure*. Ithaca, N.Y.: Cornell University Press, 1971.

Sees Hardy's poetic rendition of his story as the quality elevating Henchard's personal tragedy to mythic proportions. Traces parallels between the novel and Greek tragedy. Briefly sketches the roles major figures play in such a drama, and outlines Hardy's descriptive powers. Considers Hardy's central theme to be a demonstration of the passing of the old order in rural society.

Carpenter, Richard. *Thomas Hardy*. New York: Twayne, 1964.
Reviews Hardy's use of agricultural imagery, elements of the grotesque, and parallels with Greek tragedy to construct this portrait of Henchard as a tragic hero. Believes Henchard is driven by a need for affection and simultaneously by self-destructive impulses; notes his isolation from other characters. Suggests the novel is a presentation of the fertility myth, with Henchard as a kind of scapegoat.

Cox, R. G., ed. *Thomas Hardy: The Critical Heritage*. New York: Barnes & Noble Books, 1970.
Comments from three reviews by Hardy's contemporaries. The *Atheneum*'s reviewer praises his characterization but faults his style, especially his choice of metaphors; the *Saturday Review*'s critic finds the work less pleasing than *Far from the Madding Crowd*; R. H. Hutton, writing in the *Spectator*, comments extensively on Hardy's success in creating Michael Henchard.

Edmond, Rod. " 'The Past Marked Prospect': *The Mayor of Casterbridge*." In *Reading the Victorian Novel: Detail into Form*, edited by Ian Gregor. New York: Barnes & Noble Books, 1980.
Argues that *The Mayor of Casterbridge* is the novel that best illustrates Hardy's abiding preoccupations with the past, with history, and with memory. Sees these three elements brought together in a complex relationship with the present to give the work its special sense of unity.

Hawkins, Desmond. *Hardy: Novelist and Poet*. New York: Barnes & Noble Books, 1976.
Concentrates analysis on the character of Henchard, whom Hawkins considers Hardy's most dominant figure. Points out the pervading irony within the work, evolving from the many coincidences and reversals. Sees Henchard as a tragic hero; considers the ending deliberately contrived, however, to appeal to the Victorian audience.

Hornback, Bert G. *The Metaphor of Chance: Vision and Technique in the Works of Thomas Hardy*. Athens: Ohio University Press, 1971.
Considers the novel Hardy's finest—one in which the novelist manipulates technical details with skill to elucidate his portrait of Henchard as a tragic

hero. Devotes considerable attention to the way Hardy handles setting: shows how his ability to relate actions to locales which carry historical significance causes events of the present to take on universal significance. Claims that Hardy's compression of time has a similar impact.

Hyman, Virginia. *Ethical Perspectives in the Novels of Thomas Hardy*. Port Washington, N.Y.: Kennikat Press, 1975.
Short chapter discussing Henchard as an egotist unwilling to advance his ethical status by accepting change and developing an altruistic approach to life. Traces his decline by contrasting him with Farfrae and Elizabeth-Jane, two figures who possess more advanced ethical attitudes. Notes the psychological undertones of the novel, especially in Henchard's relationship with his daughter.

Karl, Frederick R. *A Reader's Guide to the Nineteenth-Century Novel*. New York: Farrar, Straus & Giroux, 1964.
Examines concepts of identity and isolation in the work, which Karl sees as major concerns for the novelist. Points out parallels between Hardy's world view in this novel and modern existentialism.

Kramer, Dale. *"The Mayor of Casterbridge*: The Moment as Repetition." In his *Thomas Hardy: The Forms of Tragedy*. Detroit: Wayne State University Press, 1975.
Considers the novel a highly successful attempt to present a tragedy classical in style, yet attuned to the philosophical attitudes of Hardy's day. Believes that Hardy's central concern lies in portraying the workings of the historical process and its effect on a heroic figure. Extensive analysis of the relationship between Henchard and Farfrae, exploring the shortcomings of the latter. Also examines the scene in which the Royal Personage visits Casterbridge to show how Hardy can concentrate his tragic effect in a single episode.

Levine, George. "Thomas Hardy's *The Mayor of Casterbridge*: Reversing the Real." In his *The Realistic Imagination: English Fiction from Frankenstein to Lady Chatterly's Lover*. Chicago: University of Chicago Press, 1981.
Reads the novel as Hardy's statement against conventions of realism prevalent in fiction of his day. Stresses the romantic elements of the work, including the dominance of the hero, the importance of chance, and the interference of fate. Sees Henchard's nemesis, Donald Farfrae, as representing the tradition of realism against which Hardy was rebelling.

Meisel, Perry. *Thomas Hardy: The Return of the Repressed*. New Haven, Conn.: Yale University Press, 1972.

Reads the novel as a modern tragedy: the tragic hero's fate is determined by his own character, and the tragedy results not from external forces but from the hero's inability to master his own ego or subconscious destructive tendencies. Concentrates on Hardy's portrayal of Henchard as a figure dominating every aspect of the action in the novel.

Page, Norman. *Thomas Hardy*. Boston: Routledge & Kegan Paul, 1977.
Comments on the novel are interspersed throughout Page's study of Hardy's corpus. Included are remarks about Hardy's use of factual data from Dorchester records, a discussion of Farfrae as an outsider whose presence threatens the old ways of the countryside, and an analysis of Hardy's use of techniques drawn from the visual arts as a means of presenting both character and theme.

Paterson, John. *"The Mayor of Casterbridge* as Tragedy." In *Hardy: A Collection of Critical Essays*, edited by Albert Guerard. Englewood Cliffs, N.J.: Prentice-Hall, Inc., 1963.
Argues the novel is a tragedy in the same sense as Sophocles' or William Shakespeare's works, dramatizing the conflict between two strong opposing forces: the great individual against the forces of the moral order demanding retribution for acts committed against that order. Shows Henchard's similarities to tragic figures from Sophocles and Shakespeare; demonstrates how his disruption of the moral order in selling his wife and daughter is paralleled by events in the social world of Casterbridge and in the natural world.

Showalter, Elaine. "The Unmanning of the Mayor of Casterbridge." In *Critical Approaches to the Fiction of Thomas Hardy*, edited by Dale Kramer. New York: Barnes & Noble Books, 1979. Reprinted in *Thomas Hardy*, edited by Harold Bloom. New York: Chelsea House, 1987.
Though noting Hardy's reticence to join the feminist movement of his day, Showalter explores the novelist's portrait of Henchard to show how, through the emasculation of this misogynist, the novelist displays the importance of achieving qualities of sensitivity and compassion—normally considered feminine—to become fully human.

Williams, Merryn. *Thomas Hardy and Rural England*. New York: Columbia University Press, 1972.
Concentrates on Hardy's depiction of the town of Casterbridge, a portrait Williams argues has been misread by previous critics. It is really an evolving rural locale, tied to its past but changing as new methods of farming are introduced. Notes that most of the townspeople live at the poverty level. Traces Henchard's rise and fall in this community where acceptance by others is of paramount importance. Draws parallels between Hardy's depiction of the country town and similar scenes in George Eliot's work.

The Return of the Native

Beach, Joseph Warren. *The Techniques of Thomas Hardy*. Reprint. New York:
Russell & Russell, 1962.
Reads the novel as Hardy's attempt to apply principles of drama to novel
writing. Sees the five sections of the work functioning like acts of a play.
Action is concentrated to illustrate a single theme, the tragedy of frustrated
ambitions; the limitation of all action to a single place upon the heath in the
Wessex countryside further heightens the sense of drama. Notes that the novel
gives the least weight to contrivance of any of Hardy's works.

Boumelha, Penny. *Thomas Hardy and Women: Sexual Ideology and Narrative
Form*. Totowa, N.J.: Barnes & Noble Books, 1982.
Argues that in this work Hardy attempts to deal directly with marriage. Detailed examination of the three principal female figures shows how each represents a form of female sexuality common to three different literary traditions:
pastoral (Thomasin), romantic (Eustacia), and realistic (Mrs. Yeobright).
Hardy explores the implications of female sexuality only obliquely, however; he
marginalizes this sexual energy by forcing the text into the model of classical
tragedy.

Brooks, Jean R. "*Return of the Native*: A Novel of Environment." In her *Thomas
Hardy: The Poetic Structure*. Ithaca, N.Y.: Cornell University Press, 1971.
Reprinted in *Thomas Hardy*, edited by Harold Bloom. New York: Chelsea
House, 1987.
Discusses the many ways the novel relies on techniques normally associated
with poetry to achieve its power. Remarks on how the opening chapter sets up
Egdon Heath as an elemental, almost mythical stage on which Hardy's drama
is played out. Stresses parallels between the structure of the novel and poetic
tragic drama. Views Clym and Eustacia as representatives of opposing energy
forces, light and darkness.

Carpenter, Richard. *Thomas Hardy*. New York: Twayne, 1964.
Describes Hardy's use of Egdon Heath as the most compelling image in the
work, serving both functionally (as a locale to circumscribe the action) and
symbolically (to give that action the significance of myth). Briefly notes Eustacia's failure to adjust to this locale as a cause of her tragedy; focuses on
Clym's actions, noting parallels between them and various mythic heroes.

Cox, R. G., ed. *Thomas Hardy: The Critical Heritage*. New York: Barnes & Noble
Books, 1970.
Selections from four reviews published soon after the novel appeared: a per-
ceptive assessment from the *Atheneum*, a mixed review by W. E. Henley in

the *Academy*, a sharper rebuke by the critic from the *Saturday Review*, and a critique of Hardy's pessimism from the review appearing in the *Spectator*.

Gose, Elliott B. *Imagination Indulged: The Irrational in the Nineteenth Century Novel*. Montreal: McGill-Queens University Press, 1972.
Examines three elements of Romanticism in the novel: the Byronic hero, the use of nature, and the elements of rustic society and folk myths. Extensive discussion of Hardy's use of seasonal and nature imagery.

Hawkins, Desmond. *Hardy: Novelist and Poet*. New York: Barnes & Noble Books, 1976.
Reviews the plot in some detail, concentrating on the interrelationships among the six major figures in the novel. Points out the overriding sense of irony and fatalism built around the series of misconceptions and misunderstandings that characterize so many of the relationships between the men and women in Hardy's story.

Hornback, Bert G. *The Metaphor of Chance: Vision and Technique in the Works of Thomas Hardy*. Athens: Ohio University Press, 1971.
Concentrates on the importance of setting within the novel; sees Egdon Heath as the stage on which characters must act out their parts. Notes how Hardy gives the setting significance by linking it with great events of the past and creating a sense of its universal qualities. Considers Clym the real hero of the work. Includes an extensive discussion of Clym's growing awareness of the importance of the individual life—a feeling hard to accept in the face of the magnificent and unchanging heath, where human life appears insignificant.

Hyman, Virginia. *Ethical Perspectives in the Novels of Thomas Hardy*. Port Washington, N.Y.: Kennikat Press, 1975.
Two chapters devoted to the novel explore the ways Hardy juxtaposes egotism and altruism to show how man should develop and grow morally. Extensive analysis of Clym Yeobright as the man of the future; Hyman considers him Hardy's most altruistic character, though not yet perfected. A separate chapter explores Hardy's use of minor characters as a background against which the actions of the major figures are highlighted.

Kramer, Dale. *"Return of the Native*: Opposites in Tragic Context." In his *Thomas Hardy: The Forms of Tragedy*. Detroit: Wayne State University Press, 1975.
Focuses on the qualities linking the work to the tradition of tragedy; finds that Hardy does not succeed fully in making this tale carry the universal significance expected of great tragic literature. Discusses the importance of the setting in creating the circumstances for tragedy. Faults Hardy for various techniques of presentation (such as overwriting and failure to clearly define

emotions and feelings in his characters) and for his depiction of Eustacia and Clym as tragic figures.

Meisel, Perry. *Thomas Hardy: The Return of the Repressed*. New Haven, Conn.: Yale University Press, 1972.
Discussion of the ways the novel shows an advance over Hardy's early works, as the novelist begins to devote his attention to the interactions of individuals and their community. Extensive analysis of Hardy's use of landscape; commentary on Eustacia Vye's relationship with the inhabitants of Egdon Heath.

Page, Norman. *Thomas Hardy*. Boston: Routledge & Kegan Paul, 1977.
Scattered comments in this study of Hardy's achievement outline the publication history and reception of the novel, noting the significance of its simultaneous serialization in England and America. Page remarks on the success Hardy achieved by returning to the rural setting after failing with this novel's predecessor, *The Hand of Ethelberta*. Sketches Hardy's debt to the Pre-Raphaelite Brotherhood for his portrait of Eustacia Vye.

Williams, Merryn. *Thomas Hardy and Rural England*. New York: Columbia University Press, 1972.
Argues that previous critics overstate the harshness of Egdon Heath. Notes how Hardy portrays its life-sustaining qualities, but insists people who live there must learn to accommodate themselves to this unusual environment. Examines ways characters adapt to life on the heath. Judges Clym the strongest character in the work, although he too ends up defeated by events and forced to give up his ideals.

Tess of the D'Urbervilles

Beach, Joseph Warren. *The Techniques of Thomas Hardy*. Reprint. New York: Russell & Russell, 1962.
Considers this the finest novel in English written during this time. Reads it as a story of innocence crushed by circumstance; stresses the pathos evoked by the work. Considers the structure unobtrusive and the plot relatively free of contrivances. Lengthy discussion of part 3, focusing on Tess and Angel's love. Compares the novel to others of the period to show Hardy's intent and the timeliness of the story.

Boone, Joseph A. "Trajectories of Doom: The Seducer's Plot in *Clarissa* and *Tess of the D'Urbervilles*." In his *Tradition Counter Tradition*. Chicago: University of Chicago Press, 1987.

Groups *Tess of the D'Urbervilles* with other novels in which the traditional subject of seduction is treated seriously and centrally. Shows ways Hardy's portrait of seduction perpetuates stereotypes of male domination, as the novel follows the typical pattern of such tales: continual pursuit and escape, violation of the woman, division and destruction of her life, and finally the closure resulting from her death.

Boumelha, Penny. *Thomas Hardy and Women: Sexual Ideology and Narrative Form*. Totowa, N.J.: Barnes & Noble Books, 1982.
Extensive analysis of Hardy's characterization of Tess, concentrating on her sexuality, which many critics have seen as the source of her tragedy. Reviews the narrative techniques Hardy uses to explain the nature of that sexuality, and discusses various critical responses to the work.

Brooks, Jean R. *"Tess of the D'Urbervilles*: A Novel of Assertion." In her *Thomas Hardy: The Poetic Structure*. Ithaca, N.Y.: Cornell University Press, 1971.
Traces Hardy's use of poetic devices in creating this story of a woman caught in the archetypal human tragedy of desiring the freedom to choose her own destiny but being controlled by forces outside herself. Shows how patterns of imagery and contrasting settings highlight both the naturalness of the sexual union and the stark consequences of transgression against the moral code. Briefly examines the roles of Alec and Angel.

Carpenter, Richard. *Thomas Hardy*. New York: Twayne, 1964.
Believes Hardy's careful blending of mythic qualities raises the story from the tale of a single ruined girl to one of universal significance: the tragedy of innocent humanity caught by forces over which it has no control. Delineates the novelist's use of setting and allusion to achieve the parallels to myths, especially in his description of Tess as an Eve figure. Also discusses the novel as an exposé of social injustice in Victorian society.

Cox, R. G., ed. *Thomas Hardy: The Critical Heritage*. New York: Barnes & Noble Books, 1970.
Reprints excerpts from ten reviews written by Victorian critics for important literary periodicals. Includes comments by Richard LeGalliene, R. H. Hutton, Andrew Lang, Margaret Oliphant, and Mowbray Morris. Virtually all praise Hardy's creative powers. Hutton, however, strikes a typically Victorian note: he criticizes the novelist for treating Tess as a heroine even though she has sinned.

Daleski, H. M. *"Tess of the D'Urbervilles*: Mastery and Abandon." In his *The Divided Heroine: A Recurrent Pattern in Six English Novels*. New York: Holmes & Meier, 1984.
Argues that Tess's tragedy stems from her failure to master the warring

tendencies of flesh and spirit within her; Alec and Angel represent these opposing forces. Lengthy analysis of Tess's relationship with these figures shows how each violates Tess in his way by treating her either as wholly flesh (Alec) or wholly spirit (Angel); neither is able to accept her as a person formed of both elements.

Gordon, Jan B. "Origins, History, and the Reconstitution of Family: Tess's Journey." In *Thomas Hardy*, edited by Harold Bloom. New York: Chelsea House, 1987.
Interesting analysis of the concept of history as a central concern for Hardy and for his characters. Sees Tess's actions as attempts either to reclaim her past or repudiate it. The two major male figures stand in opposition with regard to valuing the past: Alec ignores its importance, while Angel holds it in reverence.

Hawkins, Desmond. *Hardy: Novelist and Poet*. New York: Barnes & Noble Books, 1976.
Extensive summary of the action of the novel, focusing on the contrast between Alec D'Urberville and Angel Clare. Detailed discussion of Tess, whom Hawkins considers Hardy's best-drawn heroine. Notes the novelist's difficulties in finding a publisher for the work in serial form. Cites Hardy's use of descriptive techniques to create sexual symbolism.

Hornback, Bert G. *The Metaphor of Chance: Vision and Technique in the Works of Thomas Hardy*. Athens: Ohio University Press, 1971.
Examines Hardy's portrayal of Tess as a tragic heroine, giving special attention to the way the novelist uses setting to heighten the effect of the tragedy. Sketches Hardy's use of blood and coffin metaphors. Discusses in some detail the climactic scene set at Stonehenge.

Hyman, Virginia. *Ethical Perspectives in the Novels of Thomas Hardy*. Port Washington, N.Y.: Kennikat Press, 1975.
Three chapters discuss the novel as an example of Hardy's belief in ethics as an evolutionary concept. Considers Tess's moral development, showing how her values are defined by her past, yet are also shaped by the evolutionary process; explains how she is an agent of change in other characters. In a separate chapter, Hyman analyzes Angel Clare as a type of the modern man, whose relationship with Tess exposes the weaknesses of his intellectual commitment to absolutes.

Kramer, Dale. "*Tess of the D'Urbervilles*: Pure Tragedy of Consciousness." In his *Thomas Hardy: The Forms of Tragedy*. Detroit: Wayne State University Press, 1975.

Argues that Hardy's primary concern in this novel is to portray individuals creating their own tragedies. Believes the novelist stresses throughout the subjectivity of all human experience; looks at ways Tess defines herself and judges her own actions. Extensive analysis of the qualities of mysticism Hardy introduces into the text, characteristics that reinforce notions of subjectivity.

Meisel, Perry. *Thomas Hardy: The Return of the Repressed*. New Haven, Conn.: Yale University Press, 1972.
Believes that Tess's tragedy arises from the conflict between natural and social strains within her personality. Judges her to be rebellious against conventional social mores in refusing to accept her fate after Alec seduces her; instead, she asserts her independence and innocence, and maintains her right to go on with her life. Notes that, from the beginning of the story, she is isolated from the rural society in which she lives, which makes it harder for her to act as she feels she should and still be accepted by the community.

Page, Norman. *Thomas Hardy*. Boston: Routledge & Kegan Paul, 1977.
Comments on the novel are included in this study of Hardy's achievement as a writer. Remarks on Hardy's use of natural settings and on his power to write descriptive prose. Also notes that, unlike other Hardy tales, this one is set at a time close to the publication date of the story; Page traces the qualities that give the novel its contemporary flavor.

Phelps, Gilbert. *A Reader's Guide to Fifty British Novels, 1600-1900*. New York: Barnes & Noble, 1979.
Abbreviated review of Hardy's career as a novelist is followed by a summary of the major action in the work. Critical analysis focuses on Hardy's use of the locale of his birth and his general reliance on nature imagery. Emphasizes the parallels between Hardy's tale and classical tragedy.

Robinson, Roger. "Hardy and Darwin." In *Thomas Hardy: The Writer and His Background*, edited by Norman Page. New York: St. Martin's Press, 1980.
In a study of Hardy's reaction to Darwinian theories of determinism, Robinson views the novel as Hardy's most extensive examination of heredity as a stultifying force against which individuals must struggle to assert their individuality. Discusses the sources from which Hardy developed his understanding of Darwin's theory.

Van Ghent, Dorothy. "On *Tess of the D'Urbervilles*." In *Hardy: A Collection of Critical Essays*, edited by Albert Guerard. Englewood Cliffs, N.J.: Prentice-Hall, Inc., 1963.
Focuses on Hardy's use of the natural settings in which his story occurs; sees the novelist investing this natural terrain with symbolic significance, so that

Tess's story becomes the struggle of the individual of conscience against an uncaring and deterministic universe. Believes the presence of magic and folk tales reinforces the fatalism inherent in the accidents and coincidences that characterize life in the natural world.

Waldoff, Leon. "Psychological Determinism in *Tess of the D'Urbervilles*." In *Critical Approaches to the Fiction of Thomas Hardy*, edited by Dale Kramer. New York: Barnes & Noble Books, 1979.

Investigates the limits of Tess's own responsibility for her tragedy. Sees difficulties in discovering clear answers in the text, which is loaded with ambiguity; believes that the ambiguity stems from the ambivalent attitude Hardy and his Victorian contemporaries had toward women, especially with regard to sexual matters. Posits that the tragedy in the novel arises when Angel demands that Tess be ideal, because (like all men) he is unable to accept her as flawed.

Williams, Merryn. *Thomas Hardy and Rural England*. New York: Columbia University Press, 1972.

Attempts to correct serious critical misapprehensions about Hardy's attitude toward the aristocracy. Argues that the novelist's portrayal is based on a realistic view of both the upper and lower classes: the aristocracy is high-handed and rapacious, the lower classes far from idyllic. Tess becomes a victim preyed upon by both classes, as she is crushed by customs and conventions that both groups have come to accept.

CHARLES KINGSLEY

General Studies

Baldwin, Stanley E. *Charles Kingsley*. Ithaca, N.Y.: Cornell University Press, 1934.
A general review of Kingsley's achievement as a novelist. Separate chapters provide a short biographical sketch, outline the influence of Thomas Carlyle and F. D. Maurice on Kingsley's thought, and analyze Kingsley's six novels in some detail. The focus is on the social, economic, and religious issues Kingsley addresses in all of his works.

Barry, James. D. "Elizabeth Cleghorn Gaskell; Charles Kingsley." In *The Victorian Novel: A Guide to Research*, edited by Lionel Stevenson. Cambridge, Mass.: Harvard University Press, 1964.
Valuable bibliographical commentary on Kingsley's life and writings. Summaries and evaluations of important biographies and bibliographies, as well as information on editions of Kingsley's works and collections of his letters. Also provides synopses of scholarship on Kingsley written before 1962.

Cazamian, Louis. *The Social Novel in England, 1830-1850: Dickens, Disraeli, Mrs. Gaskell, Kingsley*. Boston: Routledge & Kegan Paul, 1973.
Extensive discussion of Kingsley's role as a social reformer and as a novelist. Detailed biography outlines Kingsley's development of a social conscience, his friendship with F. D. Maurice and other Christian Socialists, and his efforts to promote their cause. Excellent brief outline of the precepts and influence of Christian Socialism. Includes lengthy analyses of *Yeast* and *Alton Locke*.

Chitty, Susan. *The Beast and the Monk: A Life of Charles Kingsley*. New York: Mason/Charter, 1975.
Biography based on previously published sources and on new manuscript materials, including early letters and drawings Kingsley sent to his future wife shortly before their marriage. Argues Kingsley was a more complex figure than most previous biographers acknowledged, citing his deeply sensual private side and his carefully guarded feelings of despair.

Dawson, William J. *The Makers of English Fiction*. Reprint. Freeport, N.Y.: Books for Libraries Press, 1971.
Discusses Kingsley's motivations for writing fiction, and the causes of his relegation to the second rank of English novelists. Notes how his novels reflect his personal passion and energy, giving them a strident quality reminiscent of orations. Considers *Alton Locke* his best book, although *Westward, Ho!* is considered most representative of his powers as a novelist.

Kendall, Guy. *Charles Kingsley and His Ideas*. New York: Hutchinson, 1947.
Wide-ranging study of Kingsley's life and accomplishments in many areas. Places the novels in the larger context of Kingsley's work as a clergyman and social reformer. Individual chapters give abbreviated assessments of Kingsley's poetry, his novels, and his nonfiction.

Maison, Margaret. "Christianity Muscular and Elastic: The Broad Church Novels." In her *The Victorian Vision: Studies in the Religious Novel*. New York: Sheed & Ward, 1961.
Reviews the religious undercurrent informing all of Kingsley's novels; acknowledges that other qualities give them their lasting appeal, especially Kingsley's ability to provide realistic descriptions of places and events. Shows how Kingsley uses his fiction to further the cause of "muscular Christianity," a movement which promoted the relationship between spiritual and physical well-being.

Martin, R. B. *The Dust of Combat: A Life of Charles Kingsley*. London: Faber & Faber, 1959.
Excellent scholarly biography tracing Kingsley's intellectual development, his debt to Thomas Carlyle, his friendship with F. D. Maurice, and the influence of that powerful figure on the novelist's thought. Comments on Kingsley's fiction are included within the biographical narrative. A separate chapter discusses the religious controversy between Kingsley and John Henry Newman, whose *Apologia Pro Vita Sua* was written in response to Kingsley's criticisms of the Roman Catholic Church.

Sanders, Andrew. *The Victorian Historical Novel, 1840-1880*. New York: St. Martin's Press, 1979.
Discusses Kingsley's historical novels (*Hypatia* and *Hereward the Wake*), comparing them to similar works of the period to show how Kingsley transformed materials of history into fiction that addressed contemporary social and religious issues.

Stephen, Leslie. *Hours in a Library*. Vol. 3. Reprint. Grosse Point, Mich.: Scholarly Press, 1968.
Sweeping review of Kingsley's career and his contributions to English life and letters by a prominent nineteenth century critic. Stephen offers sage commentary on Kingsley's poetry and novels, judging *Alton Locke* the best of the author's fictional works. Outlines the influence of his highly religious nature and his deep concern for social issues on all his publications.

Thorp, Margaret F. *Charles Kingsley, 1819-1875*. Princeton, N.J.: Princeton University Press, 1937.

Biographical sketch based on manuscripts, papers, and correspondence to and from Kingsley. In the course of her narrative of Kingsley's life, Thorp examines each of the author's works to show how Kingsley faced the social, political, and moral dilemmas every Victorian confronted. Thorp considers Kingsley representative of Victorians in his attitude toward many of these problems, and notes his reliance on religion and faith as a means for confronting such issues.

Uffelman, Larry K. *Charles Kingsley*. Boston: Twayne, 1979.
Critical study of Kingsley's novels, poetry, and nonfiction. Separate chapters focus on the novels of social purpose and on the historical fiction. Includes a biographical chapter and a chronology of important events in Kingsley's life; also contains an annotated bibliography of criticism.

Wagenknecht, Edward. *Cavalcade of the English Novel*. New York: Holt, Rinehart, and Winston, 1954.
Brief overview of each of Kingsley's six novels, noting their relationship to contemporary social, political, and religious issues which occupied the novelist's thoughts and spurred his creative efforts. Cites the stylistic and imaginative flaws causing Kingsley to be rated a minor figure in Victorian fiction.

Alton Locke

Baldwin, Stanley E. *Charles Kingsley*. Ithaca, N.Y.: Cornell University Press, 1934.
Outlines the political background of the novel: the impact of the Chartist movement and its influence on England's working classes. Discusses Kingsley's use of characters to portray political and social points of view; notes the influence of Thomas Carlyle on Kingsley's thought. Also cites parallels between Kingsley's hero and Thomas Cooper, a real-life leader in the Chartist movement. Considers the novel the most representative of Kingsley's use of fiction as a means of highlighting social ills.

Cazamian, Louis. *The Social Novel in England, 1830-1850: Dickens, Disraeli, Mrs. Gaskell, Kingsley*. Boston: Routledge & Kegan Paul, 1973.
Lengthy analysis of both the plot and themes of the novel. By tracing Alton Locke's progress through the various environments in which he finds himself, Cazamian offers a careful explanation of the way Kingsley highlights the squalor of the working classes. Also discusses the novelist's techniques for representing his plan to relieve the distress of these people; notes Kingsley's sympathies with principles of the Chartists, but makes clear his aversion to radical solutions to social problems.

Chitty, Susan. *The Beast and the Monk: A Life of Charles Kingsley*. New York: Mason/Charter, 1975.
Describes the circumstances leading Kingsley to write this novel of social protest; quotes graphic descriptions by Kingsley and others of the Jacob's Island area of London, a notorious slum. While acknowledging Kingsley's claim that the novel is about the dangers of rising above one's social station, Chitty cites the biting criticisms the novelist offers of life in the London slums as a clear indication he was interested in social reforms.

Karl, Frederick R. "Five Victorian Novelists." In his *A Reader's Guide to the Nineteenth-Century Novel*. New York: Farrar, Straus & Giroux, 1964.
Reads the novel as Kingsley's attempt to promote better conditions for the working classes; notes, however, the novelist's inherent fear of pure democracy. Points out the influence of Thomas Carlyle's writings on Kingsley's thought.

Lucas, John. "Mrs. Gaskell and Brotherhood." In *Tradition and Tolerance in Nineteenth-Century Fiction*, edited by David Howard, John Lucas, and John Goode. London: Routledge & Kegan Paul, 1966.
In a general essay dealing with the failures of most authors who wrote social-problem novels in the nineteenth century, Lucas criticizes Kingsley for his inability to create a believable hero in Alton Locke; also cites the novelist's clear sympathy for the middle class rather than for the workers whom he ostensibly champions.

Martin, R. B. *The Dust of Combat: A Life of Charles Kingsley*. London: Faber & Faber, 1959.
Notes parallels between Kingsley's characters and real-life figures: the Chartist activist Thomas Cooper, model for Kingsley's hero, and Thomas Carlyle, after whom Kingsley's sage bookseller Saunders MacKaye is patterned. Points out artistic flaws: overreliance on melodrama, unmotivated actions, formlessness, signs of hasty composition. Nevertheless, considers the work Kingsley's strongest representation of his belief in Christian Socialism as a means for improving the lot of the lower classes. Briefly sketches the mixed reception of the novel by Kingsley's contemporaries.

Phelps, Gilbert. *A Reader's Guide to Fifty British Novels, 1600-1900*. New York: Barnes & Noble Books, 1979.
Biographical sketch traces Kingsley's development as a novelist of social protest. Useful plot summary, followed by critical commentary noting the propagandistic tone of the work, but remarking favorably on Kingsley's skill in creating the hero as a complex, sympathetic figure—almost too independent to satisfy the author's political purposes.

Thorp, Margaret F. *Charles Kingsley, 1819-1875*. Princeton, N.J.: Princeton University Press, 1937.

Rates the novel Kingsley's best, largely because of its accurate portrait of social conditions. Discusses Kingsley's successes and failures in presenting various characters. Sketches parallels between the novel and real-life people and events. Briefly outlines the critical reception, focusing on derogatory reviews.

Uffelman, Larry K. *Charles Kingsley*. Boston: Twayne, 1979.

Provides a detailed summary of the major action. Argues that Kingsley's purposes are to denounce physical force as a means of effecting social change and to advocate reforms based on individual sacrifice. Notes the ways Kingsley's characters become spokesmen for various social and ethical positions, often at the expense of realism. Sees Kingsley adhering to a belief in the class system while arguing for better cooperation among the classes.

Williams, Raymond. "The Industrial Novels." In his *Culture and Society, 1780-1950*. London: Chatto & Windus, 1954.

Short assessment of the work, placing it in the context of several other industrial novels. Sees Kingsley's theme as being an exploration of the development of a true Chartist. Notes the discursive nature of the narrative, and Kingsley's habit of sermonizing, which at times turns the novel into a tract.

Yeast

Baldwin, Stanley E. *Charles Kingsley*. Ithaca, N.Y.: Cornell University Press, 1934.

Considers Kingsley's thesis to be the exposition of the attitudes and concerns of Young England; notes how the author's overt political aims sometimes overshadow his artistry. Outlines Kingsley's use of characters to represent various political, social, and economic viewpoints popular in the novelist's day. Also discusses Kingsley's interest in sanitary reform and belief in the importance of the Anglican church's becoming involved in social problems.

Cazamian, Louis. *The Social Novel in England, 1830-1850: Dickens, Disraeli, Mrs. Gaskell, Kingsley*. Boston: Routledge & Kegan Paul, 1973.

Discusses the novel as a social tract, observing that Kingsley is more polemical than descriptive in discussing social injustice and the possibility for reform. Considers the novel Kingsley's search for the best way to bring about meaningful change in England. Sketches the character development of Kingsley's hero, Lancelot Smith, noting his similarity to Carlylean hero figures. Also cites Kingsley's concern for physical hygiene as a component of reform.

Chitty, Susan. *The Beast and the Monk: A Life of Charles Kingsley*. New York: Mason/Charter, 1975.
  Brief survey of the novel shows how Kingsley uses the rather weak plot as a means of illustrating his concern for social issues, especially the plight of the agricultural poor. Notes his ability to describe natural settings and cites examples of autobiographical elements that make their way into the narrative.

Kendall, Guy. *Charles Kingsley and His Ideas*. New York: Hutchinson, 1947.
  Scattered comments reflect on the success of the novel as social propaganda. Considers the characters unrealistic, often serving simply as mouthpieces for the novelist's social, religious, or political ideas. Briefly notes some hostile initial responses by Kingsley's contemporaries.

Martin, R. B. *The Dust of Combat: A Life of Charles Kingsley*. London: Faber & Faber, 1959.
  Remarks throughout this biographical study point out parallels between characters in the novel and figures whom Kingsley knew; notes similarities between the book's hero and Kingsley himself. Brief discussion of the publication of the work in monthly installments in *Fraser's* magazine. Also cites correspondence from novelist George Meredith regarding the strong positive impact the work had on him.

Thorp, Margaret. "Esau Has a Birthright." In her *Charles Kingsley, 1819-1875*. Princeton, N.J.: Princeton University Press, 1937.
  Discusses the genesis and appearance of the novel in *Fraser's* magazine and Kingsley's subsequent efforts to revise and expand the work for publication in book form. Notes the impact of the story on Kingsley's friends, on the general public, and especially on reviewers. Highlights autobiographical aspects of the novel.

Uffelman, Larry K. *Charles Kingsley*. Boston: Twayne, 1979.
  A synopsis of the plot is followed by a critical examination of Kingsley's use of autobiographical materials, his handling of plot, and his method of characterization. Finds the work's artistry subordinated to its social message, an attack on the conditions of the agricultural poor and a plea for reforms based on Christian principles.

GEORGE MEREDITH

General Studies

Bartlett, Phyllis. *George Meredith*. London: Longmans, Green, 1963.
Overview of Meredith's career as a writer. Separate sections discuss his poetry, especially *Modern Love*, and his influential essay on the Comic Spirit. Each novel is reviewed briefly, with special attention given to *The Egoist* and *Beauchamp's Career*.

Beach, Joseph Warren. *The Comic Spirit in George Meredith: An Interpretation*. Reprint. New York: Russell & Russell, 1963.
One of the first systematic studies of Meredith's artistry, exploring his use of the comic. An introductory chapter delineates the novelist's ideas on the nature of the Comic Spirit and the function of irony. Discusses several novels in detail, including *The Ordeal of Richard Feverel*, *The Egoist*, *One of our Conquerors*, and *Evan Harrington*.

Chislett, William. *George Meredith: A Study and an Appraisal*. Reprint. New York: Haskell House, 1966.
Useful collection of short essays and listings that gives a sense of Meredith's ideology and the background for his writings. Separate sections include essays assessing Meredith's personality, sketching his political views, discussing his philosophy, analyzing his artistic ideals and use of various sources, reviewing selected novels and short stories, and exploring his work as a poet.

Cline, C. L. "George Meredith." In *Victorian Fiction: A Guide to Research*, edited by Lionel Stevenson. Cambridge, Mass.: Harvard University Press, 1964.
Bibliographical essay summarizes scholarship on Meredith published before 1962. Divided into sections outlining bibliographical materials, discussing editions of the novels and collections of Meredith's letters, reviewing works aimed at establishing Meredith's literary reputation, examining special topics such as Meredith's style and his notion of the Comic Spirit, and assessing critical commentaries on individual novels.

Collie, Michael. *George Meredith: A Bibliography*. Toronto: University of Toronto Press, 1974.
Indispensable reference tool for serious students of Meredith's career. Describes in detail the contents of each of Meredith's published works, often providing commentary on the composition and publication process. Lists his contributions to periodicals and catalogs poems in various ways to aid in identification.

Cunningham, Gail. "Meredith and Gissing: Fair Ladies in Revolt and Old Women."
In her *The New Woman and the Victorian Novel*. New York: Barnes & Noble
Books, 1978.
Explores Meredith's involvement with and sympathies for the women's movement at the end of the nineteenth century. Sees him concentrating on the
problems of marriage as a result of his personal disappointments. Brief discussions of *The Egoist* and *Lord Ormont and his Aminta*. Judges Meredith sympathetic toward women but not committed to the political struggle in which his
female contemporaries were engaged.

Fletcher, Ian. *Meredith Now: Some Critical Essays*. New York: Barnes & Noble
Books, 1971.
Collection of original critical essays by diverse scholars, providing a revaluation of Meredith's stature as a man of letters. An essay reviewing Meredith's
critical reputation is followed by one assessing his poetry, and others examining each of the major novels. The focus of each essay is on critical problems
generated by the texts rather than on scholarly examinations of background,
ideology, or similar subjects.

Gindin, James. *Harvest of a Quiet Eye: The Novel of Compassion*. Bloomington:
Indiana University Press, 1971.
Surveys all the novels, focusing on Meredith's use of irony and his satiric
stance. Notes that in virtually every novel Meredith's sympathies lie with
individuals, especially women, who revolt against conventions. Meredith's
sense of pathos is sometimes obscured by his penchant for irony, but it exists
in all his best fiction. Highlights several of the techniques of style and literary
devices the novelist uses to achieve his ironic portraits.

Gretton, Mary S. *The Writings and Life of George Meredith: A Centenary Study*.
Cambridge, Mass.: Harvard University Press, 1926.
Systematic survey of Meredith's writings by a scholar who knew him. Introductory chapters set Meredith in the context of the late nineteenth and early
twentieth centuries and briefly review his earliest publications. Separate chapters examine the major fiction and poetry, integrating details of Meredith's life
into discussions of the literature.

Karl, Frederick R. *A Reader's Guide to the Nineteenth-Century Novel*. New York:
Farrar, Straus & Giroux, 1964.
Reviews the major novels to explain why Meredith has never achieved the
stature afforded other major Victorian novelists. Finds the answer in Meredith's decision to avoid the overtly dramatic in his fiction, and in his failure to
create memorable characters.

Lindsay, Jack. *George Meredith: His Life and Work*. London: Bodley Head, 1956.
Full scale critical biography, attempting to supplant earlier studies and assess the ideas informing Meredith's fiction and poetry. Detailed information, often garnered from manuscript sources, about Meredith's life. Individual chapters devoted to discussions of major works. Includes commentary on Meredith's debt to various intellectual and political figures of his day. Separate section gives an overview of the writer's concern for form and assesses the content of his works to link the nineteenth century novelist to his twentieth century inheritors.

McCullen, Maurice, and Lewis Sawin. *A Dictionary of the Characters in George Meredith's Fiction*. New York: Garland, 1977.
Alphabetical listing of every character appearing in Meredith's novels and short stories. For major characters, includes a detailed biographical sketch with some effort at analysis. Introduction explains various uses for this dictionary. Also includes listings of characters organized by individual work.

Muendel, Renate. *George Meredith*. Boston: Twayne, 1986.
Analysis of Meredith's career, focusing on the experimental nature of his novels. A chapter is devoted to an examination of Meredith's poetry; others provide analyses of the novels, dividing Meredith's career roughly into thirds and tracing his development of the complex style characterizing his writing. Also includes a chronology and a selected bibliography of criticism.

Priestley, J. B. *George Meredith*. New York: Macmillan, 1926.
This monograph in the British Men of Letters Series provides a general critical assessment of Meredith's writings. Two chapters give a brief biography; additional sections offer an analysis of the poetry, while two chapters discuss the novels. Also contains a chapter on Meredith's notion of the Comic Spirit, and one on his philosophical outlook.

Russell, Frances T. *Satire in the Victorian Novel*. Reprint. New York: Russell & Russell, 1964.
In a general study of the concept and function of satire in Victorian fiction, Russell makes frequent references to Meredith, citing numerous examples of his aims and techniques, his handling of romantic and realistic elements in fiction, his use of irony, and his creation of character types. Judges him best at dealing with the complexities of love.

Sassoon, Siegfried. *Meredith*. London: Constable, 1948.
Extended appreciation of Meredith by one of Britain's leading World War I poets. Intersperses commentary on individual novels and poems throughout a narrative of Meredith's life. Devotes attention to the novelist's relationships

with other literary figures of his age. The study focuses on the background of Meredith's literary productions.

Shaheen, Mohammad. *George Meredith: A Reappraisal of the Novels*. Totowa, N.J.: Barnes & Noble Books, 1981.
Attempts to correct thesis-bound criticism of earlier scholars who overlook or underplay the significance of characterization in Meredith's novels. Claims Meredith is interested primarily in creating individual characters rather than character types. Examines five novels to illustrate the variety of Meredith's creative genius: *The Ordeal of Richard Feverel*, *Beauchamp's Career*, *The Adventures of Harry Richmond*, *One of our Conquerors*, and *The Amazing Marriage*.

Stevenson, Lionel. *The Ordeal of George Meredith: A Biography*. New York: Scribner's, 1953.
Scholarly study accepted as the standard twentieth century biography of the artist. Carefully researched, relying heavily on primary sources (letters, reminiscences, and similar materials). Stevenson chronicles Meredith's personal life and its impact on his literary career. Comments on the novels are woven into the biographical narrative; includes details on the composition and publication history of individual works.

——————— . "Meredith and the Art of Implication." In *The Victorian Experience: The Novelists*, edited by Richard Levine. Athens: Ohio University Press, 1976.
Accounts for the difficulties readers have with Meredith's novels by exploring his use of various devices for implication. These make his works highly suggestive while denying readers the comfort of having a single standard for judging character and action. Contrasts his work with that of other novelists; sees him rebelling against conventional realism. Analyzes his handling of allegory, his deliberate attempts to mingle comedy and tragedy, his creation (or omission) of key scenes, and his use of metaphor.

Stone, Donald D. *The Romantic Impulse in Victorian Fiction*. Cambridge, Mass.: Harvard University Press, 1980.
Suggests Meredith is an inheritor of the Romantic tradition in his concentration on egoism and in his adoption of Romantic conventions. Traces the positive and negative impact on Meredith's work of literary figures from Ludovico Ariosto through Lord Byron and Percy Bysshe Shelley to Thomas Carlyle. Notes Meredith's break from these predecessors in his serious treatment of women. Discusses *The Ordeal of Richard Feverel*, *The Adventures of Harry Richmond*, and *Beauchamp's Career* to illustrate Meredith's affinity with the Romantics.

Trevelyan, George M. *The Poetry and Philosophy of George Meredith*. Reprint. New York: Russell & Russell, 1966.

Scholarly examination of Meredith's poetry by a respected turn-of-the-century critic who knew the writer. The comments on Meredith's philosophy are helpful in understanding his fiction. Includes discussion of Meredith's essay on the Comic Spirit, and comments on the novelist's understanding of the way man's physical and psychological senses work.

Williams, Ioan, ed. *Meredith: The Critical Heritage*. New York: Barnes & Noble Books, 1971.

Collection of reviews of all of Meredith's major fiction and poetry published immediately after these works first appeared. Selections from influential newspapers, periodicals, and scholarly reviews offer a range of critical responses to the novels and poems. An introduction remarks on the reception of Meredith's publications during his lifetime and assesses his reputation in England, in America, and on the Continent.

Wilt, Judith. *The Readable People of George Meredith*. Princeton, N.J.: Princeton University Press, 1975.

Engaging study of Meredith's attitude toward his audience and his methods of composition that enabled him to create and manipulate his ideal readers. Traces the novelist's concern for three major ideas—sentimentalism, egoism, and civilization—through three representative works of fiction: *Sandra Belloni*, *The Egoist*, and *One of our Conquerors*. Shows how in each Meredith makes readers become active participants in the narrative, hence making his art come alive only through each individual reading of the work.

Wright, Walter. *Art and Substance in George Meredith*. Lincoln: University of Nebraska Press, 1953.

Useful single source for critical analysis of Meredith's literary techniques and achievement. Examines the fiction to outline Meredith's growing awareness of truth and his growing mastery of the materials of his craft. Argues that Meredith was most comfortable dealing with comic materials. Separate chapters focus on *The Egoist*, *Beauchamp's Career*, and *The Ordeal of Richard Feverel*. Includes a chronology and a selected bibliography of criticism.

Beauchamp's Career

Gretton, Mary S. *The Writings and Life of George Meredith: A Centenary Study*. Cambridge, Mass.: Harvard University Press, 1926.

Demonstrates the many ways this novel is a sustained effort to deal with political issues. Notes the influence of Meredith's friend Frederick Maxse on the novelist's concept of his hero. Contains an extensive analysis of Nevil Beauchamp, along with some discussion of minor characters, to show how individuals' lives are shaped by political events and how idealism suffers in the face of everyday living.

Kettle, Arnold. *"Beauchamp's Career."* In *Meredith Now: Some Critical Essays*, edited by Ian Fletcher. New York: Barnes & Noble Books, 1971.
Claims the novel is clearly political in intent and in its realization of characters and events. Beauchamp, modeled on Meredith's friend Frederick A. Maxse, represents radical political figures. Discusses Beauchamp's relationship with the women in the novel to demonstrate the inseparability of public and private life. Concludes Meredith's conception is greater than his achievement, however, because many of the characters are not fully realized and do not arouse readers' interest or sympathy.

Lindsay, Jack. *George Meredith: His Life and Work*. London: Bodley Head, 1956.
Noting parallels between Beauchamp and Meredith's friend Frederick Maxse, Lindsay develops a detailed argument that the book is primarily a political novel concerned with the evils of capitalism. Includes careful analysis of Nevil Beauchamp, Cecilia, and Dr. Shrapnel. Concludes with selected reviews of the novel by Meredith's contemporaries.

Muendel, Renate. *George Meredith*. Boston: Twayne, 1986.
Discussion of Nevil Beauchamp's heroism, which Meredith considers ineffective in the modern world. Notes the many attractive characteristics of the hero, but points out how his uncompromising commitment to ideals leads to difficulties in dealing with others.

Sassoon, Siegfried. *Meredith*. London: Constable, 1948.
Cites Meredith's difficulties in writing and publishing this novel; explains how its success led to a general recognition of Meredith's work. Highlights both contemporary and modern reactions to the narrative techniques and to Meredith's decision to concentrate on character rather than on incident. Traces the influence of Admiral Frederick Maxse on Meredith's concept of his hero.

Shaheen, Mohammad. *George Meredith: A Reappraisal of the Novels*. Totowa, N.J.: Barnes & Noble Books, 1981.
Argues that Meredith's chief aim is to present a complex, individualized hero who is anti-Byronic; Meredith models Beauchamp on Thomas Carlyle's concept of the hero, but transcends that view by recognizing the potential for such heroism to fail in a changing society. Compares the novel with George Eliot's *Felix Holt, the Radical* to show how these authors differ in dealing with

political issues. Lengthy commentary correcting misapprehensions by earlier critics, especially Jack Lindsay.

Speare, Morris E. "George Meredith—'Beauchampism': The Idealist in Politics." In his *The Political Novel: Its Development in England and America*. Reprint. New York: Russell & Russell, 1966.
    Evaluates the novel as a political statement; considers it a satire on English conservatism. Believes Beauchamp's story is intended as a fable of modern man's struggle to master the conflicts between conservatism, England's medieval heritage, and modern democracy. The two major women in the novel symbolize the two political positions between which Beauchamp must choose.

Stevenson, Lionel. *The Ordeal of George Meredith: A Biography*. New York: Scribner's, 1953.
    Discusses Meredith's efforts to have the novel published serially, and comments about the novelist's attempts to revise the work as he proceeded with its composition. Remarks on Meredith's creation of Nevil Beauchamp as a misunderstood idealist. Compares the novel with *The Ordeal of Richard Feverel* to show both consistencies and advances in Meredith's techniques.

Stone, Donald D. *The Romantic Impulse in Victorian Fiction*. Cambridge, Mass.: Harvard University Press, 1980.
    Pithy examination of the novel as Meredith's attack on Romantic ideals. Finds Beauchamp to be an egoist living as an anti-Byronic hero. Believes the novel is influenced by Meredith's reaction to the failure of his friend Frederick Maxse to gain political office, but also sees in Meredith's portrait of Nevil Beauchamp a degree of self-criticism.

Williams, Ioan, ed. *Meredith: The Critical Heritage*. New York: Barnes & Noble Books, 1971.
    Excerpts from eight reviews published in influential periodicals such as the *Athenaeum* and the *Saturday Review*. Includes a selection by James Thomson, poet and author of *The City of Dreadful Night*, an ardent supporter of Meredith who has high praise for this and other Meredith novels.

Wright, Walter. *Art and Substance in George Meredith*. Lincoln: University of Nebraska Press, 1953.
    Judges the novel Meredith's most romantic, seeing Nevil Beauchamp as a knight whose life is a continual quest. Believes that Beauchamp is essentially comic, torn between idealistic pretensions and everyday foibles. Extensive discussion of his relationship with the four women in the novel shows how the hero grows. Argues that the lack of sympathy in Beauchamp's character is compensated for by his association with these women.

Diana of the Crossways

Beach, Joseph Warren. *The Comic Spirit in George Meredith: An Interpretation.*
Reprint. New York: Russell & Russell, 1963.
In a larger study of Meredith's exploration of the Comic Spirit, Beach briefly
notes ways this novel fails to display many qualities of the Comic that characterize Meredith's best work. Considers the story more closely allied to the
novels of George Eliot and Mrs. Humphry Ward in its treatment of the love
interest and its focus on a young girl's passage toward maturity.

Calder, Jenni. "Insurrection." In her *Women and Marriage in Victorian Fiction.*
New York: Oxford University Press, 1976.
Examines Meredith's attitudes toward marriage as exhibited in this novel.
Focuses on the heroine, a woman who lives apart from her husband and who
supports herself both financially and psychologically. Calder considers Diana
complex and contradictory, but finds Meredith's condemnation of men who
inhibit women's freedom stronger in this novel than in his earlier works.

Gordon, Jan B. "*Diana of the Crossways*: Internal History and the Brainstuff of
Fiction." In *Meredith Now: Some Critical Essays*, edited by Ian Fletcher. New
York: Barnes & Noble Books, 1971.
Focuses on the importance of the house in Victorian fiction, showing through
an exploration of this novel how the relationship of characters with specific
locales changes through the century. Believes that this offers a way of tracing
the development of English fiction from Jane Austen to twentieth century
writers such as James Joyce and E. M. Forster. Gordon reads this work as an
emblem of the movement of English fiction from epistolary modes to the
overheard gossip and fragmented conversation that make up modern fiction.

Gretton, Mary S. *The Writings and Life of George Meredith: A Centenary Study.*
Cambridge, Mass.: Harvard University Press, 1926.
Notes the immediate popularity the novel achieved; briefly traces its roots in
real-life incidents connected with Mrs. Caroline Norton, a minor novelist.
Judges the novel rather conventional and not representative of Meredith's finest
work. Extensive plot summary precedes an analysis of the heroine, whom
Gretton considers too ill-defined to be a female counterpart to Meredith's hero
of *The Egoist*, Sir Willoughby Patterne.

Lindsay, Jack. *George Meredith: His Life and Work.* London: Bodley Head, 1956.
Summarizes the major action to show the lack of political overtones, something Lindsay finds uncharacteristic of Meredith. Concentrates discussion on
the faults of the heroine, and on her relationship with Percy Dacier; finds her
self-indulgent and self-deceptive. Believes that the book is weak because Mer-

edith did not have the energy to carry his analysis of the "new woman" to its rightful conclusion, opting instead for a conventional ending that satisfied popular taste.

Muendel, Renate. *George Meredith*. Boston: Twayne, 1986.
Concentrates discussion on the heroine, whom Muendel considers Meredith's version of the "new woman": independent, sexually attractive but not conscious of the fact, and high spirited. Judges the work essentially comic, but notes the many somber incidents spoiling the purely comic effect. Argues Meredith is primarily interested in achieving psychological realism in his portrait of Diana.

Sassoon, Siegfried. *Meredith*. London: Constable, 1948.
Considerable attention devoted to tracing parallels between Meredith's heroine and Mrs. Caroline Norton, the novelist on whom Meredith based his portrait of Diana. Shows how Meredith selects details from Mrs. Norton's life and how he fictionalizes other events in the story to give his heroine a distinctive personality.

Stevenson, Lionel. *The Ordeal of George Meredith: A Biography*. New York: Scribner's, 1953.
Extensive discussion of the composition process, focusing on Meredith's use of details from the life and personality of Mrs. Caroline Norton to create his heroine. Discusses problems Meredith had in delineating Diana, especially when he resorted to recasting factual information. Sees parallels between Diana and other women in Meredith's novels, noting the author is interested throughout in showing Diana's transgressions without having readers lose sympathy for her. Concludes with several favorable comments from Meredith's contemporaries.

Williams, Ioan, ed. *Meredith: The Critical Heritage*. New York: Barnes & Noble Books, 1971.
Reprints selections from eight reviews appearing in various influential British periodicals shortly after the novel was first published. Includes a notice by the poet Arthur Symons and a lengthy assessment of Meredith's claims to eminence by journalist and critic W. L. Courtney.

Wilt, Judith. *The Readable People of George Meredith*. Princeton, N.J.: Princeton University Press, 1975.
Noting Meredith's use of a heroine who is also a novelist, Wilt carefully examines the ways the author imagines four types of readers for his work: shallow-minded critics, egoistic realists bent on seeing the impurities of human nature exposed, primitive readers glibly accepting the romantic trappings,

and finally, civilized readers sharing the author's values. Believes that in the course of the novel, Diana comes to realize she has misread herself, mistaking the reaction to her behavior by an uncomprehending public for the truth.

Wright, Walter. *Art and Substance in George Meredith.* Lincoln: University of Nebraska Press, 1953.
   Describes Meredith's novel as the story of a woman's search for male companionship, her turning away from that aim and pursuing instead an independent life, and her discovery that happiness is possible in a relationship with a man. Believes that Meredith's chief interest lies in presenting Diana as a confused, inexperienced young woman struggling for her independence; considers the ending anticlimactic.

The Egoist

Beach, Joseph Warren. *The Comic Spirit in George Meredith: An Interpretation.* Reprint. New York: Russell & Russell, 1963.
   Detailed examination of the notion of Egoism; sketches the many guises in which the Egoist is found in society. Outlines ways Sir Willoughby is representative of the typical egoist, discussing his relationships with Laetitia Dale and Clara Middleton to highlight the failure of his world view. Finds the comic element of egoism in Sir Willoughby's extreme vanity and self-esteem.

Brownstein, Rachel. *Becoming a Heroine.* New York: Viking Press, 1982.
   Points out Meredith's sympathies with women and his belief that he was championing their cause in his fiction. Believes this novel reverses the traditional story of courtship by focusing on the undoing of an engagement and presenting a hero whose qualities resemble those of the heroine of traditional courtship stories. Attention given to describing the function of Mrs. Mountstuart Jenkins, meant to represent all women; her victory over Sir Willoughby suggests the triumph of all women over men consumed by egoism.

Calder, Jenni. "Insurrection." In her *Women and Marriage in Victorian Fiction.* New York: Oxford University Press, 1976.
   Notes Meredith's continuing attack on the upper classes, a theme he pursues through several novels. In this one, he is particularly concerned with attitudes toward property and with the notion that women are a necessary part of an aristocratic man's property. Claims the notion of egoism is two-sided: both Willoughby and Clara are egoists, the latter using her egoism to establish a sense of self allowing her to rebel against the conventions constraining her individuality. Briefly catalogs the major images vivifying the theme of the novel.

Goode, John. *"The Egoist*: Anatomy or Striptease?" In *Meredith Now: Some Critical Essays*, edited by Ian Fletcher. New York: Barnes & Noble Books, 1971.

Reviews the importance of egoism for Meredith and his contemporaries, citing examples of the term's specific meanings in the later years of the nineteenth century. Reads the novel as an attack on the philosophical and sociological system proposed by Auguste Comte. Discusses Meredith's use of comic elements as a means of exposing weaknesses in a social structure whose main representative is Willoughby; argues that, rather than offering an anatomy of such a character, Meredith simply exposes Willoughby's nature to readers so that they may dissociate themselves from him.

Gretton, Mary S. *The Writings and Life of George Meredith: A Centenary Study*. Cambridge, Mass.: Harvard University Press, 1926.

Posits the aim of the novel is to expose Egoism as a vice, especially when combined with sentimentalism. Claims Meredith uses comedy as a means to achieve this goal. Argues against the notion that Sir Willoughby is a type of all men subsumed by egoism. Presents evidence to show the novel is not Meredith's greatest work. Brief commentary on minor characters.

Karl, Frederick R. *A Reader's Guide to the Nineteenth-Century Novel*. New York: Farrar, Straus & Giroux, 1964.

Considers the novel Meredith's best; discusses the author's exploration of comedy as a means of social commentary. Concentrates on the relationship between Sir Willoughby Patterne and Clara Middleton; notes how Meredith uses the conventions of classical literature to amplify the significance of his story, thereby conferring on it a universal significance.

Lindsay, Jack. *George Meredith: His Life and Work*. London: Bodley Head, 1956.

Comments on the concentration of Meredith's vision of Egoism, noting how the novel directly and relentlessly exposes the nature and effects of such a condition. Labels Sir Willoughby an extreme example of the egoist, but also considers him a type of the bourgeois man, for whom Meredith had contempt. Surveys reviews by Meredith's contemporaries, most of whom admitted the power of the work even if they objected to the novelist's ideology.

Muendel, Renate. *George Meredith*. Boston: Twayne, 1986.

Outlines parallels between the novel and classical drama. Gives a brief synopsis of the plot. Notes Meredith's conscious attempts to give the work paradigmatic significance. Traces Sir Willoughby's character in detail, citing the subtle ways Meredith displays his aversion for the hero and the many undercurrents of cruelty in Willoughby's actions. Brief sketches of Clara, Laetitia, and other minor figures.

Phelps, Gilbert. *A Reader's Guide to Fifty British Novels, 1600-1900*. New York: Barnes & Noble Books, 1979.

Explains how the novel is an example of Meredith's theory that every man is driven by egoism and must struggle to conquer this character deficiency. Includes a good plot summary and brief critical commentary defending Meredith's artistry and command of his materials.

Polhemus, Robert M. "Meredith's *Egoist* (1879): The Comedy of Egoism." In his *Comic Faith: The Great Tradition from Austen to Joyce*. Chicago: University of Chicago Press, 1980.

Believes Meredith attempts to replace traditional Christian dogma with his notion of the Comic as a guide for living. In this novel, Meredith shows how egoism stands against the growing tendencies of feminism in society. Finds the works's strength in Meredith's use and exploration of various patterns that shape life while restricting individual freedom. Examines key scenes to demonstrate Meredith's attitudes toward feminism, toward the importance of appreciating nature, and toward love. Concludes with a careful analysis of style.

Sassoon, Siegfried. *Meredith*. London: Constable, 1948.

Claims that the novel is probably Meredith's greatest, the first in the style distinctly his own and the first to focus exclusively on character from the perspective Meredith outlined in his essay on the Comic Spirit. Considers Meredith's portrait of Sir Willoughby only partially comic, however; sees a strain of cruelty in the novelist's handling of his hero. Notes parallels between Willoughby and all men; also cites similarities between several minor characters and real-life acquaintances of Meredith.

Stevenson, Lionel. *The Ordeal of George Meredith: A Biography*. New York: Scribner's, 1953.

Identifies the central theme as an examination of the horrors of incompatibility between people. Sees Sir Willoughby exemplifying two traits Meredith particularly abhorred: egoism and sentimentalism. Discusses ways Meredith's presentation of Willoughby and Clara foreshadows modern psychological fiction; sees Meredith coming to realize many of society's problems stem from the denial of freedom to women. Sketches favorable critical reactions among Meredith's contemporaries.

Wheeler, Michael. "The Bower and the World: *The Egoist*." In his *The Art of Allusion in Victorian Fiction*. New York: Barnes & Noble, 1979.

In a study of the ways Victorian novelists use allusion, Wheeler describes how the technique reinforces the central contrast between the guarded bower of Patterne Hall and the world outside its confines. Sees Meredith using literary allusions to help define his characters. Special attention paid to the use of the myth of Diana as a means of adding resonance to the story.

Williams, Ioan, ed. *Meredith: The Critical Heritage*. New York: Barnes & Noble Books, 1971.
Selections from nine reviews, all generally favorable. Includes one by R. H. Hutton, two by W. H. Henley (a strong supporter of Meredith), and one by Margaret Oliphant. Also provides laudatory comments from poet James Thomson.

Wilt, Judith. *The Readable People of George Meredith*. Princeton, N.J.: Princeton University Press, 1975.
Argues that Meredith invites his readers to engage in an elaborate game of ferreting out the true nature of the egoist, thereby involving them in actions of the mind rather than in external circumstances. Separate sections focus on the impact of egoism on Clara Middleton, one of its victims, and on Sir Willoughby, whose psychological insecurity causes him to grasp at everything around him in an effort to possess it all. Also explores ways Meredith gets readers to sympathize with Willoughby while recognizing his weaknesses.

Wright, Walter. *Art and Substance in George Meredith*. Lincoln: University of Nebraska Press, 1953.
Stresses Meredith's technical mastery in presenting characters and interweaving symbols to give his story universal significance. Extensive analysis of Willoughby, displaying the foibles of egoism and contrasting his possessiveness with the desire of most characters, especially the women, to be free of constraints. Emphasizes Meredith's belief that marriage should be an adventure shared by two equals, not the retreat from life that Willoughby imagines.

Evan Harrington

Beach, Joseph Warren. *The Comic Spirit in George Meredith: An Interpretation*. Reprint. New York: Russell & Russell, 1963.
Links this novel with others of Meredith's mid-career as works dealing with the figure of the snob. Traces the adventures of Evan Harrington from his humble boyhood through his pretentious climb to a position of social respectability, highlighting ways Meredith pokes fun at the young man's behavior. Also notes how, by getting readers to sympathize with Evan, Meredith makes his hero a mirror for all people possessing a certain streak of snobbishness.

Gretton, Mary S. *The Writings and Life of George Meredith: A Centenary Study*. Cambridge, Mass.: Harvard University Press, 1926.
Brief commentary on Meredith's ability to create characters. Analysis of

Evan Harrington as a type of young man in whom Meredith sees great potential and great energy; events and other characters mold this potential for good
or for evil.

Lindsay, Jack. *George Meredith: His Life and Work*. London: Bodley Head, 1956.
Sketches Meredith's relationship with Janet Duff-Gordon, on whom the heroine of this novel is based. Discusses the publication history of the book,
including its serialization in *Once a Week*. Considers Meredith's chief aim to
be the exploration of the qualities of a true gentleman. Sees his portrait of the
Countess de Saldar the best sustained comic touch in the novel.

Muendel, Renate. *George Meredith*. Boston: Twayne, 1986.
Argues that this novel is more conventional than its immediate predecessor,
The Ordeal of Richard Feverel. Considers Meredith's chief concern to be the
impact of class distinctions on a sensitive, immature youth. Claims Meredith's
portrait of the upper classes is generally derogatory. Points out strong autobiographical influences.

Sassoon, Siegfried. *Meredith*. London: Constable, 1948.
Briefly traces the publication history. Records Sassoon's personal reaction to
the story. Outlines biographical influences, noting how Meredith uses incidents
and figures from his life quite freely in constructing this tale.

Stevenson, Lionel. *The Ordeal of George Meredith: A Biography*. New York:
Scribner's, 1953.
Details the composition and publication history, remarking on Meredith's difficulties with serial publication. Focuses on the autobiographical elements, especially Meredith's use of the Duff-Gordons and members of his own family
as models for the main characters. Notes similarities to *The Ordeal of Richard
Feverel*, citing Meredith's continuing interest in problems inherent in England's rigid social system. Includes a brief survey of reviews by Meredith's
contemporaries.

Tarratt, Margaret. " 'Snips,' 'Snobs,' and the 'True Gentleman' in *Evan Harrington*." In *Meredith Now: Some Critical Essays*, edited by Ian Fletcher. New
York: Barnes & Noble Books, 1971.
Examines the latent conflicts present in the novel, dramatized by Evan's dilemma of having to choose between settling family debts or trying to rise in
social stature. Sees Meredith's principal sources for his ideological framework
as Thomas Carlyle's *Sartor Resartus*, William Makepeace Thackeray's *The
Book of Snobs*, and contemporary writings on the nature of the gentleman.
Reviews the roles of the Great Mel and the Countess de Saldar in highlighting
the difficulties of adopting conventional ideas about social classes.

Tompkins, J. M. S. "On Re-reading *Evan Harrington*." In *Meredith Now: Some Critical Essays*, edited by Ian Fletcher. New York: Barnes & Noble Books, 1971.
Discusses the intricacy of plotting that characterizes this novel. Suggests the full impact of its complex patterning can be realized only upon re-reading. Examines characterization and plotting in detail to dispel earlier thesis-bound readings and to show the subtlety and skill with which Meredith handles his materials.

Williams, Ioan, ed. *Meredith: The Critical Heritage*. New York: Barnes & Noble Books, 1971.
Includes material from two reviews published in January, 1861. Both praise the work, but neither suggests it is a novel of lasting merit. The paucity of selections in this volume reflects the limited notice the book received from Meredith's contemporaries.

Wright, Walter. *Art and Substance in George Meredith*. Lincoln: University of Nebraska Press, 1953.
Brief examination of the characters in the novel, especially the hero, to show how Meredith handles the comic strain in his narrative. Considers Evan Harrington an average figure whose heroics and foibles are not distinguished from those of many others in his situation in life. Notes how Meredith pokes fun at pretentiousness and at those with illusions about their self-worth.

The Ordeal of Richard Feverel

Beach, Joseph Warren. "The Wiseacre." In his *The Comic Spirit in George Meredith: An Interpretation*. Reprint. New York: Russell & Russell, 1963.
Discusses Meredith's creation of a comic situation and comic characters, which are never fully realized because of the sober undercurrents affecting the novelist's portrayal. Richard becomes an engaging figure, more tragic than comic. Extensive commentary on Sir Austin's system and on the portraits of the women in the novel.

Calder, Jenni. "Sacrificial Marriage." In her *Women and Marriage in Victorian Fiction*. New York: Oxford University Press, 1976.
Argues that Meredith is generally sympathetic to women. Believes his interest in marriage is consistent and important in virtually all his fiction; it serves as a central issue in this novel where younger characters find themselves torn between a rigid system and individual choice. Considers Richard a flawed creation because he appears too naïve about the negative influence of his father's system on him.

Gretton, Mary S. *The Writings and Life of George Meredith: A Centenary Study.*
Cambridge, Mass.: Harvard University Press, 1926.
Rates the novel Meredith's finest, praising its spontaneity and its clear statement of the novelist's belief that intellect and freedom from systems are the
cornerstones of human development. Argues for the superiority of the much-
revised second edition over the one published in 1859. Briefly notes parallels
with real-life figures. Offers analysis of Sir Austin Feverel as a figure holding
attitudes Meredith rejects.

Karl, Frederick R. *A Reader's Guide to the Nineteenth Century Novel.* New York:
Farrar, Straus & Giroux, 1964.
Traces Meredith's reliance on the Comic Spirit and the foibles of egoism as
underlying principles for creating the characters in this novel, especially Sir
Austin Feverel. Outlines the way Meredith delineates Richard Feverel as a hero
in the tradition of Miguel de Cervantes and Molière.

Knoepflmacher, U. C. "The Intrusion of Tragedy: *The Ordeal of Richard Feverel*
and *The Mill on the Floss.*" In his *Laughter and Despair: Readings in Ten
Novels of the Victorian Era.* Berkeley: University of California Press, 1971.
Compares Meredith's novel with George Eliot's story of Maggie Tulliver to
display Meredith's method of handling the tragedy brought about by the conflict between generations. Believes Sir Austin deserves blame for his insistence
on raising his son according to the dictates of an abstract system. Justifies
Lucy's death at the end of the novel as the necessary consequence of Richard's
willful actions: rejecting his father and rebelling against him.

Lindsay, Jack. *George Meredith: His Life and Work.* London: Bodley Head, 1956.
Considers Meredith's treatment of the impact of Sir Austin's educational system to be representative of a larger problem the novelist sees in his class-
conscious society: the desire to impose arbitrary restrictions on individuals.
Argues that the alienating forces of egoism are the real target of Meredith's
attack; those who fight against egoism are champions of self-determination
and brotherhood. Cites the generally unfavorable reactions of Meredith's contemporaries and speculates on the effects of such criticism on subsequent
novels and poetry.

Mitchell, Juliet. "*The Ordeal of Richard Feverel*: A Sentimental Education." In
Meredith Now: Some Critical Essays, edited by Ian Fletcher. New York: Barnes
& Noble Books, 1971.
Emphasizes the significance of Sir Austin's system as a means of dealing with
women, whom the elder Feverel sees as evil influences in society. Considers
Meredith's treatment of Richard deliberately ironic, presenting him as a ro-
mantic hero but continually undercutting those romantic tendencies which

might provoke readers' sympathies. Traces the influence of Jean-Jacques Rousseau on Meredith's idea for Sir Austin's system.

Muendel, Renate. *George Meredith*. Boston: Twayne, 1986.
Provides a brief plot summary. Focuses on Meredith's interest in the interaction of characters and ideas; notes some of the autobiographical parallels in the work. Analyzes the major action, concentrating on the psychological realism of Meredith's portraits. Also offers abbreviated assessments of minor characters.

Sassoon, Siegfried. *Meredith*. London: Constable, 1948.
While noting the novel's enduring popularity, Sassoon points out several weaknesses which detract from the work's overall effect. Nevertheless, he cites the special power of Meredith's love story to capture readers' attention. Identifies parallels between Meredith and his hero; sees Lucy as a creation intended to be the antithesis of Meredith's first wife, who had deserted him.

Shaheen, Mohammad. *George Meredith: A Reappraisal of the Novels*. Totowa, N.J.: Barnes & Noble Books, 1981.
Argues that the vitality of the narrative derives from Meredith's efforts to distance himself from his personal ordeal by transferring his energies into his fiction. Treats Sir Austin very sympathetically, claiming his belief in human perfectibility leads him to hope his system will produce good results. Extensive discussion of the function of Adrian Harley and Lady Blandish as reflections of Sir Austin's system.

Stevenson, Lionel. *The Ordeal of George Meredith: A Biography*. New York: Scribner's, 1953.
Notes Meredith's experimentation with narrative technique that gives the work a heightened sense of realism. Briefly highlights parallels between the novel and William Shakespeare's *Romeo and Juliet*. Identifies real-life figures after whom various characters are modeled. Discusses the primacy Meredith attributes to nature over artificial conventions in determining how people's lives should be governed.

Stone, Donald D. *The Romantic Impulse in Victorian Fiction*. Cambridge, Mass.: Harvard University Press, 1980.
Brief assessment of Meredith's debt to the Romantic tradition as illustrated in this novel. Argues that both Sir Austin and Richard are Byronic figures, and their adoption of such a stance leads to their misfortune. Sees Lucy as a Wordsworthian character set against these two, forced to bear the burden of their mistakes. Considers this novel a form of self-criticism, as Meredith included some of his own characteristics in both Sir Austin and Richard.

Williams, Ioan, ed. *Meredith: The Critical Heritage*. New York: Barnes & Noble Books, 1971.
Excerpts from eight reviews, including one by nineteenth century novelist Geraldine Jewsbury. Most comment on Meredith's exceptionally difficult style, and see as the principal target of Meredith's attack the educational system by which Sir Austin proposes to rear his son.

Wilt, Judith. *The Readable People of George Meredith*. Princeton, N.J.: Princeton University Press, 1975.
Intriguing assessment of the way Meredith presents characters and themes. Focuses on the role of Adrian Harley; Wilt considers him a *ficelle*, acting as an intermediary for readers. Thus, readers gain much insight and form many judgments of other characters based on Harley's mediation: he observes, records, and comments sagely on the action, consistently applying the metaphor of drama to unfolding events.

Wright, Walter. *Art and Substance in George Meredith*. Lincoln: University of Nebraska Press, 1953.
Finds the strength of the novel in Meredith's psychological portrait of his hero: Richard's story, pastoral in nature and reminiscent of romance at times, is emblematic of the experiences of all young men growing to spiritual adulthood. Sees Richard's fall into error a result of both his father's wrongheadedness and Richard's association with a series of minor characters representing various forms of evil. Considers the novel a blend of comedy and tragedy.

WILLIAM MAKEPEACE THACKERAY

General Studies

Brander, Laurence. *Thackeray*. London: Longmans, Green. Rev. ed., 1964.
Useful introduction to Thackeray's life and career. Brief biographical sketch details key events that helped to shape Thackeray's fiction. Includes commentary on each of the major novels, noting Thackeray's continual concern for personal and domestic rather than political issues. Judges him a master stylist and the greatest literary portrait-painter of English society in his own century.

Collins, Philip, ed. *Thackeray: Interviews and Recollections*. 2 vols. New York: St. Martin's Press, 1983.
Excerpts from letters, memoirs, and published sources written by men and women who knew Thackeray personally or who were touched by him in some way during the years when he was one of England's premier living novelists. Provides excellent insight into Thackeray's career as well as revealing commentary on the novels by literary figures such as Thomas Carlyle, Robert and Elizabeth Barrett Browning, and Charles Dickens.

Dodds, John W. *Thackeray: A Critical Portrait*. Reprint. New York: Russell & Russell, 1963.
Intended primarily as a critical examination of Thackeray's ideology as exhibited in his works. Traces the growth of the novelist's ideas about society, especially as they are formed in his early fiction and essays. Separate chapters are devoted to examining the major novels; includes a discussion of *The Book of Snobs*, *The English Humourists*, *The Four Georges*, and other minor works.

Elwin, Malcolm. *Thackeray: A Personality*. Reprint. New York: Russell & Russell, 1966.
An early scholarly biography attempting to assess the character of the writer and to provide a comprehensive sketch of his career as a journalist and novelist. Integrates commentary on the major fiction into the biographical context. Contains a useful chronology of important events in Thackeray's life.

Grieg, J. Y. T. "Thackeray, a Novelist by Accident." In *From Jane Austen to Joseph Conrad*, edited by R. L. Rathburn and Martin Steinmann. Minneapolis: University of Minnesota Press, 1958.
Accounts for Thackeray's inability to retain readership during the past century. Argues he was a less serious and less committed novelist than contemporaries such as Charles Dickens and George Eliot; he really wanted to be an essayist. Points out problems created by his use of the intrusive narrator, especially in

Vanity Fair (in his commentary on *Amelia*). Also discusses his narrative method in *The Newcomes*.

Hardy, Barbara. *The Exposure of Luxury: Radical Themes in Thackeray*. Pittsburgh: University of Pittsburgh Press, 1972.
Concentrates on Thackeray's subject matter rather than on artistic techniques, looking closely at the novelist's social criticism. Examines the way topics such as class, economy, insincerity and artifice, fellowship and love attract Thackeray's attention and become objects of interest for him and hence for the reader. Argues that his novels give a more accurate social portrait of his times than do the works of Charles Dickens or George Eliot.

Levine, George. *The Realistic Imagination: English Fiction from Frankenstein to Lady Chatterly's Lover*. Chicago: University of Chicago Press, 1981.
Devotes two chapters to a discussion of Thackeray's concept of realism, followed by a chapter explaining how Thackeray's theory of art is exemplified in *Pendennis*. Discusses the way Thackeray employs various literary devices, especially the intrusive narrator, and his handling of perspective within his novels.

McMaster, Juliet. *Thackeray: The Major Novels*. Toronto: University of Toronto Press, 1971.
A study of Thackeray's fiction intended to answer criticism of his artistry, this book specifically addresses his care in constructing his works, his moral stance, his intellect, and his technical skills. Uses four novels to illustrate particular strengths of intellect and craftsmanship: *Vanity Fair*, *Henry Esmond*, *Pendennis*, *The Newcomes*.

_____ . "Thackeray's Things: Time's Local Habitation." In her *The Novel from Sterne to James: Essays on the Relation of Literature to Life*. Totowa, N.J.: Barnes & Noble Books, 1981.
Wide-ranging review of Thackeray's use of objects to create an image of the past and suggest its links with the present. Discusses his use of documents (such as letters and wills), gold objects, diamonds, buttons, hands, and garments as symbols, assigning certain values or ideas to these artifacts. Notes how Thackeray blurs the line between history and fiction.

Monsarrat, Ann. *An Uneasy Victorian: Thackeray the Man, 1811-1863*. New York: Dodd, Mead, 1980.
Highly readable biography that captures the essence of Thackeray's character. Stresses his relationships with others, especially the women in his life, to explain his particular brand of cynicism and melancholy. Includes commentary on his satires and on his major fiction.

Peters, Catherine. *Thackeray's Universe: Shifting Worlds of Imagination and Reality*. New York: Oxford University Press, 1987.
Taking her cue from Thackeray's descriptions of individuals as discrete and isolated beings, and of novelists as chroniclers of the real world, Peters examines the artist's life and his major fiction to discover ways Thackeray transformed these ideas into art. Strikes a careful balance between biographical readings of the works and consideration of the novels as objects of art.

Phillips, R. C. *The Language of Thackeray*. London: Andre Deutsch, 1978.
Scholarly examination of the language of Thackeray's fiction. Concentrates on the status of language in Regency England, a period about which Thackeray writes; includes chapters on patterns of speech and differences among classes, slang, grammar, dialect, and proper names. Studies the language of *Henry Esmond* in detail.

Praz, Mario. *The Hero in Eclipse in Victorian Fiction*, translated by Angus Davidson. New York: Oxford University Press, 1956.
Reviews Thackeray's career and his writings to explain why he is so cynical; shows that, despite his egoism and desire to expose Victorian cant and hypocrisy, Thackeray remains very conventional. Ultimately judges him to be bourgeois in temperament and a traditional moralist in his approach to fiction.

Rawlins, Jack P. *Thackeray's Novels: A Fiction that is True*. Berkeley: University of California Press, 1974.
Examines Thackeray's major novels to illuminate his reasons for rejecting the conventions of contemporary fiction and explores his struggle to provide some alternatives to these conventions in his work. Surveys Thackeray's narrative methods, focusing first on *Vanity Fair*, then concentrating on his criticism and early fiction to show how these become sources of his aesthetic vision. Concludes with discussions of *The Newcomes*, *Henry Esmond*, *The Virginians*, and *The Adventures of Philip*.

Ray, Gordon N. *Thackeray: The Uses of Adversity, 1811-1846*. New York: McGraw-Hill, 1955.
Detailed scholarly account of Thackeray's early life and writings, compiled from manuscript sources which Ray edited prior to working on this biography. Attempts to account for family and outside influences that shaped Thackeray's ideas about the nature of English society and caused him to adopt the profession of letters. Contains a discussion of the composition of early works, including *Vanity Fair*.

_____ . *Thackeray: The Age of Wisdom, 1847-1863*. New York: McGraw-Hill, 1957.

Second of two-volume scholarly biography based on Thackeray's letters and on unpublished sources. Concentrates on Thackeray's literary career after he had achieved fame with the publication of *Vanity Fair*. The major novels receive considerable attention, as do several of the author's minor writings. Detailed biographical information, especially regarding Thackeray's troubled personal life and his frustrating relationships with his invalid wife and with other women, some of whom he genuinely loved.

Russell, Frances. *Satire in the Victorian Novel*. Reprint. New York: Russell & Russell, 1964.
Scattered comments in this comprehensive analysis of satire in nineteenth century literature give a sense of Thackeray's aims and techniques in holding up contemporary society to criticism. Examines his use of the romantic tradition and his handling of realism, especially in *Vanity Fair*; also discusses Thackeray's selection of the Snob as a type deserving satiric treatment.

Stevenson, Lionel. *The Showman of Vanity Fair: The Life of William Makepeace Thackeray*. New York: Charles Scribner's Sons, 1947.
Carefully researched, lively account of Thackeray's life. Excellent chapters on the early years; good accounts of Thackeray's married life with Isabella Shawe and his later affair with Jane Brookfield. Analysis of Thackeray's fiction is interspersed within the biographical narrative; particularly useful for understanding relationships between the novelist's life and his fiction.

_____ . "William Makepeace Thackeray." In *Victorian Fiction: A Guide to Research*, edited by Lionel Stevenson. Cambridge, Mass.: Harvard University Press, 1964.
Bibliographical essay summarizing significant scholarship published before 1962 on Thackeray's life and on the major novels. Also contains valuable information on other bibliographies, editions, and collections of manuscripts and letters.

Sutherland, J. A. *Thackeray at Work*. London: Athlone Press, 1974.
Focuses on Thackeray's method of composition, which many earlier critics cited as the cause for all that is wrong with the novels. Provides detailed assessments of specific passages from various novels to illustrate faults and strengths of Thackeray's inventiveness, his social vision, his transformation of autobiography into fiction, and his handling of serial publication.

Tillotson, Geoffrey. *Thackeray the Novelist*. Cambridge, England: Cambridge University Press, 1954.
Reviews the major novels to demonstrate what Tillotson believes is an essen-

tial unity to the corpus of Thackeray's fiction. Individual chapters explore the similarities among materials Thackeray uses in his works, the oneness of the form and style of his novels, the use of authorial intrusion, and the commitment of the novelist to the tenets of realism in presenting character and action. Also discusses the ideology underlying the works, and includes two appendixes providing information on Thackeray's friendships and his influence on George Eliot and Henry James.

Tillotson, Geoffrey, and Donald Hawes, eds. *Thackeray: The Critical Heritage*. New York: Barnes & Noble Books, 1968.
Collection of reviews and excerpts from published commentaries and letters recording the critical response of Thackeray's contemporaries to each of his major works. Fifty-six selections offer useful insight into nineteenth century attitudes toward the Thackeray canon. Includes general assessments of Thackeray's achievements published at various stages of his career.

Welsh, Alexander, ed. *Thackeray: A Collection of Critical Essays*. Englewood Cliffs, N.J.: Prentice-Hall, 1968.
Excerpts from thirteen previously published articles and books provide a general assessment of Thackeray's artistry and focus on specific texts which demonstrate his skills. Includes comments on Thackeray's irony and on his social criticism, remarks on his tendency to adopt a preacher's stance, a discussion of his use of neoclassical conventions, and brief analyses of *Vanity Fair, Henry Esmond, The Newcomes*, and *The Adventures of Philip*.

Wheatley, James H. *Patterns in Thackeray's Fiction*. Cambridge, Mass.: MIT Press, 1969.
Views Thackeray's work both as a product of his life and as an artistic artifact. Concentrates on Thackeray as a parodist, who first mastered that form, then gradually evolved into a moralist. Preliminary chapters focus on the early work, followed by an extensive discussion of *Vanity Fair*. Concluding chapters discuss the techniques Thackeray employs in his later fiction to comment on human nature, especially on the sense of self.

Williams, Merryn. "The Male Image of Women." In her *Women in the English Novel, 1800-1900*. New York: St. Martin's Press, 1984.
Defends Thackeray against charges by his contemporaries that he was unjust toward women in his novels. Cites examples of the novelist trying to create women who could be strong; believes he sympathized with women relegated to a bleak existence by bad marriages or family dictates.

The History of Henry Esmond

Dodds, John W. *Thackeray: A Critical Portrait*. Reprint. New York: Russell &
    Russell, 1963.
    Argues that the novel is Thackeray's most artfully constructed, and is tradi-
    tionally admired by readers and critics. Outlines Thackeray's use of historical
    materials and his ability to re-create the ambience of the eighteenth century.
    Discusses Henry Esmond in detail, showing how his heroic strain is undercut
    by hints of his dreary nature; also sketches Thackeray's handling of Rachel,
    Lady Castlewood, whose relationship with Esmond is perplexing. Concludes
    with an analysis of Thackeray's style.

Elwin, Malcolm. *Thackeray: A Personality*. Reprint. New York: Russell & Russell,
    1966.
    Abbreviated discussion of the composition of the novel, noting reasons for
    Thackeray's decision to issue it as a single book rather than in monthly install-
    ments. Traces its somber qualities to personal events in the novelist's life. Also
    provides information on financial arrangements for publication made with
    George Smith, Thackeray's publisher.

Ennis, Lambert. *Thackeray: The Sentimental Cynic*. Evanston, Ill.: Northwestern
    University Press, 1950.
    Points out the many parallels between the fiction and Thackeray's real-life
    relationship with the Brookfields, especially Jane, whom he loved. Argues
    Thackeray is less interested in the precise external relationship between a man
    and woman than he is in the psychological bond that joins them. Explores the
    way the novelist's unconscious desires for Jane Brookfield are satisfied in the
    death of Lord Castlewood and in Esmond's eventual marriage to Lady
    Castlewood.

Lukacs, Georg. "*Henry Esmond* as Historical Novel." In *Thackeray: A Collection of
    Critical Essays*, edited by Alexander Welsh. Englewood Cliffs, N.J.: Prentice-
    Hall, Inc., 1968.
    Excerpts from Lukacs' influential study, *The Historical Novel* (1962), describe
    Thackeray's ability to handle historical materials. Compares his treatment of
    the eighteenth century with that of Sir Walter Scott to illustrate how Thackeray
    concentrates less on the historical background than on the specific personages
    in whom he is interested. Considers Thackeray less true to documented facts
    than other historical novelists, but accurate in his psychological portraits of
    characters.

McMaster, Juliet. *Thackeray: The Major Novels*. Toronto: University of Toronto
    Press, 1971.

Sees Thackeray deliberately creating a double focus in the novel: one can view Esmond as a hero who possesses admirable virtues, or one may read his story ironically, finding that he tries too hard to convince readers of his goodness. Extensive analysis of Esmond's love affair with Rachel, providing evidence that Rachel loves him long before he recognizes his feelings for her. Offers a caution about interpretation: Thackeray's decision to have Esmond tell his own story in the third person introduces deliberate ambiguities.

Monsarrat, Ann. *An Uneasy Victorian: Thackeray the Man, 1811-1863*. New York: Dodd, Mead, 1980.

Calls the novel Thackeray's most complex and most carefully constructed. Praises the novelist's scholarship and his ability to evoke the eighteenth century milieu, but finds the real strength of the work in the love triangle of Henry, Lady Castlewood, and Beatrix; considers Thackeray's characterization particularly effective.

Peters, Catherine. *Thackeray's Universe: Shifting Worlds of Imagination and Reality*. New York: Oxford University Press, 1987.

Claims Thackeray intended this work to raise the level of respectability of the historical novel using Sir Walter Scott as his model. Discusses its composition and publication, and Thackeray's attempts to give it an eighteenth century flavor through dialect, spelling, and typography. Extensive analysis of Henry Esmond, who has many Victorian attributes. Careful examination of Esmond's feelings for both Beatrix and Rachel, Lady Castlewood. Argues that the plot is built on a succession of secrets revealed as the action progresses.

Phillips, R. C. *The Language of Thackeray*. London: Andre Deutsch, 1978.

Detailed analysis of the way Thackeray uses words and phrases to evoke the sense of the eighteenth century, the period in which the novel is set. Displays the naturalness of the idioms employed by the novelist, noting ways he adapts or explains archaic expressions for his contemporary readers.

Ray, Gordon N. *Thackeray: The Age of Wisdom, 1847-1863*. New York: McGraw-Hill, 1957.

Considers the novel Thackeray's finest artistic achievement; cites his aims in creating a story to answer critics' charges that he was too cynical and too haphazard. Discusses the work as an example of historical fiction and as a record of Thackeray's heartbreaking affair with Jane Brookfield. Extensive examination of Lady Castlewood. Reviews reactions by Thackeray's contemporaries, especially commentary on Lady Castlewood's unusual love for Esmond.

Stevenson, Lionel. *The Showman of Vanity Fair: The Life of William Makepeace Thackeray*. New York: Charles Scribner's Sons, 1947.

Recounts Thackeray's attempts to achieve historical veracity in the book, noting his work with eighteenth century publications and manuscripts. Also describes his efforts to pattern his heroine, Lady Castlewood, after Jane Brookfield.

Sutherland, J. A. "*Henry Esmond*: The Virtues of Carelessness." In his *Thackeray at Work*. London: Athlone Press, 1974.
Argues against those who claim Thackeray was a careful craftsman in shaping and revising this story. Proves from manuscript evidence that the novelist improvised as he wrote, altering scenes only slightly and introducing new motives and actions to account for changes in characters rather than recasting earlier sections of his manuscript. Credit's Thackeray's ability to improvise as the faculty permitting him to produce a novel that gives the appearance of overall unity.

Tilford, John E. "The Love Theme of *Henry Esmond*." In *Thackeray: A Collection of Critical Essays*, edited by Alexander Welsh. Englewood Cliffs, N.J.: Prentice-Hall, Inc., 1968.
A careful examination of Thackeray's methods of handling the relationship between Henry Esmond and Rachel, Lady Castlewood. Details the many hints and references which prepare the careful reader for the eventual marriage of this unlikely couple. Discusses the various problems Thackeray had with the intriguing affair: technical difficulties arising from the fact that Rachel's feelings had to be made apparent to readers but not to Esmond (Thackeray's narrator), and moral difficulties stemming from Rachel's avowed position as Esmond's surrogate mother had to be treated delicately.

Tillotson, Geoffrey, and Donald Hawes, eds. *Thackeray: The Critical Heritage*. New York: Barnes & Noble Books, 1968.
Seven excerpts from works by Thackeray's contemporaries. Includes comments from four British and one American periodical. Generally favorable assessments by critics George Brimley and George Henry Lewes are balanced by the harsher judgment of John Forster. A brief denunciation by George Eliot stands in contrast to Anthony Trollope's lengthy encomium from his 1879 study of the novelist.

The History of Pendennis

Dodds, John W. *Thackeray: A Critical Portrait*. Reprint. New York: Russell & Russell, 1963.
Reviews the conditions under which Thackeray wrote this novel. Calls it his most autobiographical, in that Arthur Pendennis possesses many of the character strengths and weaknesses of Thackeray himself. Extensive discussion of Pendennis' activities and motives; also includes details of the function of other

characters. Judges the novel a fair representation of everyday life, holding readers' interest because characters engage their sympathies.

Elwin, Malcolm. *Thackeray: A Personality*. Reprint. New York: Russell & Russell, 1966.
Brief comments about the composition of the novel and about Thackeray's use of autobiographical materials are scattered throughout this study of the novelist's career. Includes remarks on the illness seriously affecting Thackeray while he was writing the book.

Ennis, Lambert. *Thackeray: The Sentimental Cynic*. Evanston, Ill.: Northwestern University Press, 1950.
Biographical reading of the novel, citing ways the fiction parallels Thackeray's personal life, especially the conflict he experienced over having to balance his affection for his mother with his feeling for Jane Brookfield, whom he loved dearly. Sees Helen Pendennis modeled clearly after Thackeray's mother, and Arthur Pendennis as a close alter ego of the novelist.

Levine, George. "*Pendennis*: The Virtue of the Dilettante's Unbelief." In his *The Realistic Imagination: English Fiction from Frankenstein to Lady Chatterly's Lover*. Chicago: University of Chicago Press, 1981.
Considers the novel an excellent example of the way Thackeray deflates the conventions of the novel of his day. Extensive discussion of the hero, Arthur Pendennis, showing how he remains cynical and disengaged almost all the time—characteristics of the dilettante, a figure of growing importance in both literature and society as the century progressed.

McMaster, Juliet. *Thackeray: The Major Novels*. Toronto: University of Toronto Press, 1971.
Stresses the many tensions existing in the lives of Thackeray's characters, whose ambivalences reflect their creator's attitudes about life. Sees this novel exploring a man's struggle to live decently amid such tensions, and simultaneously analyzing the artist's struggle to portray such a life. Lengthy analysis of Arthur Pendennis' efforts to separate illusion from reality, to come to grips with the significance of experience itself, and to make that experience intelligible to himself and others.

Monsarrat, Ann. *An Uneasy Victorian: Thackeray the Man, 1811-1863*. New York: Dodd, Mead, 1980.
Demonstrates the way serial publication led Thackeray to modify his narrative in response to public outcry against certain opinions and attitudes. Traces autobiographical connections, noting especially how the novelist's feelings for Jane Brookfield influenced the tale. Also discusses how Thackeray's serious illness affected the composition of the monthly numbers.

Peters, Catherine. *Thackeray's Universe: Shifting Worlds of Imagination and Reality*.
New York: Oxford University Press, 1987.
Outlines parallels between Arthur Pendennis and Thackeray, and between
George Warrington and the author. Posits that Thackeray is interested in moral
rather than social issues, and is frustrated by Victorian conventions forcing him
to deal with some problems indirectly. Extensive discussion of the relationship
between Thackeray and Jane Brookfield, a liaison on which he based his
portrait of the heroine, Laura, and several incidents in the book. Explains how
Thackeray's serious illness caused problems in composition.

Phelps, Gilbert. *A Reader's Guide to Fifty British Novels, 1600-1900*. New York:
Barnes & Noble Books, 1979.
Brief summary of Thackeray's method of composition for this novel, followed
by a plot synopsis clarifying the major events in the work. Critical comments
focus on Thackeray's attempt to imitate Henry Fielding's *Tom Jones*, and his
failure to create strongly defined characters.

Rawlins, Jack P. *Thackeray's Novels: A Fiction that is True*. Berkeley: University of
California Press, 1974.
Briefly compares the novel to others in the Thackeray canon, especially *Vanity
Fair* and *The Adventures of Philip*. Argues that Thackeray intended the novel
as an answer to charges of cynicism leveled against him by reviewers of *Vanity
Fair*, but contends that he does not really side with either idealists or cynics.
Evidence that life is ultimately without real significance abounds in the work,
but readers' sympathies go out to characters who prefer idealism.

Ray, Gordon N. *Thackeray: The Age of Wisdom, 1847-1863*. New York: McGraw-
Hill, 1957.
Posits that Thackeray's central aim is to show his hero torn between upholding
domestic virtues and succumbing to the world's temptations. Notes how heavily Thackeray draws on his own experiences for subjects and for elements of
characterization, especially for his portrayal of the literary life. Argues that
Thackeray's illness, which prevented completion of several monthly installments of the work, also affected the overall tone and made the ending less
congenial. Sees this novel offering Thackeray's strongest protest against Victorian prudery.

Stevenson, Lionel. *The Showman of Vanity Fair: The Life of William Makepeace
Thackeray*. New York: Charles Scribner's Sons, 1947.
Describes the distressing personal conditions under which Thackeray wrote the
monthly numbers of this work: his serious illness, which interrupted the regu-
lar issue of the installments, and his growing agitation over his feelings for
Jane Brookfield. Sparse critical commentary on the work itself.

Sutherland, J. A. *"Pendennis*: The Two Thackerays and the Limits of Autobiographical Fiction." In his *Thackeray at Work*. London: Athlone Press, 1974.
Analyzes chapter 41, an exchange between Arthur Pendennis and George
Warrington, to explore Thackeray's attitudes about the use of autobiographical
fiction. In this chapter the two characters, both alter egos for Thackeray,
discuss the propriety of publishing another character's autobiography. Sutherland sees Thackeray vacillating between the realism achieved by using one's
own life as a source and the pain such exposure can cause.

Tillotson, Geoffrey, and Donald Hawes, eds. *Thackeray: The Critical Heritage*.
New York: Barnes & Noble Books, 1968.
Reprints excerpts from eight documents giving insight into nineteenth century
attitudes toward the novel. Includes Thackeray's preface, in which he laments
the strictness prohibiting frank treatment of certain subjects, a comparison of
the novel with *David Copperfield* by the eminent scholar David Masson, and
George Henry Lewes' favorable review.

Wheatley, James H. *Patterns in Thackeray's Fiction*. Cambridge, Mass.: MIT Press,
1969.
Concentrates on the early portion of the novel, specifically Arthur Pendennis' first love affair, to show Thackeray's great interest in the relationship
between the self and the roles one is forced to play—or chooses to adopt—in
society. Concludes that Thackeray saw the need for forms in shaping individuals, but feared the individual's loss of self if conventions replaced genuine
feelings.

The Newcomes

Dodds, John W. *Thackeray: A Critical Portrait*. Reprint. New York: Russell &
Russell, 1963.
Brief comments on the composition of the novel are followed by remarks on
the scope of Thackeray's vision, his use of characters from previous works,
and his handling of personal reminiscence in the narrative. Provides a brief
summary of major events. Defends Thackeray against charges that he cannot
deal with great issues by emphasizing the fineness of his observations and his
ability to delineate subtleties of character. Extensive discussion of Ethel Newcome as Thackeray's greatest heroine.

Elwin, Malcolm. *Thackeray: A Personality*. Reprint. New York: Russell & Russell,
1966.
Comments on the composition of the monthly installments of this serially
published novel are interspersed in the biographical narrative. Brief discus-

sion of the travels Thackeray planned as a means of gathering materials for the work.

Ennis, Lambert. *Thackeray: The Sentimental Cynic*. Evanston, Ill.: Northwestern University Press, 1950.
Brief remarks on ways Thackeray mined his personal experiences, especially his relationships with the women in his life, for characters and incidents in this novel. Also notes parallels between Clive Newcome and Thackeray, and between Clive and Thackeray's artist friends John Leech and John Everett Millais.

McMaster, Juliet. *Thackeray: The Major Novels*. Toronto: University of Toronto Press, 1971.
Argues against the conventional view that the novel is loosely structured. Sees Thackeray developing his story slowly and, through the various stories of the Newcome family and their associates, presenting his major theme: the pervasiveness of money in modern society and its ability to confer respectability. Examines imagery and characterization, concentrating on Ethel and Clive, to demonstrate Thackeray's mastery of literary technique.

Monsarrat, Ann. *An Uneasy Victorian: Thackeray the Man, 1811-1863*. New York: Dodd, Mead, 1980.
Notes Thackeray's decision to retreat from the controversial subjects that characterized *Henry Esmond*, but outlines the sweeping review of hypocrisy in contemporary London society Thackeray presents in this serialized novel. Argues that the story was carefully planned, and displays Thackeray's range of characterization. Briefly sketches the furor the novel caused in America because of a casual unflattering remark about the American Revolution.

Peters, Catherine. *Thackeray's Universe: Shifting Worlds of Imagination and Reality*. New York: Oxford University Press, 1987.
Discusses Thackeray's major concerns in the novel: an examination of the idea of a gentleman, and a comprehensive survey of middle-class Victorian society—especially its attitudes toward marriage. Extensive analysis of Colonel Newcome and the two female heroines, Ethel Newcome and Rosey Mackenzie.

Rawlins, Jack P. *Thackeray's Novels: A Fiction that is True*. Berkeley: University of California Press, 1974.
Uses this novel as a principal example of the ways Thackeray creates the illusion of reality by carefully representing some details while omitting many other pieces of information readers normally expect in novels. Finds Thackeray is not a conventional realist; nonetheless, he creates an illusion of the real

world. Points out many conscious violations of readers' expectations regarding plot, causation, and chronology.

Ray, Gordon N. *Thackeray: The Age of Wisdom, 1847-1863*. New York: McGraw-Hill, 1957.

Remarks on Thackeray's travels to Paris and Rome while writing the monthly numbers. Extensive discussion of the major theme: an examination of respectability in Victorian society. Comments on Colonel Newcome, whom Ray considers one of Thackeray's greatest creations; through this figure Thackeray shows how human dignity is best seen in those who suffer and are defeated in some way. Also discusses the novelist's attack on social conventions that stifle individual growth.

Stevenson, Lionel. *The Showman of Vanity Fair: The Life of William Makepeace Thackeray*. New York: Charles Scribner's Sons, 1947.

Traces Thackeray's composition of monthly installments from the novel's inception; focuses on the genesis of the work in Thackeray's mind, noting his conscious use of autobiographical materials. Recounts the furor among American readers caused by a casual remark about the worthiness of the American Revolution. Brief remarks on the reaction by some of the novelist's contemporaries.

Sutherland, J. A. "*The Newcomes*: The Well Planned Baggy Monster." In his *Thackeray at Work*. London: Athlone Press, 1974.

Observes the paradoxical nature of the novel: despite Thackeray's written plan (something he did not have for other works), the narrative seems to wander. Finds the real genius emerging from unplanned scenes; sees one exception in the death of Colonel Newcome, a sketch discussed in detail to show Thackeray's ability to create emotional reactions and evoke sympathy.

Tillotson, Geoffrey, and Donald Hawes, eds. *Thackeray: The Critical Heritage*. New York: Barnes & Noble Books, 1968.

Reprints two of the author's addresses to the reader that show Thackeray's consciousness of his method, and excerpts from five reviews by nineteenth century critics in influential British periodicals published shortly after the novel was completed.

Wheatley, James H. *Patterns in Thackeray's Fiction*. Cambridge, Mass.: MIT Press, 1969.

In a study of the way Thackeray explores various means through which individuals achieve self-expression, Wheatley gives significant attention to Colonel Newcome as a Quixotic figure with grand desires. Traces his career through the novel as he influences the lives of other characters. Posits Thackeray believed in the need for such Quixotic idealism in his own day.

Vanity Fair

Craig, G. Armour. "On the Style of *Vanity Fair*." In *Thackeray: A Collection of Critical Essays*, edited by Alexander Welsh. Englewood Cliffs, N.J.: Prentice-Hall, 1968.
   Concentrates on the crucial scene in which Becky and Lord Steyne are discovered by Rawdon, to show that in moments of moral crisis Thackeray intentionally abandons his lucid style and becomes deliberately obscure. Readers cannot be certain Becky is really guilty because Thackeray preserves the impression that she is a complex manipulator of others.

Dodds, John W. *Thackeray: A Critical Portrait*. Reprint. New York: Russell & Russell, 1963.
   Extensive analysis of Thackeray's aims and methods. Argues that his primary concern is for his characters, from whom plot emerges naturally. Stresses the realism of Thackeray's portrait of life, both in its links to the nineteenth century and in its parallels with human conduct in all ages. Considerable attention given to each of the major figures, and to the ways Thackeray achieves his ironic stance in portraying character and action.

Elwin, Malcolm. *Thackeray: A Personality*. Reprint. New York: Russell & Russell, 1966.
   Provides information on the reaction of Thackeray's contemporaries to the monthly installments, noting the novel's growing reputation among members of the literary elite. Discusses the scandal caused by Charlotte Brontë's dedication of the second edition of *Jane Eyre* to Thackeray; though spurred only by her admiration for *Vanity Fair*, some thought a personal relationship with Thackeray gave her inspiration for characters in her novel.

Ennis, Lambert. *Thackeray: The Sentimental Cynic*. Evanston, Ill.: Northwestern University Press, 1950.
   Traces in detail the biographical influences on Thackeray's characterizations. Points out similarities between Amelia and Mrs. Jane Brookfield, whom Thackeray loved; posits that George Osborne's death is the author's psychological compensation for not being able to eliminate Jane's husband. Also sees parallels between Thackeray and Dobbin, who eventually wins Amelia. On the other hand, Ennis finds Becky Sharp an original creation, drawn from many sources; provides extensive analysis of her role in the work.

Karl, Frederick R. *A Reader's Guide to the Nineteenth-Century Novel*. New York: Farrar, Straus & Giroux, 1964.
   Posits that the novel is Thackeray's exposé of snobbery and vanity in all its forms; discusses the novelist's definition of the gentleman, who is invariably vain. Notes the importance of Thackeray's moral stance throughout the work.

Knoepflmacher, U. C. *"Vanity Fair:* The Bitterness of Retrospection." In his *Laughter and Despair: Readings in Ten Novels of the Victorian Era.* Berkeley: University of California Press, 1971.
Discusses Thackeray's aim—to explore a world where illusion is paramount. Considers the effect of serial publication on initial readers. Extensive analysis of Becky, Amelia, and Dobbin shows how every character is motivated by either greed or love. Sees Thackeray vacillating between satire and sentimentality in handling his characters. Some discussion of the symbolic presentation of the world as a kind of Vanity Fair where even the good characters are motivated by self-interest.

McMaster, Juliet. *Thackeray: The Major Novels.* Toronto: University of Toronto Press, 1971.
Extensive analysis of Thackeray's use of the intrusive narrator as a means of involving readers in the life of the novel. Argues that through effective use of irony, burlesque, the mock-heroic, and similar devices, Thackeray presents a story and characters at once illusory yet believable. Notes ways he distances himself from his characters and allows certain ambiguities to remain, strengthening similarities to real life. Also points out parallels between this novel and the work of Laurence Sterne.

Monsarrat, Ann. *An Uneasy Victorian: Thackeray the Man, 1811-1863.* New York: Dodd, Mead, 1980.
Concentrates on details surrounding the novel's publication in monthly installments and the growing critical acclaim it received in literary circles and high society. Explains how Thackeray promoted his work, seeing it as a way to establish himself as a prominent writer. Notes the modest financial success the work enjoyed, despite the high praise it received.

Peters, Catherine. *Thackeray's Universe: Shifting Worlds of Imagination and Reality.* New York: Oxford University Press, 1987.
Discusses two targets of Thackeray's ironic narrative: Carlylean heroism and Romanticism. Argues that Thackeray undercuts conventional moral judgments of good and evil through the use of a dual perspective which creates ambiguities. Extensive analysis of Becky and Amelia, pointing out parallels between these characters and various women Thackeray knew. Examines the illustrations to show how they reinforce or work against the text.

Phelps, Gilbert. *A Reader's Guide to Fifty British Novels, 1600-1900.* New York: Barnes & Noble Books, 1979.
Brief summary of Thackeray's early career; points out parallels between this novel and John Bunyan's *Pilgrim's Progress.* A plot summary highlights sim-

ilarities between Becky and Amelia. Lengthy critical commentary explains the
allegorical nature of the work and demonstrates how Thackeray modifies devices of the realistic novelist to serve his thematic purposes.

Polhemus, Robert M. "Thackeray's *Vanity Fair* (1847-48): The Comedy of Shifting
Perspectives." In his *Comic Faith: The Great Tradition from Austen to Joyce.*
Chicago: University of Chicago Press, 1980.
Exhaustive analysis of Thackeray's aims; judges the work epic in scope and
considers it an attempt to unsettle readers through a series of contrasts that
give the book dramatic tension. Excellent commentary on Becky and Amelia.
Discusses Thackeray's narrative techniques, his handling of space and time,
and his insistence that all men are insignificant and doomed to a common
fate—making the pursuit of possessions and distinctions all vain. Penetrating
analysis of Thackeray's style.

Rawlins, Jack P. *Thackeray's Novels: A Fiction that is True.* Berkeley: University of
California Press, 1974.
Analyzes the work using terms from three different generic modes of presentation: drama, apologue (or moral fable), and satire. Shows how, despite similarities to each of these popular forms of fiction, the novel ultimately does not
fit neatly in any of these categories. Concludes that Thackeray consciously
interweaves all three genres to achieve a realistic portrait of life.

Ray, Gordon N. *Thackeray: The Uses of Adversity, 1811-1846.* New York: McGraw-
Hill, 1955.
Outlines the composition of the novel and Thackeray's growing awareness of
the potential the book had as a portrait both of his age and of the universal
human experience. Stresses the radical nature of the work as it appeared to
contemporaries: its heavy reliance on realism and its lack of a discernible hero.
Discusses Thackeray's mastery of stylistic devices and his understanding of the
foibles of English society. Notes how the novelist uses his characters to explore
virtually every facet of middle-class society and to comment on the weaknesses of the upper classes. Concludes with a discussion of the novel's impact
on Thackeray's contemporaries.

Stevenson, Lionel. *The Showman of Vanity Fair: The Life of William Makepeace
Thackeray.* New York: Charles Scribner's Sons, 1947.
Offers extensive details of Thackeray's trials in completing the novel, especially in his manipulation of the details of serial publication. Commentary
on the novel itself is limited to scattered observations on Thackeray's handling
of characterization and plotting, largely in response to pressure from his
readers.

Sundell, M. G. *Twentieth Century Interpretations of Vanity Fair*. Englewood Cliffs, N.J.: Prentice-Hall, 1969.
Selections from fourteen previously published studies of the novel. Six offer general critical assessments, eight concentrate on issues such as Thackeray's methods of characterization, his use of an intrusive narrator, his view of life as exhibited in the book, and his debt to the picaresque tradition. One essay notes subtle parallels between *Vanity Fair* and St. Augustine's *The City of God*.

Sutherland, J. A. "*Vanity Fair*: The Art of Improvisation." In *Thackeray at Work*. London: Athlone Press, 1974.
Examines an individual scene, a complete monthly installment, a group of installments, and finally Thackeray's handling of time throughout the novel to determine how much of the final text is the result of careful planning and how much is the product of spontaneous invention. Discusses the significance of Thackeray's additions, highlighting the notion that all of his characters live in a kind of Vanity Fair. Concludes that the novelist worked best when not cramped by strict adherence to rigid chronology.

Tillotson, Geoffrey, and Donald Hawes, eds. *Thackeray: The Critical Heritage*. New York: Barnes & Noble Books, 1968.
Eight selections from contemporary documents record the reaction of influential Victorians to Thackeray's first major work of fiction. Includes an excerpt from a review by John Forster, Dickens' biographer and no friend of Thackeray; passages from two letters by Charlotte Brontë; comments from Robert Bell's favorable review in *Fraser's* and Thackeray's letter thanking Bell for the notice; and two comments by John Ruskin on the death of George Osborne.

Tillotson, Kathleen. *Novels of the Eighteen Forties*. Oxford, England: Clarendon Press, 1954.
Sees this novel as Thackeray's attempt to avoid the conventions of contemporary novels, to portray characters and situations realistically, and to avoid the creation of traditional heroes and heroines. Analyzes the importance of the intrusive narrator, who is simultaneously moralist and satirist.

Wheatley, James H. *Patterns in Thackeray's Fiction*. Cambridge, Mass.: MIT Press, 1969.
Two chapters provide extensive analysis of Thackeray's treatment of the development of the concept of self. Sees him constantly torn between satire and realism in his portraits of complex characters. Examines the techniques that involve or distance his readers. Believes Thackeray wants to create a recognizable pattern of events, as a moralist would do, but he constantly recognizes the psychological complexities involved in any attempt at self-

expression; hence, he undercuts any generalizations by consciously introducing ambiguity.

The Virginians

Dodds, John W. *Thackeray: A Critical Portrait*. Reprint. New York: Russell & Russell, 1963.

Comments on Thackeray's inspiration for the novel and on his difficulties in composition. Brief synopsis of the major action, with some assessment of Thackeray's handling of historical figures and his techniques for creating fictional personages in the work. Judges the novel inferior to its predecessors in the canon of Thackeray's fiction.

Elwin, Malcolm. *Thackeray: A Personality*. Reprint. New York: Russell & Russell, 1966.

Briefly traces the composition of the monthly installments, noting Thackeray's habit of working in fits and starts, often waiting until his deadline for publication before dashing off the next part of the work. Attributes the novel's uneven qualities to this habit.

Ennis, Lambert. *Thackeray: The Sentimental Cynic*. Evanston, Ill.: Northwestern University Press, 1950.

Examines causes for this novel's weaknesses; finds evidence in Thackeray's personal life to suggest that both physical and psychological infirmity lay at the root of his failure to create a masterpiece. Points out parallels between characters in the work and Thackeray's various acquaintances.

Monsarrat, Ann. *An Uneasy Victorian: Thackeray the Man, 1811-1863*. New York: Dodd, Mead, 1980.

Outlines Thackeray's aims for the novel, seeing him interested in treating American and British attitudes evenhandedly and displaying both the good and the evil of the two societies. Argues that Thackeray never gained complete control over his story, but that his resurrection of Beatrix from *Henry Esmond* as the Baroness Bernstein is a stroke of genius.

Peters, Catherine. *Thackeray's Universe: Shifting Worlds of Imagination and Reality*. New York: Oxford University Press, 1987.

Highly critical commentary, claiming the work is formless and without any inventiveness or creative spark. Sees unrealized potential in Thackeray's use of two heroes—a variation on his usual pattern of focusing on two heroines. Finds him stating his positions on moral questions rather than dramatizing them through the narrative.

Rawlins, Jack P. *Thackeray's Novels: A Fiction that is True*. Berkeley: University of California Press, 1974.

Discusses the novel as a sequel to *Henry Esmond* (a work displaying Thackeray's close adherence to the traditions of romance) to show how the novelist violently rejects such conventions as antithetical to real life. Examines ways Thackeray presents the meaninglessness and triviality of modern life, which the novelist sees as devoid of heroism. Explores the author's reasons for shifting his central interest from Harry to George Warrington in the middle of the novel.

Ray, Gordon N. *Thackeray: The Age of Wisdom, 1847-1863*. New York: McGraw-Hill, 1957.

Remarks on Thackeray's original conception for the novel and the changes he made as he wrote it, shifting the emphasis of setting from America to England. Extended discussion of the major characters, including Baroness Beatrix Bernstein (Beatrix Castlewood from *Henry Esmond*) and George Washington. Considers the work highly repetitive, especially as Thackeray treats first Harry Warrington's story, then retraces many of the same incidents in telling the tale of Harry's brother George.

Stevenson, Lionel. *The Showman of Vanity Fair: The Life of William Makepeace Thackeray*. New York: Charles Scribner's Sons, 1947.

Lengthy commentary on the history of the novel's genesis and on Thackeray's difficulty in completing the monthly installments. Reviews critical reception of the work, especially in America, where readers were not pleased with the novelist's portrait of their country.

Sutherland, J. A. "*The Virginians*: The Worst Novel Anyone Ever Wrote." In his *Thackeray at Work*. London: Athlone Press, 1974.

Faults Thackeray on three grounds: diffusiveness in handling his narrative; oversensitivity to American feelings resulting in distortion of characters and events to make the American revolutionaries look good at the expense of the British; and weakness in handling moral and psychological issues. Notes instances of fine writing, but judges the novel Thackeray's least successful.

Tillotson, Geoffrey, and Donald Hawes, eds. *Thackeray: The Critical Heritage*. New York: Barnes & Noble Books, 1968.

Reprints selected passages from two reviews of the novel appearing in widely read British literary periodicals shortly after the novel was completed. The first compares Thackeray to eighteenth century masters of fiction Henry Fielding and Tobias George Smollett; the second suggests parallels between Thackeray's moral outlook and that of several nineteenth century French novelists.

ANTHONY TROLLOPE

General Studies

Bareham, Tony, ed. *Anthony Trollope*. Totowa, N.J.: Barnes & Noble Books, 1980.
Collection of nine essays reflecting the diversity of Trollope's concerns and his mastery of the art of fiction. Selections include discussions of Trollope's early works set in Ireland; comments on several of the Barsetshire novels, and on several in the Palliser series; an account of Trollope's contributions to the journal *St. Paul's*; and an assessment of *The Way We Live Now*.

Barickman, Richard, Susan MacDonald, and Myra Stack. *Corrupt Relations: Dickens, Thackeray, Trollope, Collins and the Victorian Sexual System*. New York: Columbia University Press, 1982.
Extensive analysis of Trollope's treatment of sexual relationships in his fiction. Compares him with other important Victorian novelists in his handling of the "woman question." Devotes a separate chapter to Trollope's novels, concentrating on his development of complex heroines, many of whom challenge social conventions in overt or subtle ways. Concludes with a discussion of Trollope's men, describing the limits imposed on them by a patriarchal society.

Booth, Bradford A. *Anthony Trollope: Aspects of His Life and Art*. London: Edward Hutton, 1958.
Critical examination of Trollope's achievements as a novelist focuses on those works concerning the clergy and political subjects. Discusses Trollope's theory of the novel and remarks on the background of his works to show how the novelist shaped materials he gleaned from the world around him into fiction. Analyzes several of Trollope's techniques, including his handling of plot and character, his reliance on humor and pathos, and his style. Includes a chapter on Trollope's critical reputation.

Cockshut, A. O. J. *Anthony Trollope: A Critical Study*. London: Collins, 1955.
Analysis of Trollope's achievement, arguing that in his later novels he is more gloomy and introspective than he appears in the Barsetshire series. In the first section, Cockshut examines the novelist's religious, political, and social ideas. In the latter half, he looks at several of the later novels to illustrate his thesis that Trollope gradually grew more pessimistic about the possibility of improving society or human nature.

Davis, Hugh Sykes. *Trollope*. London: Longmans, Green, 1960.
A brief biographical and critical sketch of Trollope's life and works. Discusses

Trollope's concept of the novelist's function and outlines his involvement with his characters. Considers the Barsetshire novels Trollope's best sequence; also singles out *The Way We Live Now* and *The Claverings* as meriting special attention.

Garrett, Peter R. "Trollope: Eccentricities." In his *The Victorian Multiplot Novel: Studies in Dialogical Form*. New Haven, Conn.: Yale University Press, 1986.
Argues that Trollope's multiple plots and looseness of narrative are actually strengths, giving his novels a complexity and a sense of realism in which readers find multiple perspectives from which they must discern the truth. Detailed examination of *Can You Forgive Her?*, *The Last Chronicle of Barset*, and *He Knew He Was Right*, isolating the central characters in each to show ways Trollope constructs his multiple narrative.

Gerould, W. G., and J. T. Gerould. *A Guide to Trollope*. Reprint. Westport, Conn.: Greenwood Press, 1970.
A compendium of factual information about Trollope's fiction. Includes a complete list of the novels and stories, organized both chronologically and alphabetically, and a chart dividing the works by series and by subject (political novels, social satires, and so on). Most of this guide is an alphabetical list of characters and places appearing in the fiction, with a brief explanation of each entry.

Gindin, James. *Harvest of a Quiet Eye: The Novel of Compassion*. Bloomington: Indiana University Press, 1971.
Classifies Trollope as a novelist of compassion, interested primarily in people trying to succeed in an increasingly complex society with few absolutes or moral standards. Discusses Trollope's criticism of people who have excessive intensity; these individuals often hurt others in their pursuit of personal goals. Also analyzes Trollope's heroines and his concern over the growing importance of money in society.

Hall, N. John. *The Trollope Critics*. Totowa, N.J.: Barnes & Noble Books, 1981.
Selections from important assessments of Trollope's artistry published in the century after the novelist's death. Hall's introduction provides a useful review of Trollope's literary reputation and demonstrates the sustained popularity of the novelist among general readers. Includes a selected bibliography of criticism.

Halperin, John. *Trollope: Centenary Essays*. London: Macmillan, 1982.
Collection of essays by diverse scholars providing a general assessment of Trollope's achievements. The focus is largely topical, including essays on Trollope as a traveller, on his idea of the gentleman, on the dialogue in his novels,

and on his revision of the fiction. Also contains a biographical essay and a commentary on Trollope's *Autobiography*.

Helling, Rafael. *A Century of Trollope Criticism*. Reprint. Port Washington, N.Y.: Kennikat Press, 1957.
Scholarly review of Trollope's critical reputation among his contemporaries and during the first half of the twentieth century. Examines his close relationship with the society in which he lived, and the effects of succeeding generations' reaction to Victorianism on Trollope's reputation. Includes a bibliography of criticism dealing with Trollope's works and the Victorian age.

Hennessey, James Pope. *Anthony Trollope: A Life*. Boston: Little, Brown, 1971.
Highly readable scholarly biography, the best full-length study of Trollope's life. Relies heavily on a variety of published and manuscript sources to explore the novelist's personality, describe his friendships and his career in the post office, and examine the influence of his years in Ireland on his career. Pithy commentary on Trollope's works, with special attention given to the later novels.

Karl, Frederick R. "Five Victorian Novelists." In his *A Reader's Guide to the Nineteenth-Century Novel*. New York: Farrar, Straus & Giroux, 1964.
Discusses Trollope's strengths and weaknesses, deeming him a novelist who writes competently yet predictably. Notes his insistence on highlighting the artificiality of his work. Singles out the novelist's treatment of the figure of the clergyman.

Kendrick, Walter M. *The Novel Machine: The Theory and Fiction of Anthony Trollope*. Baltimore: Johns Hopkins University Press, 1980.
Uses a close examination of Trollope's *Autobiography* to explore the novelist's theory of fiction. Surveys representative selections from the novelist's canon to show how Trollope employs his own theory, and how his novels tell the reader how to read. Includes a lengthy analysis of *He Knew he was Right*.

Levine, George. "Trollope: Reality and the Rules of the Game." In his *The Realistic Imagination: English Fiction from Frankenstein to Lady Chatterly's Lover*. Chicago: University of Chicago Press, 1981.
Considers Trollope the greatest realist among the major Victorian novelists. Argues that his works are always filled with compromises between moral imperatives and the world as he sees it around him. Judges that, in the end, Trollope has faith in arbitrary social conventions; men can survive if they simply follow agreed-upon rules of behavior.

MacDonald, Susan Peck. *Anthony Trollope*. Boston: Twayne, 1987.
Modest survey of Trollope's career and of his major concerns. Reviews approximately half of the forty-seven novels, examining the Barsetshire series in detail. Treats subjects such as love and money; Trollope's psychological studies; the social, political, and economic aspects of his works; and his perspective in the later works. Comments on Trollope's reputation in the twentieth century. Includes a brief chronology and an annotated bibliography of criticism.

Mizener, Arthur. "Anthony Trollope: The Palliser Novels." In *From Jane Austen to Joseph Conrad*, edited by R. L. Rathburn and Martin Steinmann. Minneapolis: University of Minnesota Press, 1958.
Uses Trollope's Palliser series to examine the novelist's merits. Discusses his method of composition, especially his techniques of plotting and his interest in characters who are willfully self-deceived. Notes his ability to balance summary with presentation of direct action. Some comments on his development of Plantagenet Palliser and Lady Glencora.

Polhemus, Robert M. *The Changing World of Anthony Trollope*. Berkeley: University of California Press, 1968.
Critical examination of Trollope's novels, aimed at displaying the novelist's concern for the changes occurring in society. Discusses ways these changes are reflected in the fiction. Claims Trollope is a great novelist, worthy of standing with other giants of the age, such as Charles Dickens and George Eliot.

Pollard, Arthur. *Anthony Trollope*. London: Routledge & Kegan Paul, 1978.
A survey of Trollope's canon intended to establish his contributions to the tradition of English fiction. Finds his principal strengths lie in chronicling the everyday society of Victorian England and displaying subtleties of character, which give his novels a high degree of realism despite his intrusive authorial voice. Remarks on virtually every one of the forty-seven novels and includes a brief bibliography of criticism.

Praz, Mario. *The Hero in Eclipse in Victorian Fiction*, translated by Angus Davidson. New York: Oxford University Press, 1956.
Viewing Trollope as the best representative of Victorian bourgeois attitudes, Praz examines Trollope's characters to show how he succeeds in attracting readers' attention and sympathy. Reviews several novels to illustrate Trollope's adherence to a realism grounded in the commonplace. Posits that he avoided dealing with extremes of emotion or action, and almost always opted for the comic rather than the tragic outcome a given circumstance might produce.

Quiller-Couch, Sir Arthur. *Charles Dickens and Other Victorians*. New York: G. P. Putnam's Sons, 1925.

General appreciation of the novelist, focusing on the Barsetshire novels. Discusses the many qualities which make reading Trollope's works both pleasurable and intellectually rewarding. Praises Trollope for his intimate knowledge of the society about which he wrote.

Russell, Frances T. *Satire in the Victorian Novel.* Reprint. New York: Russell & Russell, 1964.
Observes Trollope's use of satiric techniques in various works. Compares his efforts with those of his contemporaries, most of whom were less gentle in their use of satire. Discusses Trollope's use of irony. Detailed examination of Lady Carbury, a major figure in *The Way We Live Now*, who possesses traits other novelists are quick to satirize—snobbishness and hypocrisy—but which do not fully explain her behavior.

Sadleir, Michael. *Trollope: A Commentary.* 3d ed. London: Oxford University Press, 1945.
Comprehensive analysis of his life and works, arguing that Trollope must be studied both as a literary artist and as a chronicler of society. The first part deals with Trollope's youth and concentrates on the career of his mother, Frances, a popular writer in Victorian England. A lengthy section highlighting Trollope's career is followed by an assessment of his literary achievements.

Smalley, Donald. "Anthony Trollope." In *Victorian Fiction: A Guide to Research*, edited by Lionel Stevenson. Cambridge, Mass.: Harvard University Press, 1964.
Bibliographical essay summarizing Trollope's achievements as a novelist and providing details about manuscripts, editions, and collections of letters. Also reviews criticism published before 1962 of individual novels and about special subjects such as Trollope's handling of female characters, his relationship to other novelists, and his treatment of legal, political, and social issues.

―――――――――― , ed. *Trollope: The Critical Heritage.* New York: Barnes & Noble Books, 1969.
Reprints excerpts from reviews, notices, and correspondence written during the novelist's lifetime or shortly after his death; the comments cover all of Trollope's novels. Includes remarks on the man and his work by fellow writers such as Nathaniel Hawthorne, Elizabeth Barrett Browning, Henry James, Margaret Oliphant, and Edward FitzGerald. Excellent source of information on the contemporary reaction to Trollope's works. The introduction discusses Trollope's reputation and his reaction to critics.

Snow, C. P. *Trollope: His Life and Art.* New York: Charles Scribner's Sons, 1975.
Heavily illustrated biographical and critical sketch of the novelist by one of England's most influential twentieth century writers. Comments on the fiction

are included in chapters on the life; two additional chapters offer a general assessment of Trollope's achievement.

Speare, Morris E. "Anthony Trollope: The Victorian Realist in the Political Novel." In his *The Political Novel: Its Development in England and America*. Reprint. New York: Russell & Russell, 1966.
Examines Trollope's novels in which politics is a major subject. Considers Trollope more interested in portraying human nature than in illustrating the intricacies of political philosophy; claims that none of the novels displays faith in any political platform. Detailed discussion of *Phineas Finn* and *Phineas Redux*. Claims Trollope is successful in depicting three aspects of the contemporary political scene: the role of women in politics, the importance of the press, and the political atmosphere in the boroughs.

Terry, R. C. *Anthony Trollope: The Artist in Hiding*. Totowa, N.J.: Rowman & Littlefield, 1977.
Reacting to the widely differing critical opinions of Trollope's work, Terry attempts a comprehensive assessment of his artistry, examining the unchanging qualities of human nature and of domestic situations which Trollope found most interesting. Organized thematically, with extensive discussions of Trollope's interest in topics such as marriage and social issues. Argues Trollope was essentially constant in his optimism about human life and society.

——————— , ed. *Trollope: Interviews and Recollections*. London: Macmillan, 1987.
Brief biographical sketches and personal reminiscences by Trollope's family and friends offer divergent views of the novelist's personality and of his literary achievement. Includes comments by Henry James, Thomas Hardy, and Trollope's first biographer, T. H. S. Escott.

Williams, Merryn. "The Male Image of Women." In her *Women in the English Novel, 1800-1900*. New York: St. Martin's Press, 1984.
Considers Trollope the most conventional of all nineteenth century male novelists in his treatment of women characters: the best women always marry, because in Trollope's view that is the highest goal to which a woman can aspire. Traces the consistency with which Trollope applied this doctrine through his many novels.

Wright, Andrew. *Anthony Trollope: Dream and Art*. Chicago: University of Chicago Press, 1983.
Study of Trollope's artistry focuses on two series, the Barsetshire and Palliser novels, and on five additional books. Wright argues that Trollope was not simply a chronicler of everyday life, but an artist with a vision for a better world, which he portrays for his readers as an alternative to present reality.

Barchester Towers

Booth, Bradford A. *Anthony Trollope: Aspects of His Life and Art*. London: Edward
Hutton, 1958.
Focuses on Mrs. Proudie; calls her one of the great creations of Victorian
fiction. Nevertheless, Booth argues that Trollope did not take advantage of all
the possibilities such a character affords. Provides insight into Trollope's handling of satire, which seems lighthearted in this work.

Knoepflmacher, U. C. "*Barchester Towers*: The Comedy of Change." In his *Laughter and Despair: Readings in Ten Novels of the Victorian Era*. Berkeley:
University of California Press, 1971.
Sees Trollope's treatment of the changes occurring in his world as comic:
opting for the stability of an older order, he gently chides those given to the
excesses of the new. Believes the central conflicts in the novel stem from
relations between the sexes; women are the strong characters in the book.
Discusses parallels with *Paradise Lost*, which forms an ironic background for
Trollope's treatment of clerical warfare.

MacDonald, Susan Peck. *Anthony Trollope*. Boston: Twayne, 1987.
Scattered comments remark on Trollope's dramatization of the conflict between the established gentry and upstart interlopers, and on the complex
plotting which reinforces the novelist's central concern with the problem of
establishing one's place and one's values. Illuminating commentary on the way
Trollope brings this struggle to life in scenes where characters literally take
over rooms and drive others out.

Phelps, Gilbert. *A Reader's Guide to Fifty English Novels, 1600-1900*. New York:
Barnes & Noble Books, 1979.
Biographical sketch details Trollope's home life as a child and his early years
in the post office; notes the inception of his career as a novelist. A brief
synopsis of the novel is followed by critical commentary surveying the entire
Barsetshire series. Discusses Trollope's brand of realism and outlines the work
habits that allowed him to be so prolific.

Polhemus, Robert M. *The Changing World of Anthony Trollope*. Berkeley: University of California Press, 1968.
Rates the novel one of the greatest English comedies, as Trollope explores the
incongruities between the ideals of the spiritual Church and the realities of the
Church as a secular institution. Considers Archdeacon Grantly and Mrs.
Proudie the dominant characters in the book, but devotes significant attention
to analysis of Madeline Neroni and Arabin, figures whose status as outsiders
allows Trollope to highlight the foibles of social interaction in Barsetshire.

——————— . "Trollope's *Barchester Towers* (1857): Comic Reformation." In his *Comic Faith: The Great Tradition from Austen to Joyce*. Chicago: University of Chicago Press, 1980.

Sees Trollope's use of characters from other novels as an important innovation in fiction, creating a fantasy world parallel to the real one. Discusses the novelist's concern for community and social issues; shows how action in this novel demonstrates these concerns. Also examines Trollope's notions of the importance of a career. Remarks on his style, which Polhemus sees as relying heavily on understatement for its comic effect.

Pollard, Arthur. *Anthony Trollope*. London: Routledge & Kegan Paul, 1978.

Sees Trollope's support for the old order of society stated most strongly in this work; notes his satiric portrait of interlopers in Barsetshire (Mrs. Proudie, Mr. Slope). Argues that the furor over religious issues was important to Trollope's contemporaries. Describes the function of the Stanhopes as a gauge by which other characters are measured.

Sadleir, Michael. *Trollope: A Commentary*. 3d ed. London: Oxford University Press, 1945.

Discusses Trollope's negotiations with his publisher, William Longman, incident to publication of the work. Reprints correspondence from Longman's referees, who raised objections to the manuscript, and Trollope's replies to their criticisms. Illuminates attitudes of mid-Victorian readers regarding their expectations for fiction.

Smalley, Donald, ed. *Trollope: The Critical Heritage*. New York: Barnes & Noble Books, 1969.

Reprints selected comments from eight reviews and notices appearing in influential British literary journals shortly after the novel was published. Most are laudatory, although the *Westminster Review* critic chides Trollope for not involving readers emotionally.

Wiesenfarth, Joseph. "Dialectics in *Barchester Towers*." In *Anthony Trollope*, edited by Tony Bareham. Totowa, N.J.: Barnes & Noble Books, 1980.

Argues that Trollope's novel must be read dialectically to understand its significance and its power; around a spare outline dealing with the theme of ambition, Trollope organizes several series of contrasts that create dramatic tension to hold readers' interest. Believes the novel argues simultaneously for the goodness of proper ambition and for the equal goodness of the absence of any ambition.

Wright, Andrew. *Anthony Trollope: Dream and Art*. Chicago: University of Chicago Press, 1983.

Outlines the structure of the novel, especially Trollope's opening chapters, pointing out the novelist's method of advancing his story scenically. Discusses the function of the narrator, claiming Trollope has been maligned by critics for his use of the intrusive authorial voice. Believes Trollope is not arguing for the preservation of the status quo or for a return to the past; claims he actually pokes fun at those characters who are too attached to the past.

The Warden

Roberts, Ruth. "The Shaping Principle." In *The Trollope Critics*, edited by N. John Hall. Totowa, N.J.: Barnes & Noble Books, 1981.
Attempts to account for Trollope's persistent ability to captivate readers. Finds his special strength in his capacity to see complexity in situations others might reduce to simplistic moral terms. Trollope's power comes from his ability to make readers feel sympathy for people on both sides of an issue.

Booth, Bradford A. *Anthony Trollope: Aspects of His Life and Art*. London: Edward Hutton, 1958.
Reviews previous critical responses to the novel. While acknowledging its flaws and limitations, Booth argues that it displays (for the first time in Trollope's career) his superior ability to delineate character. Claims that the novel is innovative in transforming a serious subject such as the need for Church reform into domestic comedy.

MacDonald, Susan Peck. *Anthony Trollope*. Boston: Twayne, 1987.
Discusses the novel as an example of the way Trollope treats characters and incidents realistically. Provides a brief plot summary, followed by an analysis of the novelist's techniques of characterization, illustrating ways he steers away from moral extremes and provides characters with mixed motives for their actions. Also comments on Trollope's gentle satire of strident reformers.

Polhemus, Robert M. *The Changing World of Anthony Trollope*. Berkeley: University of California Press, 1968.
Focuses on Trollope's handling of the notion of change; reads the novel as an exploration of the ways progress affects both individuals and the social order. Discusses the novelist's interest in and sympathy for Septimus Harding, an unlikely hero who faces up to the problems of modern society even though events seem to overwhelm him. Insists Trollope is primarily concerned with individuals rather than social institutions.

Pollard, Arthur. *Anthony Trollope*. London: Routledge & Kegan Paul, 1978.
Notes Trollope's interest in the public theme of Church preferment and in the

private intrigues associated with young love. Although he sees Trollope siding with the established aristocratic and middle-class order over the new order of merchants and clerics with progressive ideas, Pollard acknowledges the author's intentional ambivalence: neither side is presented as unequivocally good or bad.

Sadleir, Michael. *Trollope: A Commentary*. 3d ed. London: Oxford University Press, 1945.
Brief account of the conception and publication of the novel. Discusses Trollope's ambivalence over the issue of Church preferments. Reprints a letter from one of the reader's reports sent to Trollope's publisher to illustrate the expectations Victorian readers had for novels.

Smalley, Donald, ed. *Trollope: The Critical Heritage*. New York: Barnes & Noble Books, 1969.
Excerpts from five notices published in important Victorian literary journals. All stress the satiric intent of the work, and all cite the book's strengths and its appeal to the nineteenth century reading public.

Wright, Andrew. *Anthony Trollope: Dream and Art*. Chicago: University of Chicago Press, 1983.
Discussion of the novel as an introduction to the Barsetshire series. Considers Trollope's selection of Septimus Harding as the hero and his concentration on Harding's dilemma over the position as warden to be strokes of genius. Notes how little Trollope is interested in ecclesiastical or spiritual matters; his concern is with the practical operations of the Church and the people involved in running it.

The Way We Live Now

Booth, Bradford A. *Anthony Trollope: Aspects of His Life and Art*. London: Edward Hutton, 1958.
Regards this novel as one of Trollope's best in dealing seriously with the corruption of Victorian society. Finds Trollope's portrait of Victorian business, expressed in his delineation of Augustus Melmotte, particularly bitter. Notes the hostile reviews from the novelist's contemporaries; these may have driven him back to more conventional practices in succeeding works. Points out faults in plotting, calling the work shapeless.

Cockshut, A. O. J. *Anthony Trollope: A Critical Study*. London: Collins, 1955.
Careful analysis of the novel, focusing on ways Trollope illustrates his central theme: the collapse of enduring standards of behavior as money becomes

more important than good manners and heritage. Comments on Melmotte's role in the work; examines Roger Carbury as his antithesis. Also reviews the function of the Longstaffes. Praises Trollope for technical soundness.

Gilmour, Robin. "A Lesser Thackeray? Trollope and the Victorian Novel." In *Anthony Trollope*, edited by Tony Bareham. Totowa, N.J.: Barnes & Noble Books, 1980.
Argues that the novel resists simplistic moral readings. Presents evidence about three aspects of the work which suggest a need to abandon a monistic approach: the tone of the narrator, the treatment of characters who can be classed as outsiders to the society Trollope presents, and the author's particular method of using conventions. Extensive analysis of Melmotte, noting ways Trollope deviates from conventional portraits of such scoundrels.

MacDonald, Susan Peck. *Anthony Trollope*. Boston: Twayne, 1987.
Comments on Trollope's pessimistic portrait of society; notes how his careful plotting illuminates the sham and corruption of modern society in its economic, political, social, intellectual, and religious aspects. Sees the central conflict to be the clash between old values, founded on hard work and commitment to traditional ideals, and new ideas for getting ahead in the world, symbolized by Augustus Melmotte. Shows how many characters abandon their principles in an effort to achieve either wealth or social status.

Polhemus, Robert M. *The Changing World of Anthony Trollope*. Berkeley: University of California Press, 1968.
Views this work as extremely pessimistic, a bitter satire of modern society. Shows how, through Melmotte, Trollope illustrates the depravity of a society which worships money. The portrait of the Longstaffes reinforces the central theme. Throughout the novel, Trollope emphasizes the essentially loveless character of modern society.

Pollard, Arthur. *Anthony Trollope*. London: Routledge & Kegan Paul, 1978.
Considers the work pessimistic in outlook. Notes the panoramic quality of the novel, in which Trollope examines commercial dishonesty, social scheming associated with marriage, idle youth, and pretentious authors. Detailed character sketch of Melmotte, with comments on the functions of other important figures in the work.

Russell, Norman. "Financiers (III): Trollope's Augustus Melmotte and the Corruption of the Old Order." In his *The Novelist and Mammon: Literary Responses to the World of Commerce in the Nineteenth Century*. Oxford, England: Clarendon Press, 1986.
Detailed background information on the nineteenth century financial world

is offered as a prelude to an analysis of Melmotte. Argues that Trollope pushes the notion of the moral depravity of financial speculation farther than any novelist before him; members of the upper classes know Melmotte is a swindler but still use him to gain wealth at the expense of the minor stockholders. Traces parallels between Melmotte and real-life financiers.

Sadleir, Michael. *Trollope: A Commentary*. 3d ed. London: Oxford University Press, 1945.
Summarizes the plot of the novel and compares it with events in English society which caused Trollope significant distress, such as the growing tendency to regard wealth rather than gentility as a characteristic to be valued. Points out the vitriolic qualities of the text, noting how these reflect the novelist's anger at his contemporaries' abandonment of cherished moral and social virtues.

Smalley, Donald, ed. *Trollope: The Critical Heritage*. New York: Barnes & Noble Books, 1969.
Excerpts from eight reviews by Trollope's contemporaries. Reviews are mixed: some castigate the author for what appears to be a vulgar satire, even a slander; others consider his portrait of corrupt society highly accurate.

Terry, R. C. *Anthony Trollope: The Artist in Hiding*. Totowa, N.J.: Rowman & Littlefield, 1977.
In a chapter devoted to exploring Trollope's idea of the good society, Terry discusses this novel as one of the author's best treatments of the dangers posed by modern commercialism and entrepreneurship. Provides a lengthy discussion of Augustus Melmotte as the dominant figure in the work, and of the significance of the Beargarden Club in representing the inversion of traditional values. Sees Roger Carbury as the antithesis of Melmotte, but claims Trollope's portrait of him is weak.

THE
VICTORIAN
NOVEL

INDEX

INDEX